Four Aces

Banner Books is Australia's specialist publisher of military history, committed to publishing high-quality books which add a significant dimension to the history of Australians at war.

Also available:

One Airman's War, photos & diaries of Joe Bull 1916-19, by Mark Lax

The Imperial Gift, first aircraft for the RAAF, by John Bennett

In the Ocean's Dark Embrace, RAN CDT3 Vietnam, by Lex McAulay

Endurance, RAAF Aircrew on Liberators in the Atlantic 1941-45, by Alwyn Jay

Six Aces: Australian Fighter Pilots 1939-45, by Lex McAulay

Strike and Strike Again 455 Squadron RAAF 1944-45, by Ian Gordon

Fighter Nights 456 Squadron RAAF, by John Bennett

Coomalie Charlie's Commandos, 31 Squadron RAAF, by Ken McDonald

Silent Victory, Secret Qantas Service, by Arthur Leebold

Four Aces

RAAF Fighter Pilots

Europe and North Africa 1941-44

by

Lex McAulay

BANNER BOOKS

First Published in 1998 by Banner Books
122 Walker Street, MARYBOROUGH
Queensland 4650
Australia

Design & Production by McTaggarts The Printers
63 Torquay Rd. HERVEY BAY
Queensland 4650

Cataloguing In Publication information

McAulay, Lex, 1939 -

Four Aces; RAAF fighter pilots Europe and North Africa 1941 - 44

Bibliography,
Includes index.
ISBN 1 875593 06 3

C ontents

Introduction

The flying careers of the four men in this book exemplify the wartime efforts of Australians who volunteered for aircrew service and flew fighters in North Africa and Europe. All four men joined the RAAF after war was declared against Nazi Germany, trained in Australia, were sent overseas, completed training there, and flew on operations. Only one of the four returned to Australia, and that after a series of close escapes from death. All four men were decorated and promoted to squadron command during periods of intense operations. Many other Australians served to the best of their ability, but did not receive any recognition or award in the form of decorations or promotion; many were killed in action or on active service; many spent years in prisoner of war camps; all lost friends.

The careers of these four men on operations illustrate to some degree the RAAF fighter experience in North Africa 1941-42 and Europe 1941-43. Nicky Barr, with 3 Squadron RAAF in the Desert, commanded the squadron only seven months after his first operational flights with it, and did so during a period of intense support to the ground forces while in retreat. The desert operations 1940-43 were the testing ground for the air-land support techniques which were developed and perfected for the liberation of Europe in 1944-45. The desert campaigns also were the background for what may be seen 50 years on as quaint events, perhaps episodes from the last of the 'gentlemanly' war campaigns: aircrews from both sides forced down in the desert were picked up by others who landed nearby; aircrews walked home, albeit through a merciless desert, after being forced down; columns of tanks, artillery and trucks sped off on swashbuckling forays against the enemy flanks; 'private armies' of eccentrics came and went over the desert wastes, gathering information for commanders. There was no other theatre of war like it. Nicky Barr returned to friendly lines three times after being shot down. However, Nicky's operational flying career (in North Africa) ended during a retreat, when Axis forces were surging east to Suez.

Hugo Armstrong began operational flying from England in an environment which was evolving into a modern technological battleground. Development of airframes, engines, weapons and electronics dominated air operations mounted from the United Kingdom by the RAF, Commonwealth and US squadrons. In June 1944, the Allied air forces which supported the invasion of Normandy bore only incidental resemblance to the shattered force which had been driven from Europe four years earlier.

Hugo Armstrong's operational flying began after the RAF had won the defensive Battle of Britain, and commenced learning the hard way how to conduct modern offensive operations over enemy territory. The German Luftwaffe, with all the advantages accruing from fighting over its own territory, inflicted heavy losses on attacking RAF squadrons. Hugo's career ended before this Allied campaign was successful.

Peter Panitz and Dickie Williams began their operations in what then was the most demanding and technologically advanced flying in the world: night radar interceptions in all weathers, of fast enemy bombers, flown by experienced Luftwaffe crews. Panitz and Williams formed a pilot-navigator team on 456 Squadron RAAF, completed a successful tour of operations, rested, then went on to a different but equally demanding style of wartime flying, operating at night in support of the Allied invasion of Normandy. The German forces were to be attacked by all classes of aircraft, by day and night, wherever they were found. Already well known for his success against enemy trains when with 456 Squadron, Peter Panitz took command of 464 Squadron RAAF at the height of the post-invasion flying effort, when two or three attack sorties per night were flown by many crews in their Mosquito twin-engined bombers. Dickie Williams came with him as the squadron commander's navigator. Their operational flying ended when it was obvious that the Allies were firmly ashore in France, and the Germans were facing a massive defeat. Although not 'aces' in the accepted sense of being fighter pilots who shot down a number of enemy aircraft, Panitz and Williams were just as successful in the dangerous and demanding task of navigating at night and in bad weather across Europe and attacking the trains which were an important part of the enemy war machine.

These four men, then, represent the many unsung RAAF fighter and light bomber pilots who flew in the Desert campaigns, or from England over the Channel, and in the night skies of Britain and France.

This book is dedicated to that generation of the RAAF, regardless of mustering, rank or unit, who served Australia so well in Africa and Europe 1941-45.

Chapter 1.

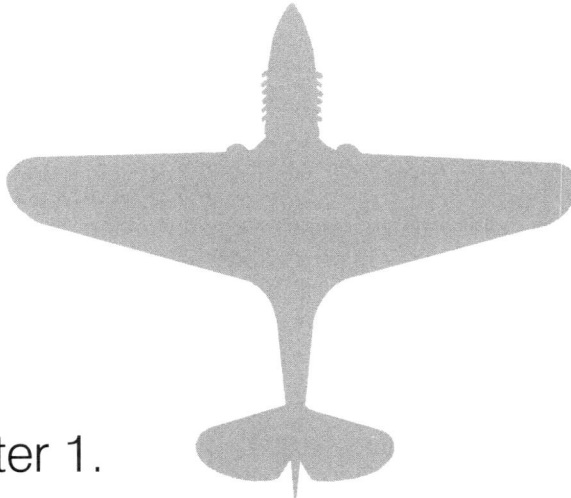

DESERT BATTLES

P-40 Allrounder

Wing Commander A.W. *'Nicky'* BARR OBE MC DFC* RAAF

Though he began operational flying somewhat later than Hugo Armstrong, Nicky Barr's experiences in the North African deserts are presented first.

* * * * * * * * * *

Andrew W. 'Nicky' Barr was born on 10 December 1915, at Lyell Bay, Wellington, New Zealand. His family moved to Australia, and he was educated in Sydney and Melbourne. In 1931, he was chosen to attend Lord Somers Camp, and subsequently became a member of its Power House organisation. Many of the staff, as well as his school teachers, were people who had served with distinction in World War 1, and who greatly influenced his life and values. After matriculation, he decided to become a wool classer, but soon saw there were more classers than sheep, so worked and studied accounting with Australian Estates Limited. Barr was a good all-round athlete, schoolboy sprint champion, Services springboard diving champion 1941, and good enough to represent Australia at Rugby. He captained the Air Force and Brisbane teams. As a sportsman, he had the desire to win, to be the first, and he later attributed his success and survival to the mental and physical toughness this training and experience produced. As Nicky's generation was growing up, during the Great Depression, the Nazis and Italian Fascists came to power, and he, like many others, was repelled by the obvious regimentation of all aspects of society under the totalitarian regimes. When war was declared against Nazi Germany in September 1939, Nicky Barr was a member of the Australian Rugby team in England.

Nicky recalled that the 1939 Australian International Rugby team was at Torquay, in Devon, when British Prime Minister Neville Chamberlain made the sombre announcement on 3 September, that, as the German invasion force in Poland had not withdrawn as requested, Britain and Germany were at war. The over-riding feeling among the Aussies was of resentment and disappointment that the war had intruded upon them after years of hard training to represent their country in sport.   The feeling must have been intense: the team was asked to fill sandbags from the adjoining beach to protect the 'Grand' Hotel, and in one day the entire beach content of sand had been bagged by the fit young footballers.   But the expected squadrons of Nazi bombers did not come while they were there.

The development of military aviation in the '20s and first half of the '30s had been relatively slow, with little difference in speed between fighters and bombers.   As the bombers were armed, and to be escorted, it came to be accepted that 'the bomber will always get through.'   Moreover, in the wars which were fought in the '30s, the bombers did 'get through', and the populations in the Western democracies were deluged with accounts of the horrors of modern bombing attacks on cities and other targets.   The Fascist forces in Spain obliterated the town of Guernica in the Civil War; Japanese bombers ranged at will over Chinese cities in their invasion of China; Italian bombers similarly attacked any chosen target in Ethiopia.   The newspapers, radio and magazines all presented detail of the terror and suffering inflicted on the populations.   Military strategists and politicians stated that future wars would be won by immense bombing fleets; civilian populations would be annihilated; poison gas would be released over target territories.

There were several results from all this.   The totalitarian regimes benefited in the short term because of the adverse psychological effect in the Western democracies resulting from the portrayal of their invincible bombing squadrons.   Further demands were met, and Italy took Ethiopia, consolidated its grip on other parts of Africa, and declared the Mediterranean to be 'Mare Nostrum' - 'our sea'; Nazi Germany absorbed parts of neighbouring countries; Japan took Manchuria and continued to expand on mainland China.   However, the successes gained by the Fascist regimes also contained the seeds of their eventual defeat.   It seemed there was no need for their air arms to develop better bombing aircraft; all that was required was to build more of the same to frighten opponents.

But, in Britain an analysis of the great danger posed by the German and Italian air forces resulted in the development and installation of the radar-controlled fighter defence, the design and production of the Spitfire and Hurricane, and the commencement of the RAF heavy bomber programme: the design, production and employment of bombing formations which would operate on a strategic basis, able to attack targets in Germany from England.   All this is well beyond the scope of this book, and has been examined in detail in other publications.   But, in September 1939, when Adolf Hitler refused to withdraw his invasion forces from Poland, and Britain and France declared war on Germany, it was widely believed that there was no effective defence against the enormous numbers of German bombers which would arrive over Great Britain.   The expected early bombing did not occur, as the German forces were busy in Poland.   The Nazi war machine swiftly destroyed the Polish armed forces in the new 'blitzkrieg' style of mechanised modern warfare, assisted by the Soviet Union under Josef Stalin, who seized the opportunity to occupy the western part of Poland.   There then came what was called 'The Phoney War', as the Germans and the French and British faced each other along the German border, with very little military activity.

Nicky Barr had for some time thought that if war did come, he would like to be a fighter pilot, so he volunteered for the RAF, trying for an arrangement whereby he could fly with an Australian squadron. But the RAF was swamped with volunteers, and the young Australian was greatly put out to be told to go away and wait, that it would be a long time before he saw an aircraft. Instead, a commission was offered as a pay officer in administration. Rather than wait, young Barr used a connection to a former Governor of Victoria, Lord Somers, and was able to return to Australia with the footballers who had not enlisted in the British forces.

31 CADET COURSE RAAF

Back in Australia, Nicky volunteered for the RAAF and was accepted on the last cadet course before the Empire Air Training Scheme commenced. Squadron Leader Roy King DFC commanded 3 Elementary Flying Training School at Essendon; Nicky reported to this unit. His flying training began on 5 March 1940, with Captain Lohse in DH60 VH-UND, and he was sent solo in this aircraft on 21 March after 9 hours 55 minutes dual instruction. Flying training continued to 2 August, when, with a total of 126 hours flying, including 71 solo, Nicky was graded as *'Above Average'* by Squadron Leader King. He then moved to RAAF Base Point Cook, and 1 Service Flying Training School, to master the more powerful Hawker Demon. 40 young men comprised No. 31 Cadet Course; successful completion of this training brought the cadets to RAAF 'wings' standard.

All the trainees, of course, wanted to feel as though they were preparing for an active role in a war, but there was almost no 'war training' - that would be done

Air Cadet A.W. Barr 'the lowest form of life', according to Nicky
(A.W. BARR, VIA RUSSELL GUEST)

elsewhere in the training system. It later became obvious to Nicky Barr that there seemed to be no centrally controlled process for taking a recruit and passing him through a system designed to produce a pilot or aircrew member ready to take his place in a fighting squadron. That did not come for some years. The pilot trainees were given various tests at times in their training intended to find those qualities and aptitudes which suited the man to a specific type of Air Force flying - and Nicky took care his bombing results were so poor that he was not considered for bombers. He was *Above Average* as a pupil pilot, as a pilot-navigator, and in air gunnery. He graduated as a Pilot Officer, with 141 hours solo flying experience, on 24 September 1940. Of the graduates of 31 Cadet Course, 12 were killed during the war, eight became prisoners of war, and seven were wounded.

No.31 Cadet Course 21 September 1940
Back row
I.N. Hamilton, I.A. McCombe, J.S. Menzies, W.M. Dempster, D.L. Pank, C.A. Greenwood,, R.H. Pope, G.W. Gibson, G. Hill, G.M. Smith, P.B. Sinnott, R.H. Tayler, J.D. Entwistle, J.H. Cox
Centre row
H.D. White, G. Turner, F.F.H. Eggleston, A.M. Greenfield, J.A.H. Parsons, J.E. Dures, C.C. Henry, C.G. Tolhurst, L.H. Bradbury, E.M. Ball, P.E. Biven, K.A. Crisp, M.H. Watson, J.N.W. Piper
Front row
D.E. Mossley, L. Bradley, D. Rutter, H.B. Dawkins, G.W. Gilbert, A.J. Rollins, D.R.A. Flach, D.E. Howie, L.W. Brickhill, J.H. Woods, A.W. Barr, T.K. Knight, H.W. Webster, F.A. McLeod *(A.W. Barr)*

Nicky was posted to 23 'City of Brisbane' Squadron, equipped with Commonwealth Aircraft Corporation Wirraways and Lockheed Hudsons. The Wirraway was a single-engined training aircraft, pressed into service as a fighter, reconnaissance aircraft and dive-bomber. It was in no way suitable for modern war, and the Japanese later found them easy prey. The Lockheed Hudson was a modern twin-engined reconnaissance bomber. The Hudson was imported from the USA, and the Wirraway was made in Australia from the basic design of the North American Company NA33 trainer. The establishment of the factory, and training of the tradesmen and other staff necessary to produce a modern aircraft was a great advance for Australia, and was one of the first steps in that aspect of national progress.

By this time, the German Wehrmacht had occupied most of Europe, Italy had entered the war on the side of Nazi Germany, and the Battle of Britain was at its height; British cities were enduring the 'Blitz' from German bombers. The theorists were wrong: bomber fleets alone could not win wars, and the British civilian population showed conclusively that it was not going to break. For the young members of RAAF squadrons in Australia, it was evident that the Wirraway could not hope to contest with the Spitfire, Hurricane or the single-engined Messerschmitt Bf109 fighter and Bf110 twin-engined 'destroyer' fighter.. The Italians were not held in high regard, and neither were their aircraft. The other possible enemy in the Pacific, the Japanese, were said by most in authority to be inept and to fly cheap copies of obsolete Western aeroplanes. One 'authority' even proved to his own satisfaction that Asians could not perform aerobatics and combat manoeuvres, as the shape of their skulls allowed the brain to be pressed upon the bone by gravitational forces during aerobatics, resulting in blackouts. Some who had read this with interest later observed the agile Japanese navy and army fighters flown by experienced pilots who prided themselves on aerobatic ability, and wished the author of the reasoning was with them as the Japanese cavorted across the skies.

However, the shortcomings of the Wirraway as a modern combat aircraft were recognised by all who flew them. Naturally enough, it was decided to exploit the points of the Wirraway which would allow for survival in the case of military operations, and this devolved to perfecting a quick and sharp spin, providing there was sufficient height in which to recover.

Murphy's Law of Marriage in Wartime

Flying Officer A.W. Barr's time with 23 Squadron was short, for in August 1941 he was appointed as an Honorary Aide de Camp (Air Force) to the Governor of Queensland, Sir Leslie Wilson. By this time, he had a total of 598 hours flying. The commander of 23 Squadron was Squadron Leader 'Dixie' Chapman, who graded Nicky as *'Above the Average'* when signing off his log-book on departure from the squadron. It soon seemed to Nicky, in the impatience of youth and the early days of the war, that this could be his entire subsequent Air Force experience, 'standing one pace back and to the rear.' It also then seemed a good time to marry his sweetheart, Dorothy Gore of Malvern, Victoria. Because of his business and sporting careers, this had been post-poned, then was post-poned again on his enlistment in the RAAF. But the decision to marry Dorothy seemed to activate one aspect of Murphy's Law of Marriage in Wartime: - Marry When Permanency Seems Sure, and a Posting Will Follow At Once. Flying Officer Barr was posted to 3 Squadron RAAF in North Africa.

3 Squadron RAAF was one of the peace time Regular squadrons, tracing its lineage to the Australian Flying Corps of World War 1. It had been an Army Co-operation squadron, and as such was included in the allocation of supporting arms and services for the 2nd Australian Imperial Force of volunteers for overseas service in World War 2. The squadron at first was to be under command of the 6th Australian Division, but this was later altered to comply with the practicalities of use of air power. The squadron embarked for overseas at Sydney on 15 July 1940, and arrived at Suez on 23 August. The first Lysander army co-operation aircraft arrived on 31 August, but soon after it was decided to form two Flights of Gloster Gladiator fighters and one of Lysanders. The Gladiator was a bi-plane fighter exemplifying the glamourous flying of the '20s and '30s, but could not perform against a modern enemy. A few earlier models, the Gloster Gauntlet, also were delivered, and in these aircraft 3 Squadron went to war.

The first tactical reconnaissance operations were flown on 13 November 1940, and the first combat followed next day - four Italian aircraft were claimed destroyed and two claimed as probably destroyed; 'probables'. A pilot was to claim a 'probable' if he was sure the aircraft was destroyed or about to crash, but because of circumstances did not actually see it destroyed, and no one else could verify the claim. A probable was not claimed if the pilot merely thought the enemy might have been destroyed. However, this fine distinction often was not observed, or even known by some pilots.   The first Hurricanes arrived at 3 Squadron on 1 February 1941, and the squadron continued to fly intensively.   On 5 April, with 73 Squadron RAF, on two patrols formations of German Junkers Ju87 'Stuka' divebombers were engaged; 14 were destroyed, 10 being claimed by the Australians.   Meeting unescorted Stukas was the dream of many fighter pilots, and the subsequent massacres became known as 'Stuka parties'.   The Curtiss P-40 Tomahawk was received in May 1941, when the squadron was in Palestine.   By late 1941, 3 Squadron RAAF had fought Italians, Vichy French and Germans, and was one of the leading Commonwealth squadrons in the North African theatre.

To 3 Squadron RAAF and OTU at Khartoum

When Flying Officer Barr and seven other replacement pilots arrived at 3 Squadron, they were lined up by the Commanding Officer (C.O.), Peter Jeffrey.   The replacements were asked if anyone was married; four men stepped forward.   Jeffrey told them bluntly that they were 'not going to be much good' to him, the leader of a fighter squadron.   Young Barr was not going to accept this, and retorted that married men had more to fight for.   He later noticed that many of the more senior and successful members of the squadron, like Lou Spence, were married.

The replacements had arrived at an opportune time.   There was a pause in operations, and it was arranged that they go on 12 October 1941 to the Royal Air Force 71 Operational Training Unit (OTU) at 'Gordon's Tree', near Khartoum.   The RAF Station there was a permanent peace-time establishment, with all that meant for civilised Service life in the 1930s: comfortable buildings and accommodation, a swimming pool, and well-trained Sudanese Mess staff and servants. There was also the historic connection with the famous defence of Khartoum against the Muslim dervishes by General Gordon.   Five more pilots for 3 Squadron arrived next day.

The aircraft at 71 OTU flown by the 3 Squadron contingent were the Curtiss P-36 Mohawk and P-40 Tomahawk.   The Mohawk was a radial- engined fighter produced in the USA, taken by the RAF from French production orders after the German defeat of France in 1940.   Though tough, it was too slow, by 1941 was obsolete, and only used operationally by the RAF in Burma.   The Tomahawk was a development of the Mohawk, powered by a liquid-cooled Allison engine which produced 1,040 horsepower, and armed with six .303-inch [7.7mm] or four .303s and two .50-calibre [12.7mm] machineguns.   These also had been originally French orders, and were taken by the RAF.   By late 1941, over 1,200 had been delivered; most were in North Africa.   At Khartoum, the sense of purpose of the six guns heightened Nicky's feelings.   The two .50-calibre machineguns were mounted along the top of the engine cowling, and the breeches protruded into the cockpit.   When fired, the cockpit filled with the smell of cordite, and to Nicky this was 'particularly helpful to me; I really felt I was at war.   It became more realistic.'

The RAF Air Commander-in-Chief, Air Marshal Arthur Tedder, recalled talking to a newly arrived Australian pilot about the Tomahawk.   The Australian was what Tedder noted as 'a little off-hand' about the Tomahawk, but broke into a grin when asked about the firepower.

The Mohawk aircraft, however, were plagued with problems and there were many forced landings. Later it was found that the piston rings had been sabotaged when the engines were assembled at the Allison plant in the USA. Nicky had to forceland Mohawk No. 2523 in the desert 80 miles (128 km) south of Khartoum: the engine seized as no oil had been replaced after servicing. But for Nicky, the Tomahawk was 'most delightful for me; I enjoyed the aircraft and felt comfortable flying it.' The syllabus at 71 OTU included formation flying, aerobatics, gunnery, line astern chases, deflection attacks, ground strafing, dog fights, and dog fights with Hurricanes. All this was invaluable to a pilot about to fly on operations, as it enabled him to master the aircraft type and gain confidence in his own ability. On leaving Khartoum on 17 November 1941, Nicky was graded as *Above Average*. He was going to take his place in an operational squadron with 639 hours flying experience.

While the new pilots at the OTU were finishing their course, 3 Squadron was engaged in some intensive operations. The squadron had moved forward from Sidi Haneish to Landing Ground (LG) 110 on 14 November 1941, and then to LG122, for the start of the 'Crusader' operation on 19 November, to relieve besieged Tobruk. Three armoured brigades advanced into enemy territory. The 19 available RAF and Commonwealth fighter squadrons had a total of about 200 aircraft. The Axis fighter force also totalled about 200, but included some 40 Messerschmitt Bf109F, which was superior in most aspects to the opposing Hurricanes and Tomahawks. Air Marshal Tedder believed the air forces were ready for the offensive, and had signalled London that his force was at full strength, had reserves, and was 'on its toes.' Tedder signalled to all squadrons, 'Good hunting.'

However, the first few days of 'Crusader' saw little air activity, due to dust storms which were followed by flooding rains. The weather also affected communications, so that the higher headquarters had little idea of the progress of the offensive. First reports, often from officers who had gone forward to the battle area and returned, were of very good air-land co-operation, and an initial superiority gained by the RAF.

On 22 November, at 09.45, 12 Tomahawks escorted twin-engined Blenheim bombers of 45 Squadron RAF to the Acroma-El Adem road area. The German Luftwaffe intercepted, and the RAAF pilots counted 15 Messerschmitt Bf109s attacking. The Luftwaffe claims by I Gruppe of Jagdgeschwader 27 (I/JG27) were accurate: four Blenheims and three Tomahawks. From 3 Squadron RAAF, three Tomahawks did not return. There was another hard combat in the afternoon, and though 3 Squadron claimed two destroyed, four probables and six damaged, six 3 Squadron aircraft and pilots were missing at the end of the day. There were four serviceable Tomahawk aircraft available in 3 Squadron at dusk.

Flight Lieutenant Bill Kloster was fortunate enough to survive a crash landing south of Tobruk at 320 kmph, his Tomahawk on fire and fabric control surfaces burned away. He was captured and sent to Germany. Harold Roberts was another who did not return. He had claimed a Ju88 probably destroyed on 14 September, and had some 70 hours operational flying. His Tomahawk was hammered by a burst of fire which shattered the windscreen and put six bullets through the oil tank; Roberts was unconscious for a few seconds.   He came to in time to forceland with the undercarriage down, about 15 miles [24 km] west of El Adem.   The Tomahawk was repairable, and he followed current instructions and left it for possible salvage.   He set off to walk back, but two days later went into an Italian camp and was captured before he could leave it.   He spent the rest of the war in prison camps.

On this day, Luftwaffe losses were heavier than those claimed by the Commonwealth squadrons, but the Luftwaffe had learned one lesson: from this day they would not engage in dog-fighting, but would keep to their successful diving attacks, using height and speed to pounce and zoom to safety again.   The RAF was much slower to learn and retained the useless restrictive formations which allowed their enemy to inflict casualties.   Rudolf Sinner, II/JG27, who eventually claimed 32 victories over the desert, later said that he lived in dread from day to day that the British would alter their formations and tactics - but they did not do so for months.

While other air forces in the late 1930s insisted on flying a tight, attractive peace-time 'V' formation, the Luftwaffe had adopted a looser formation built on pairs of fighters.   In addition, Luftwaffe tactics were superior to those of the RAF.   The invaluable experience gained flying modern combat aircraft in the Spanish Civil War had benefited the Luftwaffe in general and many individual pilots in particular.   This evolution of fighter tactics also has been recounted elsewhere, and will not be repeated here, except to add that for up to three years after the outbreak of war, some RAF squadrons failed to adopt the efficient Luftwaffe fighter formation.   Many aircraft and pilots were lost.

In the meantime, Alan Rawlinson, an 'original' 3 Squadron member, had been promoted Squadron Leader and gone from 71 OTU to take command of the squadron on 3 November.   Alan Rawlinson was only at 71 OTU for 10 days before being appointed to command the squadron.   He had joined the squadron in July 1939, and was by this time one of two survivors of the Gloster Gauntlet flight.   By late 1941, he was very experienced, and knew what he wanted in his squadron members. On 24 November, Nicky and three of the pilots who had gone to 71 OTU arrived back with 3 Squadron.   Rawlinson recalled Nicky as, 'An easy mixer, quiet, yet taking in all that was going on.'

3 Squadron RAAF on operations

The replacements found that they had joined 'a pleasant, happy squadron, with a good atmosphere'. Peter Jeffrey, Alan Rawlinson's predecessor, had been efficient and popular, and the squadron retained under Alan Rawlinson and later commanders 'a family ambience, which I think contributed to the standard of the squadron.'   Most of the squadron had operational experience, and were willing to share it, but the new pilots had to draw out this information.   This was due to the British and Australian character - the experienced pilots did not want to be thought to be 'big-noting' themselves in the eyes of the later arrivals.   One aspect of 3 Squadron organisation established by Peter Jeffrey later was adopted by other squadrons: a pilots' Mess operated, instead of the usual Service custom of Officers' and Sergeants' Messes.   'It was senseless,' Nicky pointed out, 'sharing one's life with fellow pilots during operations, recounting experiences, then eating and relaxing separately.'

There was another important part of the Squadron's life which impressed Nicky Barr and others who served in the unit: 'In 3 Squadron we were trained and had a sensitivity about flying as a squadron, not as individuals.' 3 Squadron did not devolve into an organisation comprised of a few 'aces' and 'the rest'. It was noticeable that in some other squadrons which had outstanding aces, there were also heavy losses. In the Luftwaffe and the US squadrons, aces were the centre of attention from the media, senior officers and the general public. In some Luftwaffe units, the aces controlled the flying and attacks so that other pilots protected their flanks and tail while the ace concentrated on increasing his personal score; the other pilots merely witnessed the victories. This was all very well for the propaganda machine, but an abandonment of the principles of modern fighter employment.

The Commonwealth squadrons maintained a rear base, with the aircraft deployed forward to a desert landing ground. Pilots would ferry aircraft back and forth, for major maintenance which could not be done at the forward strip. There was more fighting on the 25th, and four pilots failed to return, though some made their way back after exciting adventures with the ground forces. The squadron claimed seven destroyed, one probable and eight damaged.

The ground fighting surged back and forth, as General Erwin Rommel manoeuvred his German and Italian forces to counter the Commonwealth offensive. On the 23rd, after inflicting heavy tank losses on the British, Rommel attacked towards the Egyptian border, and for the next few days efforts were directed to stopping this offensive. Unknown at the time and for long after, Rommel's seemingly miraculous ability to counter enemy moves, to thrust and cause confusion, was based on able exploitation of information from his 621 Signals Company. This unit, of about 100 men, intercepted Commonwealth radio transmissions, sometimes so efficiently that Rommel was informed of the contents of decoded and translated enemy orders and intentions before the British brigade commanders received their copies through their own command system.

On 26 November, Nicky and other pilots flew to the advanced landing ground. That day, the squadron was informed that it was to be the first to receive the new P-40 Kittyhawk aircraft, an improvement on the Tomahawk. On 28 November, Nicky flew his first operation, from 09.30 to 10.45: a bomber escort. There was no combat, and it was a good introduction to the squadron's work. After his training, and particularly the experience at OTU, he was confident of his ability to fly the Tomahawk and felt ready mentally and physically to engage in battle.

Nicky flew again on the 29th, and on the 30th. On that day, 3 Squadron RAAF passed the '100 enemy destroyed' mark, with claims for eight destroyed and 15 damaged. During the month, the squadron lost ten pilots on operations, and as not all of the batch of pilots had returned from 71 OTU, some due to sickness which prevented them finishing the course, it was decided that the next batch of 11 replacement pilots who had just arrived would remain and be trained on Tomahawks with the squadron.

Alan Rawlinson was rested from operations after the squadron reached the '100 victory' mark. He now was the only surviving member of the Gauntlet flight, and had been in the desert longer than any other pilot in the squadron. Of Nicky Barr, he said that,

'He was a positive person and had the good fortune to survive those first few operations. Not only that, he was able to shoot down a few enemy aircraft during that early time, which is of great assistance to the newcomer, provided over-confidence is contained.'

After a few operations, the newer pilots realised that it was generally thought the Curtiss P-40 could not cope with the Messerschmitt Bf109. When the Curtiss designers were creating their fighters in the mid-30s, there was no thought given to enemy aircraft approaching the USA at high altitude, and the P-40 was designed for best performance at medium and low altitude. The Messerschmitt Bf109 had superior performance at altitude, but the Tomahawks were generally employed at lower levels, escorting bombers or on fighter sweeps over the battle front area. The standard tactic on meeting 109s was to go into a defensive circle, in which each plane covered the tail of the aircraft in front. In theory, this prevents enemy from entering the circle and shooting an aircraft down from behind. Diving attacks or accurate deflection shooting across the circle were another matter, as a young Luftwaffe pilot was soon to demonstrate. After two or three exasperating experiences of circling while the 109s were about, most of the

Nicky Barr, pensive after his second combat
(AWB, via Russell Guest)

newer pilots spoke up against the tactic, and were told by the older hands that if they wanted to lead out of the circle, to go ahead next time. This attitude, of a certain admission of superiority to the enemy, was a psychological disadvantage to the new pilots. Of this period in the Desert, Nicky Barr said that the P-40

'was a magnificent solid aircraft, get you out of a lot of trouble most times. It could handle the Macchi and Fiat, but the Messerschmitt 109 tactics were vastly superior to ours. There were heavy losses amongst all squadrons.'

It was found also that the Italians could fight well, especially if a determined pilot was in the Macchi Mc202 with the Daimler-Benz engine. When some of the Italians realised that beautiful aerobatics were of no use in combat, and then flew the aircraft as a war machine, they could be quite formidable.

Rommel's armoured force withdrew from his thrust towards Egypt, and fell back to the west.   After a pause, the Germans attacked again and captured Sidi Rezegh, which effectively isolated Tobruk again.   Ground fighting continued into December, but the Commonwealth forces were disturbed by news of the Japanese attack on Pearl Harbour, and the opening of yet another theatre of war.   Forces from the Middle East would have to be sent east, and supplies would have to be diverted there.

Air activity continued into December, with some days of heavy fighting.   On 9 December, on early operations, Tomahawks and Hurricanes engaged the Luftwaffe without loss, claiming two enemy.

At 10.35, nine Tomahawks from 3 Squadron and ten from 112 Squadron RAF swept the Tobruk-El Adem area.   Six Bf109s of I/JG27 were higher, in the sun, and successfully surprised the Tomahawks.   Sergeant Rex Wilson was killed; Sergeant Alan 'Tiny' Cameron shot down, but returned three days later; and Flying Officer David Rutter, ex-Power House and ex-31 Cadet Course, with impressive educational qualifications, also was shot down and killed, only five days after arriving on the squadron.   Rex Wilson had just been recommended for a Distinguished Flying Medal, which was gazetted in January, for his destruction of eight enemy aircraft; post-war reseach shows his score to have been five destroyed and six damaged, comprising one French aircraft and the rest German, in only nine combats.

Claims submitted by Oberleutnant Gerhard Homuth, Oberleutnant Hugo Schneider and Unteroffizier Josef Grimm were quite accurate.   Schneider and Grimm also had claimed victories in the combat on 22 November, when 3 Squadron lost three aircraft.

Wing Commander Peter Jeffrey also was hit, and had to force-land at Tobruk, while Sergeant Ken Carson's aircraft of 112 Squadron was hit.   Later, Nicky and Carson were to share a POW hospital ward at Bergamo, in Italy.

During the combat, Nicky Barr found himself alone with two 109s, who carefully maintained their height advantage while trying to get him.   Nicky was later mildly surprised to find that all the time the 109s had been hovering, he had been working in figures of eight back over friendly territory, and the combat ended almost over the squadron landing ground.   While he had been concentrating outwardly on the visible enemy - the 109s - from a lower level of consciousness he had been edging back into friendly territory. Erhard Braune, the German leader, had been aware of this the whole time, and credited Nicky with edging back on purpose.   In later studies of successful fighter pilots, this ability to consistently remain conscious of one's position in relation to the enemy, to the ground, and of directions was defined as 'situational awareness.'   This was only Nicky's fourth operational flight.   Years after the war, Braune went through Nicky's logbook and identified the operations during which they had been engaged in combat.

Fear is a normal part of warfare, and Nicky's concern was not so much that he would experience abject fear - rather, he worried for some time how he would handle it.   Once he felt reasonably comfortable about controlling it, he 'kept it inside as best I could, a personal thing.'   The worst part was waiting, on stand-by to take-off, tension caused by knowing that one was ready to go into action, but not knowing exactly when the call would come.

A 109 was claimed destroyed and another damaged by Sergeant Walter Mailey, of 3 Squadron.   His first victory had been over an Italian Fiat G50 fighter on 30 November. After a series of head-on passes, with neither doing much damage, Mailey thought that sooner or later the Italian would hit him, so instead of diving below the Italian as on previous passes, Mailey pulled up steeply, hauled around toward the Italian, his sights were on, he fired, the Italian rolled over and hit the ground.   Mailey's first thought was, 'Gee, that was easy!'.   Like almost every other pilot, he did not consider that a man had been killed - it was the impersonal aircraft which had been shot down.   Later Wally was grounded after eye problems caused by the desert dust, and ended his flying career with six enemy destroyed and five damaged in seven combats in November and December 1941 and February 1942.

12 December 1941 was a day of extensive fighting.   As the RAF radars often were not working due to the desert conditions or for other reasons, pilots could not be warned of enemy in the area, and so constantly were searching the sky for 109s.   This distracted them from other matters, such as escorting or seaching the ground below for enemy. The British 4th Armoured Brigade, with infantry, attacked the Gazala positions, and each side provided air support.

Fighters from each side met a variety of enemy aircraft types, and many pilots claimed victories.   RAF pilots claimed Ju52 transports, Dornier Do24 flying boats, Bf109s, Bf110s, Ju87s, and Mc202s, while the Axis pilots claimed Marylands, Beaufighters, Tomahawks, Hurricanes, and a Blenheim.   RAF Tomahawks and Hurricanes of 250 and 80 Squadrons strafed and bombed motorised columns in the Martuba area, but were pounced upon by 109s and Mc202s.   The RAF squadrons lost five aircraft, for two claims.   South African Hurricanes of 1 Squadron SAAF lost one to Bf109s, and 2 and 4 Squadrons SAAF also lost three aircraft, but claimed three 109s.

Just after this combat over the Derna road, 112 Squadron RAF and 3 Squadron RAAF took off to sweep the Derna area.   Nicky insisted on test-firing his guns as soon as possible after take-off.   It seemed pointless to him to get airborne, then to discover the guns were unable to fire when close to the enemy.

Tomahawk R/AN355, flown by Alan Rawlinson on a beat-up
(via Russell Guest)

A Messerschmitt Bf110

From 13,000 feet over Tmimi, a formation of enemy was seen climbing below, at the 9 o'clock position. [This was the 'clock code', in which the observer's aircraft is visualised as being on the centre of a clock face: 12 o'clock is dead ahead; 9 o'clock to the left; 6 o'clock directly behind; etc.] As 3 Squadron was making a formation turn to attack, two Tomahawks collided. Nicky saw one diving east, into cloud, and dived to escort him home. However, before he caught up with the Tomahawk, he saw a Messerschmitt Bf110 above, flying towards him, just below cloud base at 3,000 feet. Nicky swung around onto the 110's tail and fired two bursts, flames came from the wing root and fuselage and the 110 went downwards, but he did not see it crash. In the combat with the enemy formation, Flying Officer Bobby Gibbes damaged a Ju87, but Flying Officer Fred Eggleston baled out after the collision and was made a prisoner two days later. Eggleston had been at Essendon and Point Cook with Nicky, and arrived on the squadron with him. In 112 Squadron, three aircraft were lost and one damaged, for claims of a 109 destroyed and three other enemy damaged.

The Luftwaffe fighter force had increased. The experienced III Gruppe of JG27 (III/JG27) had arrived, with a total of 359 victories claimed in the campaigns for France, over Britain, Malta and Russia. JG27 now was at full strength and together for the first time since the Battle of Britain. Leaders at all levels were experienced, highly decorated, and with respectable personal tallies of enemy destroyed.

On 13 December 1941, more air operations were flown in support of the land battles. To avoid setting a pattern which could be noticed by the enemy, take-off and climb to the operational height varied in directions flown, and also the methods of gaining height (circling, flying in a straight line, or zig-zagging) varied. Experiments continued with fighter formations, particularly with three 'boxes' of four aircraft in a squadron formation.

Messerschmitt Bf109 and Junkers Ju88

At 16.00, ten Tomahawks of 3 Squadron RAAF sighted enemy at their 10 o'clock position: just below cloud base over the Derna-Martuba area, a V-formation of eight bombers and an escort of eight Bf109s. Nicky saw the 109s swing aroung to attack the Tomahawks from the left rear; a 109 had a 'sitting quarter stern position' on a Tomahawk. Nicky whipped around and attacked the 109 from above, the Tomahawk slipped to port, the 109 pulled up towards the cloud and Nicky followed; he saw no effect from his shooting. Then the 109 half-rolled and dived into the ground, close to the burning wreckage of another Messerschmitt. Nicky looked around, but the only visible aircraft were three 109s; he slipped up into cloud, flew south, then turned east.

After a time he decided to dip below the cloud, and saw that he was south west of the Gazala inlet. Well to starboard, some Junkers Ju88 twin-engined bombers were attacking a truck concentration. But a single Ju88 was flying along closer to him. Nicky quickly made a short range attack from the side, then slipped around below the tail of the 88 and fired again; the left wing dropped, it dived sharply, but he nipped up into cloud again and did not see it crash. When he did come down, there was a fire on the ground, north west of the trucks which had been bombed; almost certainly the Ju88.

Sergeant 'Tiny' Cameron claimed one Bf109 and shared a second with Flying Officer Tom Briggs, while Sergeant Ron Simes claimed one probable and one damaged, and Bobby Gibbes damaged two more. Flying Officer Tom Trimble was shot down, but came back a week later.

On 17 and 18 December, the squadron collected its Kittyhawks, and the pilots were pleased with the new, powerful engine and armament of six .50-calibre machineguns, all in the wings. On the 24th, Wing Commander Jeffrey,

Mail arrives, December 1941.
(l. to r.) Lou Spence, Nicky Barr, Jewell, Ed Jackson, Les Bradbury
(via Russell Guest)

Squadron Leader Rawlinson and Flying Officer Primrose left for Australia; command was taken by Squadron Leader D.R. 'Dixie' Chapman, formerly commander 23 'City of Brisbane' Squadron.

1942

As 1941 ended, the squadron had 29 pilots on strength, 19 serviceable aircraft, and had lost seven in December. During the year, 3 Squadron had lost eight pilots known killed, three were known to be prisoners, and ten were, at the end of the year, listed as missing. Ground fighting on Operation 'Crusader' continued, Tobruk was relieved, and operations continued through the new year, into January 1942. The Royal Navy had lost 25 ships sunk and nine seriously damaged in the effort to supply the besieged garrison. An important enemy convoy from Italy with military supplies for Rommel had reached Africa in December, and a second was to do so on 5 January.

Junkers Ju87 Stukas

On 1 January 1942, 3 Squadron claimed 5-3-4 in combats. Nine squadron Kittyhawks, flying south below 8/10th cloud, saw Junkers Ju87s at the 11 o'clock position - the Stukas were about to attack ground targets in the Agedabia area. Four Bf109s flew across the front of the RAAF squadron; two half rolled and dived, the other two climbed for the clouds; an obvious lure to distract the fighters from the bombers. The Ju87s swung into a defensive circle about 1,000 feet below the cloud, then slid out of it into a formation of pairs in a 'V'. Nicky attacked the leader of the last pair, and saw him dive, smoking, into the ground. The 87s slipped back into a circle, closer to the ground. Around him, Nicky could see other Kittyhawks attacking and the rear gunners in the Junkers firing back - a single 7.92mm machinegun against six .50- calibres [12.7mm]. Nicky made more attacks, and after one saw the Ju87 he fired at roll onto its back, smoke pouring from the tail, at only 900 feet; he did not see it crash. After using all his ammunition for no other known result, he climbed away. Nicky counted five fires burning on the ground under the air batle, in a one-square mile area. Two 109s chased him, so

P-40 Tomahawk beating up Sidi Meneish
(via Russell Guest)

he flew out to sea for a while, then returned to base. Erhard Braune flew in this combat. Nicky thought the airmanship of some of the 109 pilots in the action was 'very poor.' It was his 17th operation.

Squadron Leader 'Dixie' Chapman was shot down, probably by a Ju87 rear gunner, but the rest of the squadron claimed five destroyed, two probables and four damaged. Chapman's was the first Kittyhawk lost. Post war research showed that the Italian 209 Squadriglia had a number of Ju87s badly damaged, and the Luftwaffe I/StG3 lost three destroyed.

There were mixed feelings about the Kittyhawk expressed by the pilots. Its performance was praised, and Nicky said his 'handled beautifully, was very maneuvrable, particularly in tight steep turns,' but the new reflector sight as fitted was 'unsatisfactory': the aiming circle was not clear and visibility or clarity was lost if the pilot moved his head. Other pilots reported the same short-coming, and Flying Officer Frank Fischer, commanding B Flight, reported that he ignored the reflector and used the fixed ring and bead sight.

More combats followed on 8 January, resulting in claims for 7-5-3, which included 11 Italian aircraft, but Flying Officer Alan Baster was lost. The general opinion of the Australian pilots after this action was that the Macchi Mc200 in the hands of a competent pilot could out-turn the new Kittyhawk.

Next day, the 109s struck back. 112 Squadron RAF and 3 Squadron escorted Maryland bombers to Mersa Brega, and Oberleutnant Gerhard Homuth, I/JG27, dived on the Australians, shooting down Flying Officer Geoff Chinchen and Sergeant Ron Simes. Chinchen crash-landed at Msus, but Simes was killed. Chinchen also had arrived on the squadron with Nicky Barr. A DFM was later gazetted for Ron Simes, who had claimed five destroyed, a probable and one damaged in six combats since 20 November.

Fiat G50 and Messerscmitt Bf109

11 January 1942; Nicky's 22nd operational flight, with 586 hours solo flying.   Twenty Kittyhawks of 112 Squadron RAF and 3 Squadron RAAF escorted six 14 Squadron RAF Blenheims. At the briefing, the experienced RAF bomber leader described his intended tactics and was quite definite about his intention to adhere to them in the attack. However, he had his bombs 'hang-up' at the bomb release point over the target, could not drop them, and continued on his flight path, instead of diving for the ground and getting out of the area.   Then he turned through 180 degrees and began another bomb run - disrupting the escort formation and forcing the Kittyhawks to remain and protect him. At 13,000 feet over El Agheila, enemy were reported at 9 o'clock level, but more were attacking from 12 o'clock above.   Erhard Braune was present again in this combat.

The six RAAF fighters flying as top cover were attacked by Bf109s of I/JG27, and Flying Officer Robert 'Bob' Jones and Sergeant Alan 'Tiny' Cameron were shot down. Cameron had an incendiary round lodge in his starboard exhaust stack, which ignited the starboard wing, then the fuel tank and cockpit. As Cameron later said, the Kittyhawk 'lost its flying characteristics', and he had to bale out, 'with both eyebrows in flames.' He jumped at about 6,000 feet, and landed near an Italian camp close to the shore.   Somehow a scuffle developed, and the huge Cameron kicked an Italian soldier in the head; the man died later in hospital.

Nicky saw two Fiat G50 fighters dive past on his right, and he pulled up into the sun, to 14,500 feet.   The G50s pulled up also, but he was above, fired on one from the quarter, and saw it jerk violently upward to the right, with thick white smoke streaming from the wing root; Nicky saw a parachute open.   On the edge of his vision, he saw a Kittyhawk diving with a 109 on its tail, and dived after them; the Kittyhawk crash-landed, and the 109 circled it, the pilot waggling his wings.   Nicky flew in and shot the 109 down, south west of the Kittyhawk.   This 109 was flown by Oberleutnant Hugo Schneider, a 9-victory ace from I/JG27, who claimed victories on 22 November, and again when Rutter, Wilson and Cameron were shot down on 9 December; he was killed.

Nicky then flew back to the Kittyhawk, and noticed the squadron letters on it: CV-E. Standing by it was Bob Jones, identified by his white gloves.   The beach was not far away, so Nicky flew to it, and prepared to land, to collect Jones.   A series of such pick-ups had been made by pilots of both sides since operations began in the desert.

Nicky lined up along the beach, reduced power, lowered flaps and undercarriage, and began his landing glide.   Then he saw Jones waving him up and pointing - Nicky looked back and a 109 was there behind him, flying slowly, firing..   The beautiful characteristics of the Kittyhawk were exploited: Nicky put on full power, and pulled up the nose; the Kittyhawk surged up; the 109 sped past, Nicky lowered his nose and fired, and the 109 crashed and burned south east of Marsa El Brega.   A second 109 had pulled up and was directly overhead, still climbing into the sun.   Nicky pulled up after him and fired, hitting the belly of the Messerschmitt.   Quickly, this 109 whipped around.   The pilot was Oberfeldwebel Otto Schulz, II/JG27, who eventually claimed 42 victories over the Desert; he was about to add one more.   Nicky, still with flaps and wheels down, felt hits in the Kittyhawk, then the engine lost power, but as he was at relatively low speed, he was able to force-land safely.

He saw the 109 swinging back, and realised the pilot was going to strafe the Kittyhawk, but also knew that he had to wait a little longer before running from the aircraft, or risk being caught in the hail of bullets and cannon shells. As the 109's gun muzzles flashed, Nicky began to run towards it and to the side, to reduce the time he would be in the killing zone and to avoid the line of fire. Even so, a 20mm shell exploded against a rock in front of him, and the detonation flung stone splinters into his legs - it was as painful as being kicked in a scrum, as Nicky recalled.

The 109 flew off, one wing low and with full rudder applied; apparently Schulz had some difficulty retaining control. Schulz, from Pomerania, was one month short of his 31st birthday, had flown with II/JG27 since the Battle of Britain, and by the time he arrived in Africa, had claimed a total of nine victories over England, the Balkans and Russia. Schulz made a habit of strafing his victims on the ground to destroy the aircraft. He had shot down Tiny Cameron on 30 November; Peter Jeffrey had later landed, picked up Cameron, and flown back to base.

Nicky looked around. The Kittyhawk was burning, and 'I was there in this desert on my own.' He could not see the smoke of any of the other burning aircraft, which presumably were some distance away. He tried to tie up his leg wounds, and after a time looked up to find three Arabs had materialised from the arid surrounds; two adults and a child. They were friendly, tenderly dressed his wounds and led him away; all hid in a wadi when a German patrol was passing through the area.

Nicky was welcomed in the camp, and pleased to see that the 'gooley chit', or reward for safe conduct pass, was understood by the family, who seemed quite excited by it. Nicky slept that night in a large Senussi tent, camel on one side of the partition, family and friends on the other side with their visitor. Next morning, a 'small camel entourage' of five adults and two children was assembled, with Nicky disguised as a family member in

January 1942, on return from the desert. 'Badly in need of a warm bath, shave, hair cut and a good meal,' said Nicky.   (AWB)

burnous, and they set off for the British lines, thought to be about 35 kilometres to the east. Nicky was well aware of his own predicament, and also wondered how the notification of his 'missing in action' had been received by his family in Australia. The small party was made to resemble a small Arab family in transit as they travelled through the country, past many Italian and German units. Nicky was impressed by the large number of tanks and personnel carriers, and memorised their appearance and features.

Nicky realised that, given the many enemy in the area, and the almost total lack of knowledge of the terrain, that it would have been impossible for anyone in his situation to escape successfully. He was told that the Italians, in a brutal effort to terrorise the Senussi into submission, had taken village elders and community leaders up in aircraft, then thrown the men out over their homes. This aroused hatred, and as

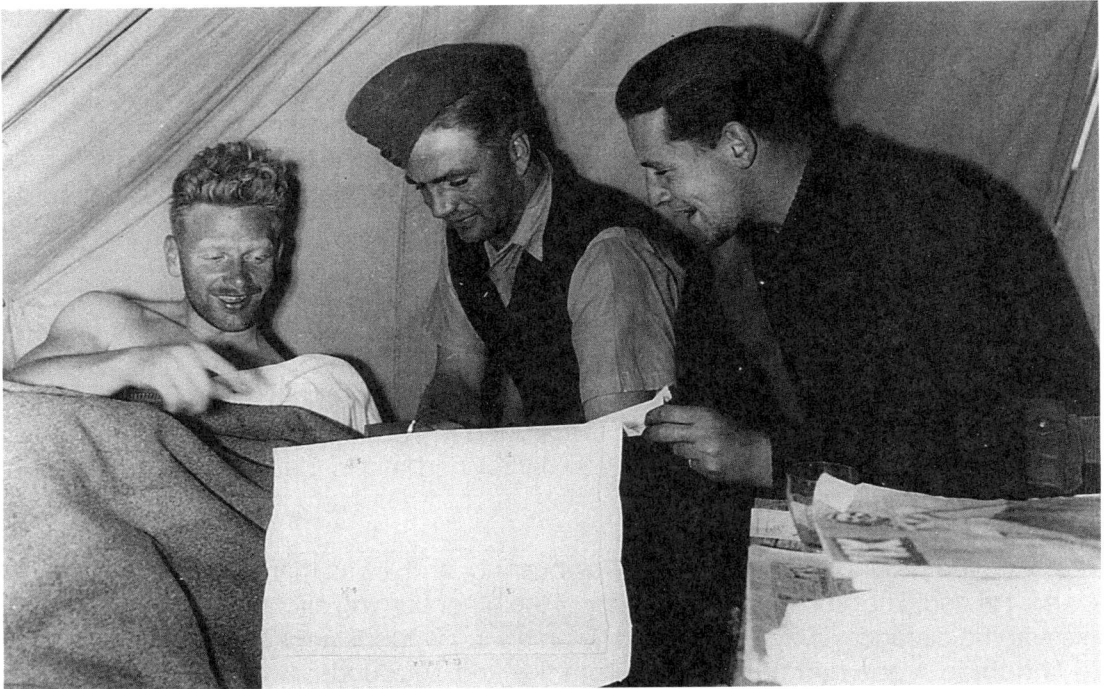

January 1942. Consulting a map with Dixie Chapman and Frank Fischer to deduce Nicky's travels in the desert.   (AWB)

the British were the enemies of the Italians, they automatically received the friendship of the Senussi. As the Germans were with the Italians, they received no assistance. The 'family' was stopped twice, but allowed to go on each time.   When the British forces were contacted, Nicky had a few bad moments, as his blond looks were exactly those of the Aryan enemy, and he had to convince British Intelligence at Army HQ that he really was an Australian ally. The Arabs had indicated a fondness for tinned fish, so Nicky saw that they were well rewarded, and also arranged for them to be given blankets, as one of the children obviously wanted one. He was surprised to learn, from the interpreter, that the Arab family also had been keen observers of the Axis enemy forces and positions, and had passed on a great amount of useful information to the British when debriefed, though the information gained would have been in direct relationship to the expertise of the interviewer. 'The last I saw of my friends,' he recalled, 'was the family disappearing over a sand dune and waving goodbye.'   He had been in the desert for five days.

Nicky now experienced, perhaps because of the release from tension due to a safe return, a great rush of self confidence: he had flown, fought, been shot down, survived and escaped from the midst of the enemy.   Later, he realised how little he did know about warfare, and that this confidence was ill-founded. None the less, he felt strongly that with the superior Luftwaffe tactics and superiority at altitude of the Messerschmitt Bf109 there were few acceptable options for countering the enemy. Aggressiveness, he decided, was the preferable, and perhaps the only, recourse available.   Often, that would seem to other people to be over-confidence.   However, Nicky was not aware of the view-point of other people at that time.   A part of this deliberate decision to be aggressive was a reaction against the deficient tactics employed against the Bf109s, such as the defensive circle.

Meanwhile, Sergeant 'Tiny' Cameron was flown to Tripoli, escaped, but was recaptured in an hour. He had flown 67 operational sorties, had received the Distinguished Flying Medal for seven victories, and already had come back twice after being shot down. It may have been Cameron who upset the chivalric Luftwaffe desert fighter pilot idea of the chap from the 'other Feldpostnummer'. Rudolf Sinner recalled a giant Australian Curtiss pilot who was captured, and entertained at a meal, but his manner and bearing were 'uncivilised', his table manners were 'horrible', and another pilot commented that he was a catastrophe, and a matter for the firing squad.

Bob Jones also was captured, by Italian troops, between Mersa Brega and Agedabia. He escaped from the truck on the night of 12 January, but was recaptured before he left the area. He was sent to join Alan Cameron in Tripoli. Neither intended to remain in captivity. They escaped again on 17 January, but were betrayed by local Arabs on the 22nd. Footsore, they were taken back and sent to Italy.

These victories on 11 January brought Nicky's confirmed victories to eight, gained in 16 combats, from a total of only 22 operational flights, in some 35 hours of operational flying. At about this time, one of the senior squadron officers said to him, 'You know, every time you get airborne, something happens.'

Until radar, electronics and missiles created an aerial battlefield in which the opponents rarely saw each other, eyesight was a vital attribute to a fighter pilot. The ability to detect and identify aircraft at long distances was crucial to the preliminary moves and hence the probable outcome of the combat. Nicky Barr was of the opinion that Bobby Gibbes had a great ability to see aircraft in the distance, while he personally could not, but he did seem to have good eyes for the actual combat, able to see and shoot accurately enough to hit the enemy aircraft.

Nicky was sent to the Scottish General Hospital in Cairo until his wounds healed, and then sent on convalescent leave, during which he met Geoff Chinchen. When he returned to the squadron, Nicky was told that Intelligence had found much of value in the information brought back by Nicky and the Arabs, three enemy had been confirmed shot down by him in the combat, and an Immediate Award of the Distinguished Flying Cross (DFC) had been made to him. 'A wonderful way to return to operations and my friends,' he recalled. He also received 'The Flying Boot' award, which indicated membership in 'The Late Arrivals Club'. This was an officially condoned morale-raising gesture, usually accompanied by Public Relations photos, and involved the presentation of a 'winged flying-boot' badge.

The citation to the DFC recounted Nicky's operational career from November, and much detail of the action in which he was shot down and returned to British lines. He 'displayed the greatest keenness and skill as a fighter pilot' and 'the greatest courage and tenacity throughout.'

On 13 January, ten Kittyhawks were flown to the new landing ground at Antelat. These sites across the region were selected by Wing Commander Fred Rosier RAF, who became Air Chief Marshal Sir Frederick Rosier. In an old Hurricane, Rosier would locate suitable landing grounds, land, and mark them out for the bull-dozers and other construction equipment, fly back and arrange for notification and what work needed to be done. There was little combat for the next week, but on the 22nd, in very wet conditions at Antelat, two aircraft were wrecked in take-off mishaps. The squadron engaged a mass of 48 enemy, claimed 3-0-4, but lost two more. In January, the squadron had lost 13 aircraft and pilots, though some pilots had returned from the desert.

Rommel, meanwhile, with the supplies from two convoys, had attacked, pushed back the Commonwealth ground forces, recaptured Benghazi on 28 January, and continued his advance to the east. Air operations again intensified, each side supporting its land and sea forces and attacking the opposing air units. Air Marshal Tedder, now knighted, thought that several opportunities to inflict a final defeat on Rommel had been missed, mainly due to what he called an excess of bravery and shortage of brains at Army field command level. Tedder was surprised to hear the British Army admit that they were still amateurs at the business of desert warfare, and that the Germans often were tactically superior. No one realised Rommel's brilliance stemmed from adept exploitation of Intelligence from his radio intercept company, linked to great personal drive and the highly developed flair for commanding well forward in the mobile battles in the desert. Rommel's early battle service had been with mountain troops in World War 1, but he began to make a name for himself when given command of 7 Panzer Division for the offensive against the Western Allies in May 1940. Rommel learned that the 88mm anti-aircraft gun made an excellent tank-killer, and in the desert time and again lured the British tanks into ambushes by the 88s, which destroyed or badly damaged the armoured units and allowed Rommel's tanks to seize the initiative. Only the Australians at Tobruk had been able to defeat a full-scale panzer attack.

On 12 February 1942, Nicky returned to the squadron from hospital, in Kittyhawk L/903. On the 14th, in combats, the squadron claimed 8.5-0-6. Sergeant Wally Mailey had been leading both 3 and 112 Squadrons, but they had not had time to take up the usual formation, and 112 was still ahead of 3 when enemy were met. 112 went for the Italian fighters and Ju87s seen, but Wally Mailey led 3 Squadron higher, despite protests from the others - he felt the 109s were nearby. Six 109s did dive from the clouds, but the Kittyhawks reacted strongly, disposed of them, then dived into the fight below. A total of 20 enemy were claimed by the two squadrons. Wally Mailey received a Distinguished Flying Medal for this action; he personally claimed two 109s.

On the 15th, two Kittyhawks were shot down as they tried to take-off to engage approaching bombers. These Ju88s already had bombed, and were returning to base. Flying Officer Tom Briggs and Sergeant Reid took off, but the escorting 109s were not seen, and pounced. Leutnant Hans-Joachim Marseille, I/JG27, saw the Kittyhawks, came down out of the sun, and first shot down Reid, who was still too low to bale out. He crashed and died instantly. Marseille went on to Briggs, now at 300 feet, and shot him down, but, though wounded, Briggs was able to bale out.

In the afternoon, 20 Kittyhawks of 94 and 112 Squadrons RAF strafed the Luftwaffe airfield at Martuba. A Bf109 of II/JG27 had just been serviced, and was ready to fly. Oberfeldwebel Otto Schulz, Nicky's opponent of 11 January, climbed in and was airborne in 30 seconds.   Schulz attacked the newly-arrived 94 Squadron RAF, shot down four, then destroyed another of 112 Squadron.   All this was witnessed by people on the ground.   One victim was the commander of 94 Squadron, Squadron Leader E.M. 'Imshi' Mason DFC RAF, with 17 victories in earlier campaigns.   Schulz reported that he thought the Kittyhawks were flown by novices - no evasive action was taken.   His score now was 44 in 332 operational flights, and on the 22nd he received the Knight's Cross.   Leutnant Marseille also received the decoration at the same ceremony, for 50 victories.

Nicky flew his next operation on the 18th.   Squadron Leader Dixie Chapman was posted to command 451 Tactical Reconnaissance Squadron RAAF, and was replaced by Bobby Gibbes.   Gibbes assumed command on the 26th.   He and Nicky had known each other at Point Cook and on 23 Squadron, and Nicky 'knew we were going to make a great team.'   Nicky became senior flight commander, which meant leading the squadron when Gibbes did not fly.   Nicky did not aspire to command - it just seemed to happen. He had decided to be a fighter pilot because the prospect of survival was better than most alternative wartime occupations.   Altough a component of a squadron formation, there was a strong individual element and responsibility about the role of fighter pilot which appealed to him.   He thought that, for his survival, much more would depend upon himself.   Now he found himself leading formations and responsible for those men in their aircraft.   'I never considered I was a hero of any sort.   I was simply hell-bent on surviving as best I could.'   Medals did not sit large in his estimation, and even 50 years after, he still is mildly reprimanded, by those who notice such matters, for having his decorations and campaign medals in the wrong order.

New pilots were arriving from the training units, and one of these was Sergeant Ross Biden, who left 71 OTU at the end of January with an *'Above Average'* grading, but with only 190 hours' total flying experience.   On 1 March, Sergeant Biden flew his first Kittyhawk solo.   He arrived at the squadron base on 3 March with a total of 4 hours 15 minutes experience on the Kittyhawk, and flew his first patrol on 8 March.

A Macchi Mc202

At 17.00 on 8 March, 12 Kittyhawks from 450 and 3 Squadrons, led by Nicky Barr, intercepted enemy aircraft about 15 miles [24 km] north of Tobruk.   The enemy were seen at the 11 o'clock position, 2,000 feet below the Kittyhawks: 15 Ju87s escorted by two Bf109s and Italian fighters.   The Macchi fighters were in two tight echelons of five and of four aircraft - too close for correct operational flying.   Nicky placed 450 Squadron above, as top cover, and attacked.   The Italians thought the Kittyhawks were friendly aircraft, and made no move to counter their approach.   Nicky swung in behind them and shot down a Macchi Mc202, which poured black smoke and dived into the ocean, witnessed by Nicky's No. 2, Sergeant Allen Beard.   Beard himself climbed and dived on four Mc200s flying echeloned right; they did not see Beard.   He came in behind, on the port quarter, fired, and watched the Macchi fall in a flickering falling-leaf descent.   Beard fired three more short range bursts into two other Macchis, but saw no results.   While other Kittyhawks were attacking the Ju87s, Beard saw the first Mc200 hit the sea.   Six Italians were destroyed, with two probables and two damaged claimed.   Later, 112 Squadron met what were obviously the survivors of this combat: all 15 Stukas, the two 109s, but only two Macchis.   112 claimed a Stuka and a Mc200.

On 12 March, another rising star of the squadron was killed. Peter Giddy had claimed his first victory, a MC200, on 22 January, and in February and March claimed another four destroyed and two damaged in five combats. He was performing aerobatics over the airfield when a panel flew off the Kittyhawk and the aircraft crashed, killing him.

On 14 March, the squadron claimed 1-2-0; there were no other combats that month. Sergeant Ross Biden flew his first five operational sorties.   Nicky Barr 'formed a very high opinion of Ross.   I remember wondering why he was a Sergeant; who were his assessors? He was intelligent, capable, and most likable even though laconic in style. His combat reports also were brief and concise.'

Air cover was flown over Convoy MW10, four freighters carrying 26,000 tons of vital fuel, ammunition and food to beleagured Malta. Nicky's 39th, 40th and 41st operations were flown in support of these ships.   Quite long flights of 3 hours 15 minutes, 2 hours 50, and 4 hours were made, over the Mediterranean.   The last flight went 230 miles [370 km] from the coast.   However, when he returned, Nicky was told he was to go on two weeks leave, which caused the comment in his logbook, "Yippee!" He was now a Flight Lieutenant, commanding B Flight. Coincidentally, Otto Schulz also was sent on leave to Germany, was commissioned an Oberleutnant, and did not return to Africa until late May.

Nicky had found the desert arena to have its advantages.   The almost limitless spaces were an excellent place to fight, if fighting was necessary, as mimimum harm was inflicted on non- combatants and their property by the battles which flowed back and forth along the coastal regions for three years.   He thought it an
'impressive place.   It has its own form of beauty.   There are ethereal qualities about it, which, especially at dusk and dawn, are very impressive.'   At those times of day, he found it *'so remote from war that it is a form of - or it was to me, any way - a form of therapy in its own way.'*

He would stand and look around; the only movement was of the wind raising small whirls of sand.   This moved him to write a short poem of the scene, with only the wind dancing by.   Nicky would go for walks, to enjoy the solitude, or stroll around the airfield perimeter and chat with members of the various units and organisations working or guarding the landing strip.   Some of these were quite interesting people, and included the famous Gurkhas.   All this was a valuable refreshing break from the tensions of combat.

3 Squadron RAAF was out of operations in April, retraining and re-equipping.   Allan Beard crashed and was killed on 16 April. The war went on regardless, so squadrons in turn were sent back to the established base areas.   A needless complication for squadrons on the various far-flung fronts was caused by a certain pedantic mentality at the Air Ministry in England.   When new equipment, such as the Curtiss P-40 Kittyhawk, was ordered from foreign factories, the RAF insisted on producing its own user handbook or manual, even though one was available from the original supplier.   This insistence on bureaucratic procedure resulted in aircraft and other items of equipment arriving for operational use without a manual for use by maintenance staff or aircrew.   Air Marshal

Tedder, not an overly patient man in such matters, had enough of needless losses caused by simple lack of information, and finally signalled the Air Ministry in London to ask that the original handbooks be packed with the equipment, as 'We can now understand American language, and need not wait Air Ministry interpretation.'

Early in May, General Rommel began preparations for another offensive, with the intention to beat the British to the punch. Rommel had detailed information on his enemy's preparations, because as well as the flow of accurate and timely reports from 621 Signals Company, the Axis were intercepting and reading the reports sent by the US military observer in Cairo. Colonel Bonner Fellers, US Army, received full briefings and information from the British, and passed on this information by radio. The Axis were in possession of the US codes, and were able to read everything sent by Fellers. Rommel received this Intelligence, plus that from his own 621 Company. He decided to attack before the British launched their offensive on 15 June. Rommel's Luftwaffe fighter and bomber units were strengthened, but this relaxed the intense pressure of attack on the vital British-held island of Malta. The battered but tenacious RAF squadrons on Malta almost at once re-commenced attacks on the precious Axis ships bringing supplies to the African battle front. The Axis powers could not manage to maintain adequate and simultaneous pressure both on Malta and in North Africa to achieve victory at either. Malta and the North African front were inter-dependent, each striking at the Axis enemy to assist the other. Air action in the Mediterranean battle areas intensified as May passed, each side enjoying success and enduring losses. Rommel's Luftwaffe formation increased its number of Bf109s to about 130, when III/JG53 returned from Sicily and Crete.

Air Marshal Sir Arthur Tedder estimated that by 15 June, he would have available 49 Commonwealth squadrons with 800 aircraft, against an Axis total of 1,200. He also had enough personnel for another 18.5 squadrons, but no aircraft. Tedder put little value in simple numbers of machines on opposing sides. He believed that the true worth could not be presented as statistics: aircraft capabilities, training, leadership, reserves, location and available alternates for withdrawal were the important factors in his opinion. Taking these into account, he believed his force was sufficient to support the land offensive.

3 Squadron, meanwhile, returned to operations, flying sweeps and escorts over the battle areas and enemy territory. Ross Biden, in Geoff Chinchen's C Flight, met his first enemy aircraft on his 11th operational sortie, and on his 13th sortie, on 16 May, was shot up by a 109. He noted that bomb-racks were fitted on 21 May.

On 22 May, Kittyhawks from 112 and 250 Squadrons were to escort nine Bostons of 24 Squadron South African Air Force (SAAF) to bomb Martuba. Three other Kittyhawk squadrons were sent out ahead, to divert attention from the main formation. 3, 260 and 450 Squadrons provided the diversion force. Nicky, on his 52nd operational flight, was leading four Kittyhawks in the 12-plane squadron formation. They climbed to 11,000 feet north west of El Adem. When the formation was 15 miles [24 km] east of Bomba diving 109s were engaged, but with no result.

A Messerschmitt Bf109

32 miles [50 km] east of Tmimi, four Bf109s of II/JG27 dived on 450 Squadron, the top cover, and shot down Sergeants Quirk and Williams.   Nicky climbed, and saw a 109 also climbing in a spiral below him. He dived and in a steep turn raked the 109 with fire; it slowly rolled over and fell onto its back. Nicky did not see any actual damage from his fire, but the 109 was confirmed destroyed.   When he arrived back at base, he was forced to use the auxiliary pump to lower the main wheels, and in the landing damaged the tail and engine cowl.

In the combat, Squadron Leader Gibbes claimed a 109, which later was confirmed, while Flight Lieutenant Rose claimed one as a probable.   Gibbes' victory was identified as Unteroffizier Sdun, who was wounded.   Meanwhile, I and III Gruppen JG27 had attacked the other RAF formation, and claimed six, but actually three were lost; a single 109 was claimed.

On 26 May, General Rommel began a series of attacks which eventually drove the British forces back to Egypt and to the El Alamein position. The official British view was that the moves back were a 'strategic withdrawal', but those involved knew it was a retreat forced by German successes, and sometimes a retreat which verged on chaos, with large quantities of supplies simply abandoned to Rommel's forces.

At 07.20 on the 26th, in an attack on four Ju88s and six Bf109s, Bobby Gibbes shot down a 109, and turned for the bombers, but a rear gunner hit the Kittyhawk, it began to burn, and Gibbes was forced to parachute. He injured his ankle, and until he returned from medical attention, Nicky assumed command of the squadron, with the rank of Squadron Leader.   In the combat, Nicky himself fired at five enemy, with no result.

On this day, 3 Squadron flew its first operation as fighter-bombers, with 250-pound [113kg] bombs under the fuselages of the Kittyhawks. The bombs had extended nose fuses, so they would detonate above ground rather than bury themselves before exploding.   At 19.00, 12 squadron aircraft, six carrying bombs, attacked the enemy airfield at Tmimi; four scored direct hits in the dispersal area.   This was Ross Biden's 15th sortie.

The British forces were in retreat, and the air units were given a rather simple directive: to make as many attacks as possible against the defined enemy targets, particularly the supply line along the coastal road.   This had to be done while the squadron forward bases themselves were moving back.   A period of intense bombing and strafing operations began on 27 May, when five operations were flown, totalling 19 sorties, against Axis forces in the Bir Hacheim area.   The Free French formation in the British desert armies was holding a southern position there, which Rommel had to destroy before he could force his way around that flank. The embattled French fought bravely, the Germans persisted, and dubbed the battle area 'the Cauldron'.   Nicky flew one sortie, but had to force land at Sidi Rezegh, and clear a rough runway to take off again, while the German forces were actually visible on the horizon.

Warrant Officer Harold Norman, on his fifth operational sortie with the squadron, learned that the Fighter Command adage 'do not straggle' was based in truth. He fell behind the squadron while strafing enemy motor vehicles and suddenly was hit from above and behind by a volley of shot which smashed through the cockpit and instruments into the engine, then from port into the wingroot and engine, which died at once. Two 109s were behind him. At 1200 feet, Norman baled out and was taken prisoner.

On 28 May, 35 sorties were flown; on the 29th, 17. Ross Biden flew four sorties, in different aircraft, on the 28th. The targets were so close that the last two flights were of only 45 minutes and 35 minutes each. Nicky recommended Biden for a commission at about this time.

Shot down

On 30 May, intense air attacks were made on Axis forces in the 'Cauldron' battle area, and the Luftwaffe reacted strongly. 19 RAF aircraft were lost, for three Luftwaffe claimed destroyed and two probables. Bf109s of III/JG53 and I/JG27 engaged Bostons escorted by South African Kittyhawks of 2 Squadron SAAF, but also fought 250 and 3 Squadron RAAF. Feldwebel Kaiser of I/JG27 claimed two Kittyhawks: Nicky Barr and Sergeant Colin McDiarmid.

3 Squadron had attacked its ground targets, and climbed to cover 250 Squadron while they bombed in their turn. Enemy aircraft were reported 2,000 feet above, in the sun. Pairs of 109s, enjoying the advantage of height and speed, made diving attacks on the Kittyhawks. While one pair was climbing after their lunge, another pair would be coming down. Colin McDiarmid was shot down and killed; Nicky, now at ground level, turned into another diving 109 and quickly swung after it, looking up at the belly and tail of the Messerschmitt; fired; the 109 dived earthwards but no crash was seen; Nicky's Kittyhawk was thumped and flung half onto its back, one wing past the vertical. He thought it was a hit by anti-aircraft, possibly blast from one of the many 88mm gun batteries in the area, rolled upright - 'very close to the ground indeed' - and the propellor hit the earth.

Nicky crash landed and looked around:- other 109s were still at height, and Ju87s were bombing. The Kittyhawk later was classified as being Category 2 damage. Nicky was in the actual battle area.
'I've never been in a place so nasty and noisy in my life... War in a fighter cockpit had been relatively quiet for me, but this was frightening.'

For about an hour, he crawled and evaded some Afrika Korps motorised units which were about to capture him. Then someone shouted to him through a loud-hailer that he was in a minefield, and not to move. Finally, after he spent two hours in the crossfire, the 7th Hussars and Gloucestershires forced back the Germans far enough that Nicky could make his way across the two hundred or so metres of mined ground to friendly territory. An Army doctor noticed blood coming from Nicky's nose and ears, so he was sent to the Army hospital in Tobruk, and spent the night there under observation for concussion. It had been his 60th operational flight. Nicky returned to 3 Squadron next day. The whole incident resulted in a second award of 'The Flying Boot'.

'For me, that day was the most concentrated and extended period of abject fear in all my life.   To me, air-to-air combat, strafing and dive-bombing were relatively quiet and acceptable by comparison with the hell, noise and terror of ground battle.   I hoped I would never ever be exposed to ground fighting again.'

The squadron flew 12 sorties on 31 May.   During the month, eight aircraft had been lost or written off.   Ross Biden was hit by anti-aircraft fire, but returned to base.

June 1942

On 1 June 1942, Nicky returned to the squadron.   Sandstorms in the morning held the air forces on the ground until the afternoon.   At 18.30, 3 Squadron RAAF and 112 Squadron RAF took off, Nicky leading five aircraft from 3 Squadron, and there were four from 112.   Enemy were reported by ground control 'Turtle' to be 17 miles [27 km] south south east of Gazala, and they flew there, and then further, another 17 miles.   The radar was not accurate.   Then enemy were seen above at the 3 o'clock position: four Ju88s of I/KG54, four Bf110s, and Bf109s of III/JG53.   The 109s and 110s attacked from the 5 o'clock direction, almost directly astern.

A Messerschmitt Bf110, a Bf109

The Kittyhawks whipped around to face them, and Nicky fired at a Bf110 from the front quarter, saw strikes and flames from the port engine, and the wing dropped; by the time he turned, the enemy aircraft were out of sight, up-sun in the haze.   A 109 dived through the top cover - 112 Squadron - but did not pull up; Nicky was behind it, on the port quarter; a long burst set it on fire.   Pilot Officer Coward and Sergeant Neill also claimed a Bf109 each; Leutnant Karl Heinz Quaritsch of III/JG53 was shot down, crash-landing in Axis territory.   III/ZG26 lost three Bf110s, reportedly to ground fire.

There was little flying on 2 June because of sandstorms, but on the 3rd there was a resurgence of activity.   3 Squadron carried out one ground attack operation.   Elsewhere, 5 Squadron SAAF engaged Ju87s of I/StG3 near Bir Hacheim, and claimed nine destroyed.   Leutnant Hans Joachim Marseille, I/JG27, demonstrated his masterly air to air gunnery, claiming six Tomahawks in 11 minutes, and the South African squadron did lose six destroyed or force-landed after damage in the action.   Marseille's cannon jammed after ten rounds, and he carried on with only the two 7.9mm machineguns mounted over the engine.

3 Squadron pilot strength was badly reduced.   Nicky wrote in his log book, "Desperately short of pilots."   Some had been stood down from operations for return to Australia, and others had been removed from operational flying on the orders of the squadron doctor, who was alert for signs of exhaustion.   Nicky remembered that about seven pilots who had come as far as 3 Squadron, had gone to Khartoum for the course there, but had not rejoined the squadron.   He enquired of RAAF HQ, but no one knew of these pilots, nor seemed to care much.   Curious, he persisted, and eventually discovered that some had not flown on operations at all, had returned to Australia and even been promoted!   Much later, he learned that some were presenting themselves as experienced operational pilots

from the Desert.   Nicky then made it his business to locate these men and inform them that due to the pilot shortage in June 1942, and the vital need to halt Rommel's forces, pilots had been required to fly intensively despite tiredness and despite being due for rest; several had been killed.   Nicky made it clear to each of the men concerned that he held them personally responsible for the losses - they had shirked their responsibility. He believed that in this case and in others, there had been a poor selection of pilots, and some men were wrongly cast as fighter pilots.

Nicky also came to believe that another aspect of Air Force assessment was incorrect. 'Many postings and even promotions were assessed predominantly upon how many hours the person had flown, because that was the inevitable question asked in order to determine experience.   I was more pre-occupied in finding out what pilots had done in the hours they had flown.   That was much more relevant.'

As his Service experience broadened, Nicky came to the opinion that in many instances the best people for a particular job were not employed in it.   In a broader sense, the nation at war was not making best use of its assets.   Not only were the best people for particular jobs employed elsewhere, but in many cases the wrong person for a particular job was performing it.   This, of course, has been noticed by many in all walks of life and in all eras.   Nicky also formed the opinion that, while there were some notable exceptions who made it difficult to generalise accurately, many pre-war RAAF permanent officers failed in war service, and many others with opportunity to do so did not get onto operations. Nicky believed that the peace-time selection of personnel was basically flawed, with promotions based on seniority, not merit.

In the distant wastes of the Pacific, at Midway Island, the US and Imperial Japanese Navies were about to engage in a decisive battle.   A Japanese victory would have resulted in their domination of the entire Pacific and Indian basins.   The balance between victory and defeat was to be tilted by the 70 men of the US Navy dive-bomber squadrons led by Lieutenant Commander Wade McClusky.   Well conscious of the inherent dangers in taking heavily-laden single-engined aircraft on long flights over the sea, aware that he was leading the only dive-bomber force available in the battle area, McCluskey went on beyond his briefed search range, and found the Japanese aircraft carriers at the most opportune time to attack.   Three carriers were sunk in the attack, and a fourth next day. The balance of power in the Pacific had been tilted in favour of the USA, and the Western democracies.

On 4 June, 3 Squadron flew 16 sorties over the North African battle area; on the 6th, 39 sorties; and in the next ten days, flew another 300 sorties.   These attacks were made by pilots living in primitive conditions in the desert, in aircraft maintained, fuelled and armed by crews existing in the same conditions, with men and machines subjected to the stresses of operational life, enemy air attack at night, strafing by day, and the dust, grit and relentless heat of the region.   Heavy ground fire was a constant threat to the pilots on the bombing and strafing sorties, added to the ever present danger from fighters. On 12 June, in attacks on three large concentrations of enemy troops south west of El Adem, Sergeant Bray was hit by anti-aircraft fire, but landed in a mine-field; the tail of the Kittyhawk was blown off, but he survived.   Stevens crashed in the squadron dispersal area; Finlayson's aircraft was damaged; Sergeant Ross Biden was hit by anti-aircraft fire, and he made his first forced-landing on his 32nd operational sortie; Alderson's aircraft was damaged on landing.

Nicky's logbook contains numerous short entries evocative of the sorties.
6 June: 'Direct hits on one tank, armoured cars, and motor transport. Heavy ack-ack.'
7th: '20-25 tanks bombed and strafed; three fires; heavy ack-ack.'
8th: 'Motor transport; strafed two staff cars; Hurricanes two missing.'
9th: 'Motor transport; six guns, 15 tanks.' 'Seven 109s intercepted at El Adem, got a burst at one, but they all dived away.'
11th: 'Cauldron area, 30+ enemy aircraft seen but did not attack; bombed with Bostons.'
12th: 'El Adem area, heavy anti-aircraft; Biden hit, but OK!' **Later:** 'Results excellent on motor transport and tents in thick concentration; Geoff Chinchen missing.'

Chinchen was shot down in flames by ground fire, but parachuted from only 700 feet, and was taken prisoner by a patrol of German panzer troops; he remained with the panzers in the battle for a few days. Thomas' aircraft was damaged; Biden again force-landed. Tomorrow, and the day after, and the day after that, meant more of the same.

On the tenth day of such operational flying, 16 June, 3 Squadron set a record, flying 69 sorties in the Sidi Rezegh area; Nicky alone flew six and Lou Spence flew five.
The terse logbook entries from Nicky are:
'With Lou Spence. Bombed motor transport behind 15 heavy Jerry tanks; two direct hits.' Later: *'Hurricanes accounted for six tanks and numerous motor transport.' Later still: '10 aircraft dropped bombs in the centre of Italian lorried infantry - yippee!' And later, at 14.50: 'Bombed motor transport and troop carriers. Four 109s attacked, damaged one - pieces of tail flew off.'* South west of Sidi Rezegh, seven Kittyhawks led by Nicky

June 1942. 'After a scrap. Looking very jaded,' commented Nicky. The P-40 was hit in the tail.(AWB)

had been attacked head-on by four 109s. He fired at one, saw two flashes on the engine cowling, but the 109 dived away into the haze and was not seen. Later, at 16.20: *'Bombed Rommel's HQ. Six fires. Four 109s attacked; Sergeant Donald wounded, Sergeant Ryan killed; Sergeant Biden killed. Heavy ack-ack.'*

Nine Kittyhawks on the way back to base were attacked; Sergeant Ryan failed to return. Ross Biden made his third forced landing in five days, but this time the 250-pound [113 kg] bomb was still attached; it exploded, killing him. Nicky saw the tragedy, and later 'Located and identified Sergeant Biden. 109 chased me home.' Ross Biden had a grand total of 262 flying hours, and had flown at least 36 operational sorties, with over 20 against the Axis forces advancing in the offensive. To Nicky, Ross Biden was 'just one of the many fine young men I would have wanted to survive and be with throughout the peace. He made a lasting impression on me.' Biden's commission was notified after his death.

A 3 Squadron Kittyhawk with bomb visible under fuselage
(RAAF Museum)

However, this 16 June 1942 saw a tremendous day's flying by a squadron of 14 aircraft: 69 sorties flown, 61 bombs dropped. Air Marshal Sir Arthur Tedder sent a personal hand-written note to Nicky, the squadron commander:
"Congratulations on most efficient and successful fighter operations past two days. The bombers did very well because of the secure protection by 450 and 3 Sqns. The fighting by 3 Sqn was grand. You have put the Germans back a good pace and we must keep them there."

Nicky went to all three Messes in his squadron and read out the message. He thought that Australians did their best when the situation was at its worst.
'I know, convincingly, there is a gene in many Australians called Fighting Spirit. It shows up on sports fields, in business and in war. It is at its best when situations are at their worst.'

While the media regaled the general public with accounts of the exploits of pilots who shot down enemy, this ignored the vital work required of all squadron members in successfully escorting the bombers, and accurately carrying out ground attack sorties. These two aspects of operations were of more importance to the overall plan of battle. The Nazi propaganda machinery quite actively sought out and identified to the German public 'aces' in all parts of the fighting: fighter pilots, U-Boat commanders, tank-commanders, anti-tank gunners, dive-bomber pilots and so on. Another serious weakness in the direction of the Luftwaffe was not rectified until it was too late: the standing of fighter pilots was determined by the number of enemy fighters destroyed, not by the destruction of the more important Allied bombers.

What was being forged in these desert battles were the techniques for provision of close and sustained air support to the ground forces, to the limits of available technology and tactics.   In two years, in June 1944, the Allied forces which landed in Normandy would have at their disposal the most modern and effective organisation for detection and identification of enemy positions and units, and for speedy application of firepower onto those targets.

June 1942.
Taking off on yet another sortie.
(AWB via Russell Guest)

On 17 June 1942, nine sorties were flown in two operations by 3 Squadron.   Near El Adem three aircraft were hit by anti-aircraft fire, and one Kittyhawk was shot down.   Otto Schulz, now an Oberleutnant, with the Knight's Cross and 51 victories, shot down a 274 Squadron Kittyhawk, flown by the Canadian Wally Conrad, who force-landed successfully.   Schulz, as usual, swept in to strafe - but another Kittyhawk was there, fired, and Schulz was killed.   Schulz' victor was the Canadian J.E. Edwards, then a sergeant, who went on to score aerial victories of 15 destroyed and eight probables, with 13 damaged, plus another 14 destroyed or damaged on the ground.   Oberleutnant Marseille shot down six aircraft in the Gambut area to bring his score to 101, and he was at once called to Berlin to receive the Oak Leaves to the Knight's Cross.   Most of Marseille's victories can be identified in RAF, RAAF and South African Air Force records.

On the 18th, 3 Squadron moved to Sidi Azzeiz, and flew 34 sorties to the end of 23rd June.   As the squadron now was engaged in close support operations for the army, air-to-air combat was incidental.   However, the Australian squadron had been the leading unit in air victories in the desert theatre.

The sky over the German and Italian forces was rarely free of British, Australian or South African aircraft which bombed and strafed any visible target.   The cumulative effect of a month of battle on the Axis forces was extremely wearing.   Great advances had been made, great successes achieved, but the attacking infantry, armour, artillery and engineers simply were being driven to destruction.   Rommel's battlefield brilliance, his personal reputation, and the willingness of his troops, had combined to defeat the mediocre British command time and again, but human flesh, spirit and nerves could go on only for so long.   Tobruk had been held determinedly in 1941 by General Morshead's 9th Australian Division AIF, but now was captured from the South Africans on 21 June, and Rommel's forces crossed into Egypt on 24 June.   Morshead's men were appalled and contemptuous.   British Prime Minister Winston Churchill was enraged, and began a series of sackings of his senior commanders in the Middle East. Churchill was well aware that the 'Ultra' signals intercept system gave the British high command in Cairo excellent information on the Axis forces. Despite this, when the fighting began, the British command in the Middle East seemed unable to cope with Erwin Rommel.

Rommel's forces received a great boost to morale by capturing Tobruk, and Rommel was promoted Generalfeldmarschall. But, ever aware of the battle requirements, he confided in a letter to his wife that he would have preferred an extra division. Also ever the opportunist when his foe was in disarray, he decided that the supplies captured in Tobruk would be enough to sustain a further attack through to the Suez Canal. The weak point in all this was petrol. To Rommel's fury, most of the fuel supply at Tobruk had been destroyed as his forces entered the town. It was imperative that tankers from Italy come safely to Africa. A touch of light comedy was provided by Italian Dictator Benito Mussolini, 'Il Duce', who arrived at Derna with resplendent uniforms and a white horse, for the expected victory parade through Cairo.

The fortunes of the Western democracies in the Pacific basin had been decided at Midway by a few US Navy dive-bomber aircrews. Now, three weeks later, the balance between success and defeat in North Africa, and so in the Mediterranean, with all that implied for the entry of Turkey into the war, for the progress of the German forces in Africa and southern Russia, and possibly through Iraq and Persia to India, was to be tilted by a few Commonwealth personnel: the British Commonwealth 'Ultra' Intelligence teams and aircrews of the reconnaissance and torpedo strike aircraft on Malta. The RAF torpedo squadrons, because of the short-comings of the aerial torpedo, were required to fly directly at their target, to go in to less than a kilometre, at relatively low speed and low height, in the face of fire from automatic weapons and anti-aircraft artillery, plus cope with enemy fighter interception. The torpedo strike aircrews suffered frightful losses, and only a handful survived as few as five operational flights. Land and air battles raged over the El Alamein positions, but all depended on the destruction of the ships from Italy. The RAF torpedo squadrons were sacrificed, but Rommel never received enough petrol or other materials to enable him to push through the El Alamein position, and then go on the remaining mere 100 kilometres to the great prize of Alexandria, and further east to Cairo and Suez. Mussolini and the white horse returned to Italy - but not before he was seen at close range by Nicky Barr.

A Fiat G50

On 24 June, Nicky was leading four Kittyhawks at 3,200 feet, just below patchy 6/10th cloud. They were looking for Rommel's spearhead and any Commonwealth forces escapees from Tobruk. Four 109s, probably from II/JG27, on a 'free hunt', attacked from behind. Nicky whipped around in a turn, and dodged a 109, then found himself behind a Fiat G50 itself shooting from behind at Sergeant Fox, who was in CV-N. The G50 was in a steep turn, but Nicky stayed with it, fired and hit it, and saw it hit the ground inverted; other pilots reported seeing it burst into flames. Off to a side, Nicky saw Sergeant Lloyd Boardman firing at close range into a 109. Nicky turned to leave the area, but saw below the battle three fires burning on the ground; heavy anti-aircraft fire peppered the sky around the planes.

On the way back, Nicky's engine seriously overheated, so he selected a suitable convenient claypan and landed, to allow the engine to cool.   Lloyd Boardman had destroyed the 109 with two bursts, while ignoring the anti-aircraft fire, and also left the battle area.   He counted five burning aircraft on the ground in an area of one square mile [2.5 sq.km].   He noticed a Kittyhawk on the ground, so landed alongside, and found it was his Commanding Officer.   Nicky assured him all was well, so Boardman took off and returned to base.

In less than a month after taking command of the squadron, Nicky had led 37 operational missions, including air to air combat, dive-bombing, and strafing, at a time when the squadron was involved in frequent moves during the retreat.   As he was on the sports field, so with the P-40 was Nicky an 'all-rounder'.

The matter of fighter pilot victories has been of great interest since the beginning of air combat, and is a subject well beyond the scope of this book.   However, as an experienced pilot of the 1941-42 Desert campaigns, Nicky Barr made several points.
'Without cameraguns to support pilot claims in their combat reports, results of air battles relied upon cross-referencing with other squadrons and pilots, RAF Headquarters Intelligence and Army reports.   During a prolonged retreat, with combats predominantly over enemy territory, confirmations became infrequent.   It is of passing interest to note that I only claimed six aircraft destroyed which were confirmed.   Another six were claimed as "probable or damaged" but were officially confirmed as "destroyed" through RAF Headquarters.   In combat, there was no merit whatsoever in hanging around or being preoccupied about whether you had a claim or not.'

The squadron operations record noted that four pilots had been shot down during the day, and stated that this was due to tiredness.   By this, it meant 'operational tiredness.' Nicky, and Bobby Gibbes, had tried to have people posted from the squadron on medical grounds, rather than wait for tragedy to occur.   It was at this time that he decided to try to find the pilots not seen since the OTU period.   Nicky also had protested in diplomatic service terms to the RAF about the fact that 3 Squadron RAAF, with the highest number of air-to-air victory claims, had been employed on ground attack operations while squadrons with lesser tallies had been employed against the Luftwaffe.   Air Commodore George Beamish was a huge man who had played Rugby for Ireland.   When Nicky was introduced to the gathered officers as another international Rugby player, Beamish placed a huge hand on the shoulder of the young Australian squadron leader, and boomed, 'I always eat little boys like you!'   However, Beamish listened, spoke to Air Marshal Tedder, and the squadron role was changed back to air combat.

On 25 June, 42 sorties were flown by 3 Squadron RAAF, but this was surpassed on the 26th, when 61 sorties were flown.   3 Squadron was not alone in achieving such high sortie rates in the desert conditions, as 112 Squadron RAF flew 69 sorties, and 450 Squadron RAAF flew eight bomber escorts.

Shot down in flames

The first 3 Squadron operation on 26 June was at 09.10, a bomber escort, with the Kittyhawks carrying bombs for their own attacks.   In his logbook, Nicky noted that they bombed the enemy spearhead, but then were chased home and strafed on the ground. On the next operation, the 109s struck well, shooting down two Bostons and two Kittyhawks, for no loss.   At 12.05, five Kittyhawks took off to escort Bostons to attack over 100 enemy transport vehicles at Mingar El Amar.   It was Nicky's 90th operational flight, and his third that morning.   109s had attacked three times during the operation. As the bombing attack closed and the Kittyhawks were leaving the target area, Nicky found his engine was over-heating and losing power, so decided to dive steeply in the hope that the cooler engine would provide greater power.   Then Murphy's Law came into force: two 109s pounced and attacked Nicky.

'It was no surprise to see a pair coming through on me.   I evaded one attack, before being hit in the port wing and fuselage by a good burst of cannon.'

One 109 pulled away, but the second closed to 30 yards [metres] and hit the Kittyhawk.. The other Australians saw a big flash on the Kittyhawk, and it dived steeply, on fire. Nicky knew that he was being hit from above and rear, knew there were hits on the engine and wing, and on the tail; he lost fore-and-aft control; he was hit in the leg; flames were licking around his legs and arms, and parachute pack, and filling the cockpit; airspeed was so high the cockpit canopy was hard to open.

'Compared with the previous two occasions, this was a truly hairy situation.   I've no idea of my dive speed, but suddenly, in a flash, the canopy shot back to the armour-plate and I was sucked out of the cockpit with such force that the flames on my arm, hand, trouser leg and parachute harness were extinguished. My vision was now impaired and I had no idea where the ground was.'

He thought about opening the parachute at once, but did not want to do so, as there had been known instances of German pilots machinegunning people in their parachutes. While this was denied by the Luftwaffe, Nicky himself had seen it happen when Bobby Gibbes was C.O., Peter Jeffrey had seen it, and another squadron also had reported it. Realising that he might not have been as high as he thought, Nicky pulled the rip-cord, and floated down safely enough.

'My attempted one leg landing was abysmal, but I recall feeling euphoric about everything when releasing the parachute harness.   Then came oblivion.'

Nicky was shot down by Oberleutnant Werner Schroer, III/JG27, who claimed a total of 61 victories in Africa, including one victory at the time and place Nicky was hit.   Schroer survived the war, as a Major with the Oakleaves and Swords to the Knight's Cross, and 114 victories.

Nicky had been flying Kittyhawk CV-N.   As the squadron was returning, a Kittyhawk was seen on the ground - it also was lettered CV-N, but was the aircraft of Sergeant Fox, who was last seen with a Fiat G50 shooting at him on the 24th.

Nicky could not see very well, as his eyelashes had been seared, in addition he had third-degree burns to his legs and arms and wounds to his leg and foot. He passed into and out of a coma, and has fragmentary memories of the next days. At one time, he heard someone speaking in Italian, saying that he was dead. The man had felt for a pulse, but a piece of shrapnel was pressing on the vein, and no pulse was evident. After many hours of 'no dreams, no lights, just nothingness', Nicky arrived by stretcher at a German casualty clearing station, where his burns were dressed and his badly injured leg put in plaster. Later, due mainly to neglect, on three occasions, amputation was seriously considered; the wounds troubled him well after the war. Nicky, with others, then lay for two days in the open.

Near by was a friendly German officer, a native of Hamburg, who was an amputee. However, the rigours of the journey by road were too much, and this officer, and six Allied prisoners, died en route to the hospital in Tobruk. The iron tray of a captured 8th Army truck was not suitable for use as an ambulance, but nothing else was available. All the dead were cremated by the roadside. The survivors were put in an Italian hospital on the outskirts of Tobruk, and on 6 July were visited by Benito Mussolini. Nicky's comment on the event was 'very impressive little man.' But he also knew of about 40 deaths in the past three days, from a combination of dysentery and mis- or ill-treatment. His leg was so badly injured that doctors in Africa, then in Italy, seriously considered amputation, but always were refused permission by Nicky. On 7 July, in company with two wounded Afrika Korps officers and other patients, he was put aboard the hospital ship *Citta di Trapani*, for Naples.

Also aboard was Rudy Leu, an RAAF pilot on 112 Squadron RAF, suffering from burns to both hands and arms. Leu flew Tomahawks and Kittyhawks, and since 20 November 1941 claimed six destroyed, a probably and a damaged, plus a share in another destroyed, in seven combats. Later, Leu described the vessel as 'a misery ship, taking ages to go anywhere.' The ship was crowded, but with no visible medical support provided. They arrived in Naples on the 12th - after a torpedo from a British submarine was seen crossing the bows. Nicky was moved to a hospital at Caserta, near Naples, where his wounds and burns were dressed once in six days, and dysentery cases were dying at the rate of 35 a day. On 24 July, he was graded as a serious case - he believes due to neglect - and put on a train to Bergamo, to the German-controlled 'Hospitale Clementino'. Food provided for the journey was one piece of bread and two bowls of boiled rice. Near Rome, bricks were thrown through the train windows. Four patients died on the trip, through sheer negligence. On arrival though, the quality of treatment improved markedly - a number of Allied doctors and medical staff had been sent there after being captured in North Africa. Some of the hospital staff were nuns. One of these, for no particular reason, one night at 2.30 a.m. decided to look in on the prisoners, and discovered Nicky was haemorrhaging severely. She raised the alarm, help came, and his life was saved. She was known as 'The Sister with the kind heart.' Nicky did not forget this, and on visits to Italy after the war always found and hugged the nun, somewhat to the surprise of onlookers.

Meanwhile, in early July, Rommel's thrust into Egypt had been halted, mainly by the fresh 9th Australian Division making strong attacks on the Italian forces in the northern coastal sector, at Tel El Eisa. Here, the Aussies destroyed 621 Signals Company, closing Rommel's window into the British command and operations rooms. Field Marshal Claude Auchinleck, the British commander, took command personally of the land fighting, refused to allow Rommel to bounce him eastwards, and laid the basis of Rommel's eventual defeat in Africa. Unfortunately, Auchinleck also refused to allow Prime Minister Winston Churchill to bounce him in any direction, and was relieved of his command. On 30 September, Hans-Joachim Marseille, the leading Luftwaffe fighter pilot in Africa, died when he had to bale out of his Messerschmitt after what was reported to be engine failure, but struck the tail and fell without opening his parachute. The 22-year old Berliner had claimed 158 victories in 382 operational flights in the Battle of Britain and Africa. Rommel also was unable to bend to his will the new British army commander, General Bernard Montgomery, and by early November, after another decisive battle, was in retreat from the El Alamein position. On 8 November 1942, Allied forces landed in Morocco, and Rommel was forced to fight on two fronts. Far too late, the extra units he had asked for were sent from Europe. By early December, the outcome was plain to see, as the Axis forces in Africa were squeezed from east and west. In winter-bound Russia, the encircled German 6th Army fought on at Stalingrad. Disasters were developing for the Nazi regime in the East and the South.

Meanwhile, some of the captured pilots had been having their own adventures. Geoff Chinchen, after parachuting from 700 feet and spending a few days with the panzers, had been sent to Derna and to Benghazi, and flown to Italy. On 12 September, a train-load of prisoners was sent north through Italy. Chinchen had a table knife, and laboriously cut a hole in the wooden door of the wagon, through which the bolt was manipulated, the door opened, and about a dozen men escaped near Trento early in the morning. Among them were Bob Jones and 'Tiny' Cameron, on his 31st birthday. There was no plan, and the escapers had only the clothes they wore. The guards fired on the tumbling figures, but hit no one. Chinchen did not manage to get out before the escapes were halted.

Cameron was captured, and spent the rest of the war in captivity, until liberation by US forces in April 1945. Bob Jones found himself to be some ten kilometres from Trento, swapped his extra clothes for food with the peasants, and walked to Switzerland in a week. Geoff Chinchen, meanwhile, had been placed in Fort Bismarck with other prisoners. When it was learned that all the inmates were to be moved in October 1943, Chinchen and another man hid. The guards thought they had escaped, and both men remained in hiding until the prison was emptied, then cautiously executed their real escape. They contacted the French Resistance, and were guided to Switzerland in November 1943. There, Chinchen again met Bob Jones. Life in Switzerland began to pall.

On 4 December 1942, with an escort of an officer and three soldiers, Nicky was taken by train from Bergamo to Milan, for interrogation by Luftwaffe officers. On 10 December, he was sent to Gavi prison for six and a half months. This prison had a very high mortality rate, and Mussolini closed it in 1932, but re-opened it for wartime requirements. It then was titled *No.5 Punishment Camp*. The prisoners were 'dangerous enemy officers', murderers, hardened criminals, those with religious beliefs who opposed the Fascist regime, and similar people. Nicky spent six and a half months in the castle. On 20 June 1943, he was sent back to the Bergamo hospital, and his entire right leg was cased in plaster, to prevent his escape.

POW Camp No.5, Ligure. The 'X' marks Nicky's cell.
(AWB via Russell Guest)

An amusing incident transpired during his stay in hospital. The Italians were told of a new method of performing an appendectomy, using the then-new modern cross incision on the patient, and it was arranged that a captured Allied doctor would demonstrate the technique. The prison hospital's operating theatre was carefully prepared, with an imposing array of cameras and arc-lights to record the procedure for other doctors. One item which had been difficult to keep cleaned to the operating room standard was the crucifix, one of which hung in every room. Nicky, with an armed guard, was brought in to interpret; an Italian Major supervised the entire room. The patient was brought in, the Allied doctor, a Protestant, prepared to begin, when an Italian staff member tripped on a power cable, and the entire array of cameras and lights was dragged down in the collapse; lights crashed over the operating table, doctor, staff and patient. The captured Allied doctor had sufficient Italian to shout, "*Basta!!*" ('Enough!!'), and strode through the wreckage to the crucifix. He clasped his hands and prayed, "*Oh God, send your son down to see what these bastards are doing to me!*"

The supervising Major asked Nicky what the doctor had said, but, looking at the armed guards, Nicky was a little doubtful that a full translation should be given. The Major insisted, and Nicky mentally shrugged, then repeated the doctor's prayer. "*Did he really say that*?" demanded the Major; Nicky assured him it was true. The Major promptly shouted the translation to all in the room, and collapsed with laughter. The story flew round like lightning: a Protestant doctor had prayed to Our Lord!

Then, in August, with a five-man Italian escort, Nicky was sent to Milan. He did not want to spend the rest of the war, however long that might be, in a prison camp and away from his wife. At that time, his wife was 'the image, the focal point' of his life, and returning to her was the main point of his efforts when in enemy areas. Allied forces had totally defeated the Axis in Africa in May, and in July had invaded Sicily. An invasion somewhere on the Italian peninsula was imminent, but where this was to take place was unknown to those in captivity.

Nicky escaped from the Italians and almost reached Switzerland, in fact, was in sight of Lake Como, when caught by border guards. Nicky hit one man on the head with a rock, but his companions, with dogs, re-captured Nicky and gave him a severe beating. He was sent back to hospital in Milan, and needed some weeks to recover. Then he was court-martialled, as the injured border guard allegedly had died. The penalty for murder was death, but Nicky was not found guilty, mainly due to the efforts of a Swiss Colonel who represented the Protecting Power under the Red Cross agreements. Nicky was sent back to Gavi, sentenced to 90 days solitary confinement, but the Geneva Conventions allowed only 30. This barrier was overcome by awarding three consecutive periods of 30 days, separated only by a single 30-minute period in the camp yard. *'I was a loner before that,'* said Nicky, *'but it made me more so. I learnt a lot about myself.'* The last 30 days were spent with a Croatian professor of languages, who helped Nicky improve his German and Italian.

Nicky also had reinforced his opinion about 'Fighting Spirit.'
'It was evidenced so many times during my POW hospital and prison days. Chaps with shocking wounds, many double amputees, fighting on, while others with relatively minor problems without the will to live were not with us next morning.'

The prisoners were to be moved, under German SS guard, to another camp. All were warned that those remaining in a carriage after any escapes would be shot immediately after 'Appell', the roll-call. This caused great resentment in the carriages when some people made it clear they were going to escape, regardless of the danger to themselves

Roccapretura (L'Aquila) - Veduta parziale

L'Aquila, the area where Nicky operated with the guerrillas. He sheltered in the square-fronted house with single door and narrow upper window, facing camera.
(AWB via Russell Guest)

and the threat to those who remained.   Nicky did leave the train, between Piacenza and Bologna, despite the efforts of those who did not wish to go, and who hindered those who did.   As promised, the SS did shoot some of, but not all, the prisoners who remained. Nicky, for a time after escaping from the train, was in company with Captain Ray Conway AIF, who had been captured on Crete in 1941.   Conway was much fitter than Nicky, and it was decided they would go their own ways, so, after shaking hands, Conway left. Nicky went into the Emilia Toscanna mountains to recuperate.   He then spent 2 1/2 months with the partisans, but the group was betrayed, and he was captured again. Near Verona, SS guards used rifle butts, pistols and boots to inflict another severe beating. Once more he escaped from the prison train.   Five escapers were successful; another 23 were caught and shot by the Germans.   Alone, Nicky made his way south through the Brenner Pass in early Spring 1944, through Italy towards the battle area at the Allied landing at Salerno, and contacted a Special Operations Executive [SOE] group in the Abruzzi, who were operating in the Pescara-Chieti areas.   Nicky worked with them for three and a half months, but then contracted malaria, and went through the German lines near Campo di Giove to return to the Allied ground forces.

The simple phrase *'I escaped from..'* was, in Nicky's opinion,
'an over simplification of events before, during and afterwards.   None could have been successful without the warmth, courage and co-operation of many people who became involved in my doings.'

Nicky had been away from the Allied forces for 21 months, and was thoroughly debriefed by a British Colonel.   However, no one from the RAF or RAAF at senior level showed the slightest interest in his experiences.   It was evident that the Permanent Air Force perceived the information gained by a junior wartime officer to be of little value.

Nicky had been awarded a Bar to his DFC on 5th February 1943.   The citation stated that, since the award of the DFC, Nicky had destroyed a further four enemy aircraft, and assumed command of the squadron 'during the critical period of the German advance'. Mention was included of his six sorties in one day, of the forced landing and return flight to the squadron, and being shot down later.   The citation concluded, 'This experience in no way diminished Squadron Leader Barr's zeal to engage the enemy.   Throughout his operational career this officer has displayed outstanding qualities of leadership and devotion to duty.'

Nicky also was awarded the Military Cross, a decoration for action against the enemy on the ground.   The lengthy citation gave a resume of his experiences, from being shot down on 27 June, and first trying to escape from the Italian dressing station, to the escape attempts in Italy.   The citation mentioned that while in the mountains, he organised other escaped prisoners so that many were able to reach Allied lines, and after recapture, escaped again when it was discovered the key to the cell was in the lock on the other side of the door - it was pushed out and dragged inside by a wire.   The citation concluded, *'Squadron Leader Barr acquired a radio transmitter and continued his good work among the prisoners.   Towards the end of February 1944, he obtained guides and brought 10 prisoners through to the Allied lines.'*

Nicky spent the next weeks in an Indian Army hospital, and eventually made his way to 3 Squadron RAAF late in March 1944 - returning 20 months late from his sortie of June 1942. Nicky flew on operations again as early as 21 March, in a Mustang of 603 Squadron, as target marker for 42 Martin B26 Marauders which bombed a fuel and stores park near San Demetrio; many bombs, he noted, fell in the town. He returned to the UK in April, reported to RAAF Headquarters, and in May did a Spitfire conversion course at the Central Gunnery School, Sutton Bridge, from 8 June to 8 July 1944, graduating as an *Above Average* Instructor and Marksman. Later he did a parachute course. On 16 July, Nicky flew a Typhoon of 258 Squadron on a rocket-firing attack on a V1 site in the Pas de Calais area, as his 93rd operation. Nicky asked if he could go to France as an air-to-ground controller, but was told that as an escaped Prisoner of War, this was not allowed. His operational flying against the enemy in Europe was over.

In July, at the Brandesburton Officers' Mess, he was presented with his third 'Flying Boot', an event he recalled as *'a wonderfully happy, low-key affair about a meaningless piece of metal.'*

Nicky returned to Australia through the United States. *'It was sheer delight,'* he recalled of his return. *'It was the most euphoric feeling anyone could have. Anything that happened was a blessing after that.'* In October 1944, he was posted as Chief Instructor, Fighter Training, at Mildura, and found the syllabus needed to be changed. The pilots were being taught what was relevant to the European and Mediterranean theatres, not the South West Pacific Area (SWPA).

Meanwhile, unable to remain in Switzerland any longer, Geoff Chinchen and Bob Jones had again contacted the French Resistance, gone back into France on 1 September, and were taken to Grenoble, where they met US troops, and then went on to the UK.

March 1944. On return to Allied lines; 'still frail'. (AWB)

On 6 November 1944, Nicky flew to New Guinea to gain first- hand knowledge and experience of the operational flying there.   He flew four operations before returning to Mildura. It became obvious to Nicky - and many other people - that Australia and its war effort in the Pacific was being by-passed.   The US forces, led by General Douglas MacArthur, did not want Australian forces in the final campaigns, and certainly not in the final victory over Japan. The RAAF fighter training effort gradually wound down. By the end of the war, in August 1945, Nicky had 1175 hours, in 20 different types of aircraft. On 30 August he was graded as *Exceptional* by Group Captain Peter Jeffrey, CO 2 OTU Mildura. Nicky then went to Heidelberg Repatriation Hospital for three and a half weeks, 'for an overhaul', as he put it.   His war service on discharge totalled five years seven months.   About three years had been overseas service.

In 1949, 1950 and 1951, Nicky was among several experienced RAAF pilots in the Reserve recalled for flying after a break from service, to establish just how much training would be necessary to bring such men up to an acceptable standard in time of emergency. This allowed him to again fly the Wirraway and Mustang, and to convert to the jet-powered De Havilland Vampire.   After the war, Nicky resumed his business career, and became one of Australia's most successful men. He also enjoyed friendship with several of the leading Luftwaffe fighter pilots, including Adolf Galland, Wolfgang Spate and Erhard Braune. Nicky was inducted into the USAF 'Eagles' fraternity, and has attended reunions and ceremonies in Europe, the USA and Australia. At time of writing, he lives in retirement in south-east Queensland with Dot, the girl he married in 1941, and for whom he endured so much in Axis captivity.

* * * * * * * * * *

Peter Jeffrey, Nicky's first CO on 3 Squadron, was awarded the DSO and DFC for his service in North Africa, and returned to Australia to become first CO of the newly raised 75 Squadron RAAF in March 1942, which received P-40 Kittyhawks and moved to defend Port Moresby alone against superior Japanese forces for 44 days, followed by a similar command of 76 Squadron RAAF, and more command postings. He gained five enemy destroyed in the air, plus others strafed on the ground, all in 1941.

Alan Rawlinson, CO of 3 Squadron RAAF when Nicky began operational flying, first engaged enemy in the biplane Gloster Gladiator in 1940, before the Hurricanes and Tomahawks arrived, in which he claimed eight destroyed, two probables and eight damaged. After commanding fighter training units in the Middle East and Australia, he formed 79 Squadron RAAF and led it on service to New Guinea in 1943.   Command of other units followed, and after the war he served in the RAF, before retiring and returning to live in South Australia.

Walter Mailey flew Tomahawks and Kittyhawks with 3 Squadron, and claimed six victories and five damaged German and Italian aircraft, before going to Rhodesia as an instructor and thence back to Australia.

Alan 'Tiny' Cameron claimed six destroyed, one probable and seven damaged before capture.

Appendix 1

Logbook details; selected aircraft flown by Nicky Barr.

71 OTU   Hurricane 2640, 2674, 4782, 4850
                    Mohawk 2507, 2523
                    Tomahawk 386   [first flight]

3 Squadron RAAF

28 November 1941	first operation	Tomahawk AM392
9 December 1941	fourth operation	Tomahawk AN336
		attacked by Bf109s, Rutter & Wilson KIA
12 December 1941	7th operation	Tomahawk AN336 Bf110 destroyed
13 December 1941	8th operation	Tomahawk AN336 Bf109 & Ju88 destroyed
1 January 1942	17th operation	Kittyhawk AK599 Two Ju87 destroyed
11 January	22nd operation	Kittyhawk AK645 Two Bf109 & one G50 destroyed; Shot down near Brega; escaped.
20 February 1942		Received new Kittyhawk, AK903; flew 14 ops in it to 18 April.
9 March 1942	35th operation	Kittyhawk CV*L AK903 One Macchi Mc200 destroyed, one probable, two damaged.
7 May 1942		Kittyhawk AK902; 13 ops in it to 27 May.
22 May 1942	52nd operation	Kittyhawk AL199 One Bf109 destroyed.
30 May 1942	60th operation	Kittyhawk AK889 Shot down at Knightsbridge.
1 June 1942	61st operation	Kittyhawk CV*W AL178 One Bf109 destroyed, one Bf110 damaged.
24 June 1942	84th operation	Kittyhawk AK756 One Fiat G50 destroyed, Bf109 damaged.
26 June 1942	90th operation	Kittyhawk CV*N ET873 Shot down.

258 Squadron RAF, England

16 July 1944	93rd operation	Typhoon AT477 Rocket attack, V1 site, Pas de Calais.

RAAF Kittyhawk squadrons, New Guinea

9-13 November 1944   94-97th operations in Kittyhawks 531 and 806.

Appendix 2
Text of Citations to Awards

Citation to Award of the Distinguished Flying Cross, date 20 February 1942, London Gazette No.35463.

This officer, who commenced operational flying in November, 1941, has displayed the greatest keenness and skill as a fighter pilot.   In December 1941, during a patrol over the Derna area, he shot down a Messerschmitt 110; the next day in the same area, he destroyed a Messerschmitt 110 and a Junkers 88.   One day in January 1942, his squadron formed part of an escort to bomber aircraft operating over El Agheila.   Enemy aircraft were encountered and, in the ensuing engagement, Flying Officer Barr attacked 2 Italian fighters, one of which he shot down.   He then observed one of his fellow pilots, who had been shot down, waving to him from the ground, but, when preparing to make a landing in an attempt to rescue him, Flying Officer Barr was attacked by 2 Messerschmitt 109s.   Although the under-carriage of his aircraft was not fully retracted, he immediately manoeuvred to engage the attackers, only to find that his guns had jammed.   Quickly rectifying the fault he delivered an accurate burst of fire which caused one of the Messerschmitts to disintegrate in the air.   A further 2 enemy joined the combat and Flying Officer Barr was wounded and forced down.   While on the ground he was further wounded by the enemy's fire but, despite this, he made his way through the enemy's lines and rejoined our forces some 3 days later.   He brought back much valuable information regarding the dispositions of enemy tanks and defences.   Flying Officer Barr displayed the greatest courage and tenacity throughout.   He has destroyed 8 enemy aircraft.

Citation to Award of a Bar to the Distinguished Flying Cross, date 5 February 1943, London Gazette No.35891.

Since being awarded the DFC Squadron Leader Barr has destroyed a further 4 enemy aircraft.   In the absence of his Commanding Officer in May, 1942, he assumed command of his squadron and continued to lead it with courage and distinction during the critical period of the German advance.   On one day alone he flew on 6 fighter-bomber sorties and on another occasion he force landed during an operation, but after overhauling his aircraft and preparing a runway, managed to fly back a few minutes ahead of the incoming enemy.   Some days later a formation led by him was attacked by enemy aircraft.   In an effort to save one of his pilots from an attack, he was himself shot down.   This experience in no way diminished Squadron Leader Barr's zeal to engage the enemy.   Throughout his operational career this officer has displayed outstanding qualities of leadership and devotion to duty.

Citation to Award of the Military Cross, date 1 December 1944, London Gazette No.36820.

Squadron Leader Barr was wounded and his aircraft shot down in North Africa on 27th June, 1942. A few hours after being captured, while the Italians were attending to their wounded, he hobbled 1/4 mile in an unsuccessful attempt to escape. He was transferred to Italy and sent to hospital at Bergamo. Four and a half months later he escaped and had almost reached Switzerland when he was recaptured and sent to Gavi. When prisoners were being evacuated from this camp to Germany, Squadron Leader Barr managed to unfasten the door of the waggon and, after organising the escape of the other prisoners with him, jumped from the train. He soon met another officer who had injured himself when jumping, and after the latter had received medical attention at San Lorenzo they both travelled to Monastero. Eight days later, Squadron Leader Barr left his companion and went on to Corianna Valli. Here, finding himself too weak to cross the mountains, he organised prisoners in the district and, as a result, many of them were able to escape to the allied lines. Squadron Leader Barr was again captured by Alpine troops, and, after being ill-treated, was handed over to the Germans, who imprisoned him with another re-captured escaper in a prison cell. Discovering the key of the door to be on the outside they managed to escape, with the aid of a piece of wire, and returned to Coriana. Here, Squadron Leader Barr acquired a radio transmitter and continued his good work among the prisoners. Towards the end of February, 1944, he obtained guides and brought 10 prisoners through to the allied lines.

Appendix 3

Nominal Roll of 31 Cadet Course RAAF

E.M.	Ball	
A.W.	Barr	survived, W/C/dr OBE, MC, DFC, CO 3 Sqn RAAF
P.E.	Biven	survived, S/Ldr
L.	Bradley	
L.W.	Bradbury	to 3 Sqn RAAF in Desert
L.W.	Brickhill	
K.A.	Crisp	
J.H.	Cox	KIA 14/12/44, 43 Sqn RAAF, Phillippines
H.B.	Dawkins	died, 22/7/44, POW of Japanese, F/Lt 22 Sqn RAAF, N. Brtn
W.M.	Dempster	
J.E.	Dures	
F.F.	Eggleston	to 3 Sqn RAAF, POW, to Europe, survived
J.D.	Entwistle	
D.R.	Plach	
G.W.	Gibson	
G.W.	Gilbert	
A.M.	Greenfield	KIA 22/7/42, 158 Sqn RAF, Germany
C.A.	Greenwood	
C.C.	Henry	
I.N.	Hamilton	killed 13/8/43, 1OTU East Sale, Victoria
G.	Hill	
D.E.	Howie	
T.K.	Knight	to 3 Sqn, F/O, KIA 13/12/41
I.A.	McCombe	survived war, S/Ldr DFC
F.A.	McLeod	

J.S.	Menzies	
D.E.	Moseley	
D.L.	Pank	
J.A.	Parsons	
J.N.	Piper	
R.H.	Pope	KIA 10/12/41, N.E.I.; F/O 13 Sqn RAAF
A.J.	Rollins	
D.	Rutter	KIA 9/12/41, F/O, 3 Sqn RAAF, Middle East
P.B.	Sinnott	
G.N.	Smith	
R.H.	Tayler	
C.G.	Tolhurst	
G.	Turner	
N.H.	Watson	
N.W.	Webster	survived war, S/Ldr GM, CO 35 Sqn 1945
H.D.	White	survived war, S/Ldr
J.H.	Woods	

Sources:

Nicky Barr's log-book, interview and comments;

RAAF squadron operational records at the Australian War Memorial and the RAAF Historical Section; Roll of Honour at Australian War Memorial.

Details of the shooting down, POW incidents and escape details of Cameron, Chinchen, Eggleston, Kloster, Jones, Norman and Roberts from AWM 54 collection, 81/4/135 and 779/3/129 files.

The Barr, Mailey, and other interviews with former members of 3 Squadron RAAF in the Murdoch Sound Archives, Australian War Memorial;

Ross Biden's flying detail from his log-book at RAAF museum.

Correspondence with Alan Rawlinson;

Detail from Chris Shores and Russell Guest for Luftwaffe identifications.

Official History Volumes.

"With Prejudice"; Lord Tedder, Little, Brown & Co., 1966.

"The RAAF POWs of Lamsdorf"; Editor J.E.   Holliday, Brisbane 1992.

chapter Two

COMBAT OVER THE CHANNEL

Spitfire Leader

Squadron Leader Hugo Throssell Armstrong DFC* RAAF

Hugo Throssell Armstrong was born in Perth on 9 June 1916.   He was a nephew of Captain Hugo Throssell VC, 10th Light Horse Regiment, and named for his uncle, who won the Victoria Cross on Gallipoli..   Mr. Armstrong senior owned the Armstrong Cycle Company in Hay Street, Perth, and the family lived in a big house at Mount Lawley.

The Armstrong family can be traced back as far as 1376, to Liddesdale, Scotland. The family originally was 'Fairbairn', and a Fairbairn was Chief Armourer to a Scottish king.   During a battle, the king was unhorsed, but Fairbairn, of enormous strength, leaned over, grabbed the king by his thigh and lifted him onto Fairbairn's own horse. For this feat of strength, the king gave the man the name of 'Strongarm', and land on the border between England and Scotland.   At one time the Armstrongs could field 3,000 men.   The first Armstrong of Hugo's branch to come to Australia was his great-grandfather, Louis, who married Martha McGonigal in Bairnsdale, Victoria.   Louis and his family were engaged in sugar production on Fiji, but the family fortune was lost when German scientists found a way to produce sugar from beets in Europe.   With the family finances gone, Hugo's father, 'PW' Armstrong, worked at labouring jobs in Queensland, went to New Guinea looking for gold, and left just before his two companions were killed and eaten by local people.

'PW' made his way to the West Australian goldfields, saw his chance and seized it. Telegraphic communication with the financiers and London Stock Exchange was possible only from Perth; telegrams were sent in written form to and from the goldfields by camel train.   This took a week or more.   The constant thudding of broad camel feet had created smooth continuous hard-surfaced tracks right across country from the fields to

Perth.   'PW' had one of the first bicycles in the area, and opened a courier service for telegrams at 10 cents a mile [1.6 km] for same-day delivery.   The new business was an immediate success.   With 50 telegrams in the courier bag, 'PW' earned $5.00 per mile.   In six months, 'PW' had $10,000.00.   He bought more bicycles and hired riders at the excellent wage then of $10.00 per week.   'PW' expanded into bicycle agencies in Perth, and later imported US and British cars.   The Throssell side of the family included George Throssell, Premier of West Australia in 1903.   Hugo Throssell, Hugo Armstrong's namesake, was a well-known sporting figure in his school days and after; feats of strength and stamina were almost common-place before the action against the Turks in which Throssell won the Victoria Cross.

Frank Lawson, a school mate of the young 'Hoogie', recalled that 'frequent children's parties were held on a grand scale in the large garden, with sack races, treasure hunts and other delights, and prizes for all'.   Hugo attended Hale School 1925-1932, and was a member of the 1932 shooting team, which was second in the annual competition.   Hugo also took part in cycle races in his teens, but was beaten in one by Clarry Herbert, who received the prize - a valuable bike frame - from Mr. Armstrong.   Hugo joined the RAAF on 25 May 1940, and was a member of the First Course of the Empire Air Training Scheme (EATS).   Along with the other West Australian recruits, Hugo travelled by train to No. 1 Initial Training School (ITS), at Somers, in Victoria.   Aboard the train was a fellow he'd not seen since the jostling at the end of a bike race: Clarry Herbert.   As would be expected, friendships blossomed among the trainees, some friendships continuing through all phases of training and eventual squadron postings in England.   Clarry and Hugo were in different Flights at Somers, so, while friends, had closer mates in their respective Flights.

Later, when training with Canadians, Herbert found that 'Clarry' was a girl's name in Canada, and after some discussion it was decided to call him Gary.   The name stuck through his RAAF and post-war careers.   Looking back, Gary Herbert realised that even at Somers Hugo was more mature than the others on course, that probably he was more conscious of upholding the family name, and probably also aware of upholding the honour of the name of a Victoria Cross winner.   Gary considered that he personally did not acquire that degree of maturity for another three years, by which time he was on his second tour of operations.   Some people were commissioned on a probationary basis before the initial training course actually ended, and Hugo was one of these.   The young and inexperienced Australians generally did not attach much importance to rank, but later in the UK they saw that, in English society, unless one was commissioned, 'you were nothing,' as Gary recalled.

Hugo graduated 24th of 98 on the first EATS course at Somers, on 23 June 1940.   The course then started flying training, first at Mascot, at 4 Elementary Flying Training School from 27 June to 9 September, and later to Wagga Wagga, to 2 Service Flying Training School (2SFTS), from 23 September to 12 January 1941.   37 members of the 2SFTS course were commissioned as Acting Pilot Officers or promoted to Sergeant, and prepared to move overseas.

No.1 Empire Air Training Scheme Course, May 1940, Somers, Victoria.
A nominal roll is in the appendix.   Hugo Armstrong is third from right in the rear row and
Gary Herbert is second from the right in the front row.
(Gary Herbert)

By this time, the Germans had invaded and defeated all the countries of Western Europe and commanded the coastline from the tip of Norway to the border of Spain.   France had fallen in 12 weeks.   The only setback suffered by Germany had been the failure to destroy the Royal Air Force and achieve air superiority over southern England to allow an invasion force to cross from France.   London, Coventry and other British cities had felt the full fury of the German Luftwaffe.

Hugo's first flight was in DH-82 VH-UVZ, with M.W. Bateman, on 27 June 1940   He soloed on 8 July, after 11 hours.   On 9 January 1941, on graduation from 2SFTS, he had a total of 155 hours, and was assessed *'Average'* as a fighter pilot, *'Average'* as pilot-navigator, but *'Above Average'* in bombing and air gunnery.   'Wings' Parade was at Wagga Wagga on 14 November 1940, and the members of the course were officially promoted Sergeant or commissioned as Pilot Officers on 12 January 1941.   Hugo was commissioned as a General Duties Pilot on that date.

The West Australians on the course were sent home, posted to 5 Embarkation Depot in Perth for leave.   Officially, they reported every day, but were not required for duty.   On 3 March 1941, the ship *Ulysses* departed for the UK with aircrew from 1 EATS Course.   Also aboard were the first staff for RAAF Headquarters in London, to be at Kodak House.   The ship's departure was at 10.15 p.m., in secrecy, with no family members to make a last farewell.   The only exception was Gary Herbert's father, responsible for supplying fresh water to shipping.   As the ship pulled away from the darkened wharf area, only Mr. Herbert was visible, standing under a light.   His enlarged silhouette was reflected in the black waters below the wharf, and every movement by him was magnified in the reflection.   Gary, and all the other young Aussies lining the rail, watched as the lone figure grew smaller.   The thought then struck that this might be the last time he would ever see his father, and Gary wondered if similar thoughts were passing through other minds nearby.   When the ship was at sea, Gary found a remote dark corner and wept.

The voyage to South Africa was pleasant, but boring. Apart from watching dolphins racing alongside and cavorting, the only amusement was playing cards. Playing for money was, of course, against Service regulations, but few Australians obey every regulation.

The ship reached Durban on 18 March. The Aussies were impressed by its beauty, and more so by the friendly reception provided by the townspeople, who extended invitations to homes, dinners, dances and night clubs. The staid nature of South African society was reflected on the beaches, where behaviour was more sedate and formal than the Australian experience at home, with little sky-larking and outright fun. 'The girls,' recalled Gary Herbert, 'were very hospitable.' Hugo successfully used a ploy with the local girls. At dance or nightclub, with a merry group at a table, Hugo gradually would become withdrawn and pensive, until one girl would ask why he was so quiet. Hugo's reply was that the place and company were fine, very enjoyable, but it was sad to be so far from home and family on one's birthday. This always resulted in sympathy and a closer relationship. 'Hugo had five or six birthdays in Durban,' said Gary, 'and another four or five in Cape Town.'

Cape Town also showed the young Aussies something of a different way of life. They were surprised to find that in hotels no 'shouting' was allowed - everyone paid for his own drinks. If there was singing or other exuberant behaviour, the hotel closed for an hour. The South Africans, for their part, could not understand the easy-going relationship between the Australian officers and junior ranks, with first names used casually. This was 'never done in South Africa,' said Gary Herbert, 'nor in England.'

The first Australians to train in Rhodesia left the ship at Durban, and after departing Cape Town the ship turned north along the west coast of Africa. Again the voyage became boring, with the only entertainment gambling and playing records on a gramophone, forerunner of today's cassette- and compact-disc players. A popular song of the time was *'A Nightingale Sang in Berkely Square'*, particularly poignant because British cities, and London especially, were being heavily bombed by the German Luftwaffe. To this day, that song brings to Gary Herbert memories of the voyage from Cape Town. The boredom was soon to end, as the ship approached danger areas closer to England, where German U-Boats and aircraft attacked British shipping.

At Freetown, the *Ulysses* joined a convoy of 30 ships with four destroyers and a cruiser escort. Here the inexperienced Aussies had their first taste of war. A Vichy French reconnaissance aircraft flew over, obviously checking on the assembling convoy, and the six or so British anti-aircraft guns opened fire. This was interesting, and all the RAAF ignored orders from the ship's captain to take cover, preferring to stand outside and watch. The captain was concerned that falling shell splinters would injure his passengers, but they instantly assessed as negligible the odds of being hit by anything from the few shells exploding above the anchorage. Later, some were to see very intense anti-aircraft barrages, but this was the first, and it was all new and exciting.

The ship's passengers were allowed ashore at Freetown, and Pilot Officer Armstrong was responsible for ensuring the EATS people were back aboard by the appointed time.

Hugo had some difficulty with this, as there had been no shore leave since Cape Town, and would be none until arrival in England, so the most was made of the opportunity to enjoy this part of Africa, so different from the cities in the south.

The convoy sailed, with *Ulysses* in the lead, providing a spectacular view back over the powerful assembly of ships bound for the embattled United Kingdom.   The ship's sole armament was a single .303-inch Hotchkiss machinegun, from the era of the Boer War or earlier, mounted on the bridge.   The Australians were given training in its use.   On 11 May, the gun was actually used.   A Focke-Wulf FW200 *'Condor'* four- engined bomber attacked, hit *Somerset* missed *Scottish Star*, but flew so close to *Ulysses* that Leo Hanley, at the gun, hit it with some .303-inch rounds.   However, the big Focke-Wulf flew away. *Somerset,* loaded with meat, halted, the crew abandoned ship, and the derelict was left behind, sinking by the stern.   The Aussies had seen a small act in the war.   They were unaware that the previous night London had been heavily attacked, with over 2,500 fires started, 1,500 people killed, and great destruction inflicted when 570 Luftwaffe bombers dropped over 1,000 tonnes of bombs on London in the latest of a series of heavy raids.

Embattled Britain

On 14 May, the convoy sailed up the Clyde to Glasgow.   The Aussies stared at the seemingly endless shipyards, all apparently working at full speed.   There was little obvious bomb damage in the industrial areas, but many tenements on the hillsides had been wrecked.   Next day, the RAAF contingent arrived at the London personnel reception depot, Uxbridge, to await posting to Operational Training Units.   Gary Herbert noted that it was 'very cold.   The women are not so good.'   The women, of course, were showing the effects of the nightly bombing campaign by the Luftwaffe.   Thousands of people had been killed, thousands more wounded, homes and businesses destroyed; destruction was everywhere.   Yet, London carried on with 'Business as usual', and 'London can take it!'

Hugo, Gary, the other aircrew volunteers and RAAF HQ staff had arrived at the heart of the Commonwealth in its darkest hour.   Companionships were broken as men went to scattered bases for their next stage of training.   The Observers in the contingent were deemed fully qualified, and went almost at once to RAF bombing and coastal reconnaissance squadrons; few survived more than a few months. On 24 May, Gary went to 17 Operational Training Unit (OTU) at Upwood, for conversion to the twin-engined Bristol Blenheim bomber.   Hugo went to fly Spitfires.

The staff for RAAF Headquarters went to Kodak House, and it was only long afterwards that Gary Herbert found that all those non-operational Kodak House staff were promoted to senior Non-Commissioned Officer or Officer rank before any of the RAAF aircrew who actually flew against the enemy received promotion.   He remained a Sergeant through his first tour of operations.

Hugo joined No.20 Course at 55 Operational Training unit [OTU], Usworth, Durham. Here he flew Miles Masters, Magisters and Hawker Hurricanes in June and July, and was assessed *'Above Average.'*   By the end of July, Hugo had 209 hours, and was posted to 257 Squadron RAF at Coltishall, where he flew his first operational sorties on 4 and 5 August: a convoy patrol and an unsuccessful search for a missing aircraft. He was deemed satisfactory in handling the Spitfire, and posted to 129 (Mysore) Squadron at Leconfield. Except for one convoy patrol on 26 August, all Hugo's flying was training. Then the squadron moved to Westhampnett. Of his 265 hours total flying experience, Hugo had 26 hours on the Spitfire MkI and two hours on the Spitfire MkV.

Hugo Armstrong's operational flying with the RAF was during the two year period after the Battle of Britain, when the British Commonwealth air forces maintained an offensive against the Germans on the Channel coast. Every advantage except numerical superiority was with the German Luftwaffe. For a better understanding of the achievements of Hugo Armstrong and squadrons with which he flew, some background to the cross-Channel operations of 1941-42 is necessary.

RAF commanders assumed that the spring of 1941 would see a resurgence of heavy Luftwaffe attacks on Great Britain, a second 'Battle of Britain' to follow that of 1940. However, the Nazi regime turned its attention to the east, and attacked the Union of Soviet Socialist Republics [USSR] in June 1941. RAF senior ranks, almost without exception, accepted that offense was better than defence, and this had resulted in actions over France as soon as the RAF had time to draw a breath after the great exertions in France and over England between May and November 1940. After June 1941 the RAF increased offensive operations in an attempt to assist the USSR, to force the Luftwaffe to retain in France and Belgium the maximum strength necessary for defence of the Channel coast region. It then was found that the RAF had to solve many of the problems which beset the Luftwaffe in the Battle of Britain in 1940 - how best: to escort a bomber force; to operate an efficient air sea rescue service; to exercise command and control in actions against an enemy perfecting a modern defensive network which included anti-aircraft guns, radar control and fighter units; to sustain and replace loss of pilots and leaders over enemy territory. The full ramifications of the RAF's 1941-44 cross-Channel operations are beyond the scope of this book, but a generalisation is that the RAF suffered considerable losses by persisting with offensive operations, did achieve a measure of air superiority, evolved tactics and formations, and trained pilots and leaders from section to wing level. RAF higher command belief was that losses were acceptable for the advantage of holding the initiative.

Instructions were issued that RAF aircraft could attack only targets which did not contravene the Red Cross or civilians. The first official cross-Channel flight was made by two aircraft of 66 Squadron on 20 December 1940, the first fighter sweep on 9 January 1941 and the first 'Circus', a bomber force with fighter escort, was made next day, when six twin-engined Bristol Blenheims of 114 Squadron attacked a target in the Foret de Guines, south of Calais, under the protection of six fighter squadrons. A Circus operation was designed to bring the Luftwaffe fighters into action, so a small bomber force was accompanied by a large force of fighters, but they did not penetrate far into enemy territory. The targets selected were those of which loss or damage was intended to hurt the enemy as well as bring up the fighters.

Other types of operation were 'Ramrod', in which the primary aim of the fighters was to protect the bombers; 'Rhubarb', in which small formations harassed aircraft and ground targets; 'Roadstead', anti-shipping attacks with fighter escort; 'Rodeo', fighter sweep without bombers; and 'Jim Crow', a reconnaissance to find suitable shipping targets. There were many other types of operations not relevant to this account.

By mid-June 1941, all types of RAF offensive operations had resulted in claims for 44 enemy destroyed, while 50 RAF pilots had been lost. Circus operations resulted in claims for 16 enemy, against a loss of 25. However, the moral ascendency and experience gained was deemed of more importance than losses. In fact, but not known until the end of the war, Luftwaffe Quartermaster records showed that 58 Luftwaffe day fighters had been lost, 14 more than claimed by the RAF.

On 10 July 1941, Hauptman Rolf Pingel, commander of the First *Gruppe* of *Jagdgeschwader* 26 (Kommandeur I/JG26), was captured when he force landed in England. During his interrogation, he said that the bombing was not a serious worry, the Luftwaffe fighter pilots were pleased the RAF was on the offensive and coming to them in France, and that RAF claims were far too high. Operations intensified in July, reached a peak in August and early September, then slackened to the end of the year. By the end of July, the RAF had lost 123 pilots, but claimed 322 enemy. This later was found to be far in excess of actual Luftwaffe strength, which was about 200 fighters. Luftwaffe units continued to move from the Channel region to other theatres, but two fighter formations - JG2 *'Richthofen'* and JG26 *'Schlageter'* - remained in place.

An immediate problem, and one which never was fully rectified, was that of range for RAF fighters. The Hawker Hurricane and Vickers-Supermarine Spitfire were designed to protect Great Britain against raiders coming across the sea from Germany. An hour or 90 minutes flying was adequate for such operational use, but not nearly enough for penetration into Occupied Europe, for combat, and then for return to England. Even use of external 'drop' tanks was only partly successful, as fighters had to release these when engaged, and immediately were governed by the amount of internal fuel carried. This problem plagued the Luftwaffe Messerschmitt Bf109s in the Battle of Britain, and for lack of fuel many aircraft from each side were lost in the English Channel.

During the latter stages of the Battle of Britain, RAF Fighter Command had formed 'Wings' of several squadrons, named for the airfield from which the flying headquarters and leaders operated, though some attached squadrons operated from neighbouring airfields. Consequently, there were, among others, the Duxford Wing, the Biggin Hill Wing, and the Tangmere Wing. The famous Wing Commander Douglas Bader led the Duxford Wing in the Battle of Britain, took command of the Tangmere Wing in March 1941, and led it until his capture in August 1941. It was decided that some squadrons in the Wing would be rested, and moved from the Channel coast to a quieter sector in the north. 610 Squadron, second of the 'original' Tangmere Wing squadrons under Bader, left on 30 August. It was replaced by 129 (Mysore) Squadron. The other squadron in the Tangmere Wing was the experienced 616 (South Yorkshire) Squadron of the pre-war Auxiliary Air Force.

First Operations

129 Squadron was raised in June 1941, equipped with Spitfire Vb aircraft. The squadron was commanded first by Squadron Leader D.L. Armitage, but in September he was succeeded by Squadron Leader R.J. Abrahams. The Tangmere Wing, including 129 Squadron, flew two operations on 30 August, the first being a straightforward fighter sweep and the second a bomber escort to a target on the Continent. Only 616 Squadron had contact, with a claim for a Messerschmitt Bf109 destroyed and one damaged. The Bf109s opposing the wing were flown by the experienced pilots of *Jagdgeschwader* 26 (JG26), based in the Pas de Calais.

A potent new German fighter had arrived - the Focke Wulf FW190. Powered by a 1700 horse-power BMW 801D radial engine, armed with four 20mm cannon in the wings and two 7.92mm machineguns in the upper engine decking, the FW190 was superior in every aspect to the Spitfire V, except turning ability. Designed, tested and developed in secrecy, beautifully designed to facilitate the role of the fighter pilot, the arrival of the FW190 was a complete surprise to the RAF. Employed within the defensive tactical policies of the Luftwaffe fighter command in the West, the FW190 was to inflict severe losses on RAF squadrons executing the policy of non-stop attack across the Channel.

129 (Mysore) Squadron RAF Fighter Command, Autumn 1941
On Spitfire cowling are the squadron doctor and Hugo Armstrong; standing are, left to right, Sgt Ramsay RCAF, Ted Hall RAAF, Sgt Irish RCAF, unknown, Sgt Tucker Jamaica, Sgt Frith RCAF, P/O Whalen RCAF, Sgt Hardy Rhodesia, Sgt Ted Hiskens RAAF, S/Ldr Abrahams RAF, F/Lt Cunliffe RAF, Sgt McPhee RCAF, F/Lt Thomas RAF, Sgt Wilson RAF, Sgt Drew RAF, Sgt Davies RCAF, unknown. Seven of these pilots were killed in action. (Ted Hall)

After arrival on 129 Squadron, Hugo flew several sorties, but did not regard them as offensive operations. His personal Spitfire Vb was 'N'. However, on 17 and 18 September, he flew on Circuses 95, 96 and 97, escorting Blenheim bombers, and then as cover to a Walrus air-sea rescue aircraft in the Channel. He noted, *'Glorious day. No 109s near us at all.'* These sweeps were numbered from '1' in his log book.

On 18 September a German ship passing through the English Channel was attacked by Blenheims of 88 Squadron, with an escort of Spitfires and Hurricanes from 41 and 615 Squadrons; one Blenheim was shot down by a FW190 of II/JG26. The Focke-Wulf leader, Hauptmann Walter Adoplh, circled the ditched bomber and was himself shot down by a Spitfire. The rest of the JG26 formation had no idea of what happened to their leader. Adolph had flown in the Spanish Civil War and with JG1 in 1940, and claimed 28 victories with II/JG26 since October 1940. Experienced leaders on both sides would be lost throughout the war, killed or captured when making some seemingly innocuous departure from standard procedures.

First Victory

On 21 September 1941, 129 Squadron was tasked for Circus 101, in which 11 Blenheims were to bomb Gosnay power station. 129 Squadron was part of the close escort wing; Pilot Officer Hugo Armstrong was detailed as Green 2. At 15.10, 129 Squadron crossed the French coast at 18,000 feet. Over Le Touquet, 109s dived on the squadron; the Spitfires broke right.

In the turn, Hugo saw two 109Fs flying in line astern at the same height. The second 109 crossed through his sights. At only 100 metres range; from slightly to one side and astern Hugo fired; strikes flashed on the starboard wingtip of the Messerschmitt; the tip and aileron peeled away. The 109 flicked onto its back due to aerodynamic forces, but Hugo half-rolled with it, and at 50 metres range dead astern fired; the 109 flicked again and started down in a 'flip-flop' vertical spin. It was obviously out of control, and was seen going down by two other members of the squadron.

As Hugo broke away, he saw a Spitfire with a 109 behind it, shooting, so he swiftly fired in front of the 109 to scare it off; this worked. As Hugo climbed to join his leader, he fired at another 109, but missed. By this time all his guns had ceased to work because of low air pressure. The 109s chased them close to the English coast before turning back, and Hugo landed, almost out of fuel, at Friston. He fired 92 cannon and 160 machinegun rounds; one cannon stoppage was caused by problems with the magazine spring. This was Hugo's fourth offensive sweep; he had only 53 hours on Spitfires, and 228 as a solo pilot.

At the rear of his log-book, Hugo began a series of small cartoon drawings to mark his victories. This one was headed '109F Dest', and beneath was a small cross with the name *'Hans'*, the date, and a few flowers at the base of the cross.

Hugo's victim might have been Leutnant Ulrich Dzialas, 8th Staffel JG26 (8/JG26), who is noted in the geschwader history as lost on the afternoon of this day, diving into the Channel south of Boulogne, during a combat with about 25 Spitfires.

The two Luftwaffe fighter units claimed a large number of victories on this day - 19 for JG26 and ten for JG2. Fighter Command admitted loss of 12. Donald L. Caldwell, the US historian of JG26, author of *JG26 - Top Guns of the Luftwaffe* and *JG26 War Diary,* stated that 12 victories were awarded JG26, 'confirmed' by the official Luftwaffe office for such matters, and that JG2's claims were for a time of day when the RAF formations would have been at Dover on their return. The only admitted Luftwaffe loss against Circus 101 was Leutnant Dzialas.

Hugo wrote about the combat to his brother.
'It was quite an interesting show. We were jumped over the French coast on the way in by about one hundred 109s. It developed into the most glorious shambles, with aircraft falling out of the sky all over the place. After I knocked my bloke down, I joined up with another Spit to try and get home. It took us about fifteen minutes to get out. At one time we were engaged by two whole squadrons, but with a lot of luck managed to get through.'

Later, he wrote of returning from six days in London, and being 'pretty crook in the gut,' but as there was 'lovely cloud all over the place, it don't [sic] look like work today.' Unfortunately perhaps, there was squadron practice flying.....

Hugo was nominated as a section leader towards the end of September, often flying as leader of Blue or Green Section.

Sweeps as part of Circus operations continued in October, with Hugo often leading Green Section.   Circus 104 was on 2 October, to Le Havre, but Hugo noted, *'did not cross the coast owing to bombers messing about - decided to go - decided not to go - came home!'*

On the 2nd, JG2 claimed eight Spitfires and Hauptmann Johannes Schmid of 8/JG26 claimed his 39th victory, a Spitfire, followed on 3 October by his 40th, also a Spitfire. Schmid had received the Knight's Cross after his 25th victory in August 1941.

Gary Herbert flew his first operation as a bomber pilot on 12 October, and Hugo flew in the escort.   24 Blenheims bombed Boulogne from 12,000 feet.   129 Squadron flew rear cover, and was not engaged in combat; Hugo counted it as his sixth offensive sweep. Gary thought it a good operation, with no losses, though the plentiful anti-aircraft fire - 'flak' from the German '**fl**iege**r a**bwehr**k**anone' - damaged many aircraft.

'Surprised I was not more excited than I was.' noted Gary, adding, 'Been more excited at a bike race.' Gary also noted the calm atmosphere in the Mess, with people relaxing over a beer or reading magazines or newspapers, and hardly a sign that they were actively involved in a war.   The crews knew nothing of the results of the raid, until they listened to the 9 o'clock BBC radio news, and learned that two Spitfires had been lost, but four Messerschmitts claimed.   JG2 and JG26 each claimed two Spitfires, and the only admitted Luftwaffe loss was one from JG2.

Soon after this date, however, the news began to arrive of losses and deaths among the first Australian graduates of the EATS courses. At least nine members of the course had been killed by this time in the Middle East - North Africa, Libya and Syria. Pilot Officers

Jim Kent, Reg Lea and Don Munro, and Sergeants Norm Evans and David Gale were killed in June, and Felix Clowry in July, then Cecil Berriman in August, and Rowland Secomb in September.

Leutnant Dzialas' body came ashore that day, 12 October, and he was buried next day. His friend, Leutnant Peter Goering, nephew of the Luftwaffe Reichsmarschall, performed the last honours. Peter Goering was killed later on 13 October, attacking Blenheims with Adolf Galland, the commander of JG26. Hugo flew on the operation as part of the escort, as Blue 2, and noted they were engaged until ten miles off Boulogne; two of the 129 Squadron Spitfires were missing.

Hugo then flew a series of aircraft and cannon tests in 'N', and on the fifth flight noted of his cannon, *'Both fired at last.'* More local flying and testing followed, with another sweep, over St. Omer on the 21st, from which Hugo *'came home at zero feet.'*

On 20 October, Pat Nangle of the first EATS course died in an accident in the UK, flying with 88 Squadron RAF.

On 25 October Hauptmann Franz von Werra was drowned when his Messerschmitt went into the sea near Vlissingen. Von Werra was the only German serviceman in World War 2 to escape from Allied capture. He had been shot down during the Battle of Britain, sent to Canada, and escaped over the border to the then-neutral USA. He returned to Germany, fought in Russia, but was lost when the engine of his 109 failed. On 26 October 1941, Major Walter Oesau, commander JG2, claimed his 100th victory. However, the Luftwaffe was suffering losses also. On 6 November, Hauptmann Johannes Schmid, commander 8/JG26, was lost, reportedly when his wingtip hit the sea while he circled a shot-down Spitfire of 452 Squadron RAAF. Schmid claimed 45 victories.

129 Squadron moved to Debden for night-flying training on 1 November, and to Sutton Bridge on the 15th, for air-to-air gunnery. On 7 December, Hugo collided with the angle of glide indicator when making a night landing. He noted, *'Prang.'* However, he received a red ink endorsement in his log-book for 'Error of Judgement'. All through this time, Hugo led either Green or Blue Section. On 24 December, the squadron returned to Westhampnett. But, on the only sweep before the New Year, the squadron saw *'no enemy aircraft whatsoever'*. Hugo ended 1941 with 313 hours as a solo pilot, including 138 on Spitfires. (From this point, hours quoted will be those as a solo pilot.)

On 4 November, a Blenheim strike from Tangmere was cancelled by bad weather. Here, at the airfield, Gary Herbert met Hugo, and they exchanged news. Two days later, Gary began preparations to go to Malta, and arrived there on 1 December. He survived the frightful losses suffered by Blenheim squadrons on anti-shipping strikes in the Mediterranean:- 57 aircraft and 199 aircrew. Gary flew another tour of operations, survived the war, and returned to Australia as one of the few survivors of the first EATS course. On 8 November, Bill Hopkinson of the first course was killed in action in Greece, with 107 Squadron RAF.

Hugo and Pilot Officer E.S. 'Ted' Hall RAAF, called 'Sammy' in 129 Squadron, were the Australians on the squadron. They flew together on many practice and training flights, and Ted later acknowledged the benefits he gained from Hugo's teaching.

Despite the hard-won practical lessons which began in May 1940, of over 18 months of relatively intense aerial operations, in late 1941 some RAF fighter squadrons still flew sections in 'Line astern' formation, despite the advantages demonstrated by Luftwaffe use of twos and fours in the 'finger four' formation, which had been adopted by some RAF squadrons as early as the Battle of Britain. 129 Squadron persisted in the tactically unsound line astern formations.

'It was a frightening thing for the last man of the line, the Number 4, or "Arse-end Charlie"', recalled Ted.

On one sweep, he and Hugo became separated slightly from the rest of the squadron by enemy action, and were somewhat vulnerable. Ted, concentrating greatly, clung to Hugo's turns, anticipating the

'vicious weaves, and often turned inside Hugo's turn. Once, with my thumb on the centre gun-button, I yanked the stick back sharply and hit my stomach with force. The plane shook as all guns fired, and with great concern I noticed the yellow tracer bullets searing in Hugo's direction. I heard him yell, "Break fast, Sammy!"' Later, in the Mess, Hugo asked, 'Did you see the bastard that shot at us?'

Before Ted could reply, he was called over by the Commanding Officer, and then went on leave. By the time he returned, Hugo had forgotten the question.

Hugo himself went on leave, and returned from London quite excited about a girl he had met, called Jacqueline, but 'Jonnie' for short. Jacqueline's father was English, her mother French, was born and educated in France and had escaped before the German invasion was

Hugo in the Spitfire marked for 'Jonnie' the Free French girl Hugo met in London. (Ted Hall)

complete. Hugo, said Ted, 'was overjoyed with their friendship, and decided to inscribe an insignia on his plane, to show her on his next leave. After much trial and error and much discussion we came up with the Cross of Lorraine on the side and "Jonnie" to the front of his Spitfire.'   Ted was the cameraman, the results were good, and later he was told by Hugo that the photo 'was well received.'   Now it can be revealed that the decorations were all in chalk, and did not last beyond the next rain shower...

By the end of 1941, RAF command accepted that the Luftwaffe on the Channel coast had not reacted as desired to the RAF offensive, and had not moved substantial reinforcements from Russia or the Mediterranean back to the Channel coast.   The bombing campaign in the coastal region could not be shown to have slowed the German war effort, but anti-shipping attacks seemingly had more positive results.   Little enemy coastal traffic was seen in daylight in the area of operations.   Actually, as shipping losses rose, the Germans simply used the network of roads, rail, canals and rivers which covered Europe.   Later, it was realised that railways carried a significant part of German war production all over Europe.

Unknown to the RAF, by late August 1941 the available German fighter strength on the Channel coast was reduced to about 90, and if pressure had been maintained the Luftwaffe units on the coast would have been destroyed.   It was information such as this which was not available through the 'Ultra' radio intercept and decoding system, nor from the daily translations of radio interception of local Luftwaffe transmissions, known as the 'Y' Service.   Adolf Galland later said that the strain on the two units defending northern France was greater than that imposed by operations during the Battle of Britain, but morale was high and pilots knew that if they baled out or force landed they would be safe.   However, with the easing of intensity by the RAF, Luftwaffe strength was built up again to normal levels by the end of September.   Experienced pilots had been brought in to replace a proportion of pilot losses, and some independent fighter units, formed from reserves, had been committed to operations.

German records show that admitted Luftwaffe aircraft losses in northern France in 1941 totalled 135, but RAF claims were for 731 enemy destroyed.   JG26 lost 63 pilots killed to all causes, including three of the rank of Hauptmann.   Total RAF losses for 1941 were 462 pilots killed or captured.   But the RAF and Commonwealth air forces now were able to sustain such losses and accept them as part of the price for expansion and development of a force intended to play a major role in the future liberation of Europe. For the intense fighting of the Battle of Britain period, July-October 1940 alone, RAF losses were 448.   At the end of 1940, RAF Fighter Command comprised 67.5 squadrons, including 55 single-engined fighter squadrons.   By the end of 1941, strength in the Command was 105 squadrons, including 71 single-engined.   Expansion of the RAF fighter force in the year had been more than shown by these figures, as squadrons had been committed overseas as well.   The Mediterranean and Pacific theatres made great demands, and Air Marshal Arthur Harris, when commanding RAF Bomber Command, protested at the constant drain of trained crews from the UK, stating that 1,000 bomber crews had gone overseas in a year, which left his force at the same size as in 1939.   By May 1942, 53 squadrons of all types were in the Mediterranean, with enough aircrews for a further 18 squadrons.

It should be kept in mind that the Luftwaffe, despite the great German victories of early summer 1940 and despite the defeat in the Battle of Britain, contented itself with defending Germany's territorial gains in France and the rest of Western Europe. By the end of 1941 it was the RAF which flew over German-occupied areas when and where it wished. The RAF was developing into a modern offensive air arm, while the Luftwaffe merely reacted to RAF operations. The Luftwaffe fighter leaders built up big personal scores and were showered with medals, but made a negligible contribution to the development of their arm of service as an instrument of air power.

Three Aussies on 129 Squadron - Ted Hiskens, Ted Hall, Hugo Armstrong.
(Ted Hall)

In November 1941, the British War Cabinet had decided on the expansion of Fighter Command for use in the spring of 1942, and the RAF was warned that the fighter force was not to be hazarded. Particularly to be avoided was a constant drain of losses from minor operations which were only a nuisance to the enemy.   This aptly described 'Rhubarb' operations.   There was little activity over the winter months, and large scale operations did not commence until March 1942.

1942

In January 1942, meanwhile, Squadron Leader R.H. Thomas, Hugo's commander in B Flight, succeeded R.J. Abrahams in command of 129 Squadron. The Tangmere Wing now consisted of 129 Squadron and 41 Squadron, commanded by the dynamic South African Petrus 'Piet' Hugo, who had four confirmed victories at this time.

Hugo Armstrong's log-book entries for January 1942 reflect the lack of offensive operations, with local flying, formation practices or defensive patrols or scrambles, with no contact.   Early February saw more of the same.   Of a convoy patrol on the 11th, Hugo noted, *'Foul weather.   Found them by balloons.'*   The foul weather was just what the Germans wanted.

The Channel Dash

On 12 February 1942, the German Luftwaffe co-operated with the Kriegsmarine in the successful dash by the battle cruisers *Scharnhorst, Gneisenau* and *Prinz Eugen* from Brest north through the English Channel to home ports in Germany.   This was the latest in a series of defeats for the Royal Navy and for British prestige.   A German conference was held earlier to discuss the situation of the ships, and if a dash through the Channel could succeed, or if a circuitous route out into the Atlantic and then north of Scotland would be preferable.   Adolf Hitler decided on the Channel dash.   In his opinion, the British could not react quickly enough to a daring surprise charge through the Channel. He was correct.   The Royal Navy and RAF response was piecemeal and a failure, well described in John Deane Potter's *Fiasco*, (William Heinemann, 1970).   Despite having Plan "Fuller", to attack the ships if they did leave Brest, and despite unmistakable signs that the Germans were about to force a break-out, the British commands were taken by surprise.   They then exacerbated matters by failing to co-operate, failing to inform the piecemeal attack forces which were committed of the real situation, and failing to observe one of the Principles of War: Concentration of Force.

The German ships were well away from Brest, moving north at 30 knots under bad weather, before they were first seen by any member of the British forces.   Squadron Leader Bobby Oxspring, commander 91 Squadron, was called by the Biggin Hill Operations controller, Squadron Leader Bill Igoe.   Oxspring was told that a large formation of enemy aircraft was active over the Somme estuary, not moving much, and possibly covering shipping. It was decided that Oxspring and Sergeant Beaumont would fly over for a look.   The first indication of enemy presence was bursting flak in the clouds.   The Spitfire pilots looked down and saw three large ships surrounded by escorts, a total of 20 or 30 ships; Oxspring's first thought was that the Royal Navy was well off course.   He then realised the ships were enemy, and decided to break the enforced regulation about radio silence while on reconnaissance, to radio the information.   The time was just after 10.20.   Bobby Oxspring, a lowly squadron commander, knew nothing of Plan "Fuller". He flew back, landed at 10.50, and reported.   Nothing had been done about his radio report.   It then was decided to consult a recognition book of German ships, and Sergeant Beaumont, with pre-war service in the RAF Marine Section, identified *Scharnhorst*, which he had seen at a naval review.   This report was not believed at higher levels.

But at about the same time Oxspring had seen the ships, British radar on the south coast detected ships in the Channel.   Murphy's Law came into effect.   The telephone system was engaged and other related telephone delays meant that the report was not received at naval headquarters at Dover until 10.40.   At 10.50, confirmatory further radar reports were received from a different site.

Then, 30 minutes after Oxspring's radio message, at 11.09, two more Spitfires landed, and two pilots more senior to Oxspring and Beaumont also independently confirmed the sighting.   These were the Kenley Station Commander and Wing Leader, Group Captain Victor Beamish and Wing Commander Findlay Boyd.   Bored with the inactivity caused by bad weather, and with his paper-work done for the day, Beamish had taken Boyd along to beat up the casino at Le Touquet, and strafe enemy there.   They also found the German ships, and, also ignorant of "Fuller", they kept radio silence until they landed.

It is difficult now, well after the event, to understand the reasoning behind an order not to use radio to report enemy strengths and locations, but to fly back to base and report. Possibly the quality of radio equipment at the time had resulted in radio transmissions which were garbled and resulted in wasteful responses, and the ability of reconnaissance pilots and crews to properly identify what they saw, rather than what they thought they saw, was not high at that stage of the war. The reasoning for the ban on radio warnings might not be known, but the results of the order were spectacular.

The full story of the prolonged refusal to accept facts by the Royal Navy and RAF, failure to react in time, repeated instances of incompetence and staff failures, and the post-event cover-up of British failure ordered by Winston Churchill, are beyond the scope of this book. However, as usual, young men in fighting units paid in blood for shortcomings of commanders and staff. For example, RAF squadrons were not told the truth, that capital ships were in the English Channel, and one torpedo squadron was sent after 'three merchant ships'. This incredible blunder resulted in attacks on Royal Navy ships in the battle area.

825 Squadron of the Fleet Air Arm was to make a torpedo attack under escort of five Spitfire squadrons. 825 Squadron had only six Fairey Swordfish aircraft and crews. The squadron commander, Lieutenant Commander Eugene Esmonde RN, had been awarded the Distinguished Service Order (DSO) for his part in the squadron attack on the German pocket battleship *Bismarck* in May 1941. Esmonde, a 33 year old Irishman, had over 6,500 hours flying time, and was a leader his crews would follow anywhere. Only two squadron crews had operational experience.

The Swordfish can be briefly described as of World War 1 type of design, provided for aircrews on operations 25 years later. A single engined biplane, of wood, canvas and bracing wires, the Swordfish had open cockpits and the crew communicated by shouts or speaking tubes. A gunner protected the rear with a .303-inch (7.7mm) magazine-fed machinegun, while the observer and pilot concentrated on finding the target and dropping the torpedo. The observer stood in the centre cockpit, held by a wire to a waist harness to prevent him being thrown out in manoeuvres. The Swordfish had a range of 200 miles [320 km], and a top speed of 90 mph [140 kmph]. If a ship was sighted in the distance, was steaming away at 30 knots, and the Swordfish had to battle a 30 knot headwind, the aircraft would be unable to catch it before being forced to return through lack of fuel. Yet the Swordfish was very agile, and crews believed they could out-manoeuvre modern fast fighters close to the water. In addition, bullets simply punched through the canvas, and if the crew and engine were unhit, the aircraft often passed through incredible volumes of fire.

825 Squadron was preparing for practice flying when word came of the German ships, and for an attack. The Spitfires would meet the Swordfish over Manston, and the force would go out together. When the position of the ships was plotted, their speed deduced, and weather conditions taken into account, Esmonde knew the worst possible situation confronted him: heavily armed fast-moving ships, almost past his station, and a headwind. He could only afford to circle for two minutes, and if the fighters were not on time, he had to go on regardless. It was tantamount to a death sentence, and Esmonde knew it.

Wing Commander Tom Gleave, present at Esmonde's briefing, was shocked at Esmonde's appearance in the last few minutes before take-off. Gleave understood that he was looking at a man fully aware he was going to destruction because duty required it.

The Swordfish circled, but no Spitfires arrived. Esmonde continued circling, then ten Spitfires of 72 Squadron, led by Squadron Leader Brian Kingcombe, arrived from Gravesend. The weather was so bad they had been stood down, but then three times called to scramble, cancelled each time. Finally, they were sent to Manston to escort the Swordfish, and assist in a battle between British and German torpedo boats - what Kingcome thought was 'a small naval scuffle.' No more Spitfires arrived, because of flying conditions, and, with time running out, Esmonde dived to 50 feet and set course for the German ships. 72 Squadron, still ignorant of the true situation, went ahead as escort. It was over two hours since Bobby Oxspring had reported the ships, and all that time the Germans had been waiting for the expected heavy British attacks. Nothing had happened. Hitler had been right: the British command was not able to react swiftly and correctly to a sudden change in the situation.

129 Squadron, including Hugo Armstrong, with Ted Hall as his Number 2, was scrambled to escort Hurricane bombers, but the target was unknown. The Hurricanes were met at Manston, and the formations set off into the very bad weather over the sea. Hugo led A Flight on the right of the Hurricanes, Flight Lieutenant Bowman led B Flight.

'Suddenly,' recalled Ted, 'on our right, not far away and barely visible in such terrible weather conditions, was a warship escorted by E-boats. Violent weaving and luck helped us escape the flak coming our way from Gneisenau. We overtook two Swordfish biplanes which were lumbering slowly ahead. The one nearest me, perhaps 50 yards [metres] away, blew up! Seconds later, the other was hit and cartwheeled over the water. Scharnhorst was almost in front of our weave-line. In the semi-darkness, the yellow flashes of the massive guns and many anti-aircraft guns could be seen along the whole side of the battleship [sic]. The concentrated firepower was horrific, so the Swordfish flying straight and level had no chance. I watched a third bi-plane visibly disintegrate, almost at the battleship.'

All six Swordfish of 825 Squadron were shot down by flak or fighters. None of Esmonde's crew survived, but some of the next two crews were rescued and reported the heroic charge at the big ships, at pitifully slow speed, over grey winter seas, under low cloud, past destroyers and torpedo-boats, among Messerschmitts and Focke Wulfs, into anti-aircraft fire, to destruction. Some FW190s dropped flaps and undercart to stay behind the slow torpedo bombers, and one was shot down by a Royal Navy gunner. The second flight of three Swordfish simply disappeared in the action, last seen by members of the leading flight, already shot down themselves and in the water. Over their heads, dodging flak and fighters, the second flight went roaring past the crashed Swordfish towards the German capital ships; no one survived. Ted Hall's description is all that is known of their fate. The German sailors and officers watched the slaughter of the biplanes and were aware of and deeply impressed by the bravery of Esmonde's crews.

'Still weaving violently,' Ted continued, *'we passed within 30 yards [metres] of the ship's stern.   Tracer from the other side was nearly as heavy, but in seconds the darkness of the weather hid us from view.   Sergeant Wilson RAF, flying as Number 4, was hit badly, but was rescued from the sea.   B Flight was too far left of the action and were jumped by 109s. Pilot Officer Davis RCAF was shot down; 'Bowie' damaged a 109.   The official loss of Allied planes for the day was 42!'*

Later, in the Mess, a grinning Hugo asked Ted, 'Did you see that shell go past, "Made in Hamburg 1938"?'

Lieutenant Commander Esmonde was awarded a posthumous Victoria Cross. Decorations were received by many other participants, on both sides.   Though the British had been shocked by the daring voyage, and the German ships reached safety, both *Scharnhorst* and *Gneisenau* were damaged by mines, and played little further part in the war.   The threat they posed to Allied Atlantic convoys while at Brest was removed. Hitler had made a correct tactical but a wrong strategic decision.

The German fighters from JG2 and JG26 claimed 13 Swordfish, ten being 'confirmed' by the official Luftwaffe system and a victory credit given the relevant pilots.   The German ships also were credited with destruction of six Swordfish.   It is acknowledged by all concerned and accepted by historians and enthusiasts that almost all victory claims for intense combats were exaggerated, but to the author of this book there seems to have been a disproportionate effort directed to disparaging Allied claims, while Luftwaffe claims have been accepted, partly due to the allegedly thorough verification into each claim by relevant Luftwaffe authorities, and the issue of a confirmatory document for an individual claim.   These documents appear to have taken on the halo of irrefutable historical fact. Events such as the Channel Dash call into question the accuracy of the Luftwaffe system. Only six Swordfish took part; Ted Hall alone saw three shot down by ships' fire; but ten were officially credited to fighter pilots by the German system.   This was a battle fought at sea, by forces moving south to north, in abominable weather conditions and with no wrecked aircraft on land to be counted.

Next day, 13 February, a fighter sweep was made over France.   Hugo's No.2 on this operation spun in over Berck, possibly due to oxygen failure.   Another sweep was flown on the 15th, and on a formation practice on the 16th, Hugo was *'shot at by a Spit over Worthing.   Missed!'*

Deaths among the first EATS course continued, with Sergeant Frank Reid killed in North Africa, with 3 Squadron RAAF.

The British forces, still smarting from the German success in the Channel, did strike back.   On 23 February, off Trondheim, *Prinz Eugen* was torpedoed by HMS *Trident,* and suffered severe damage to her stern.   *Prinz Eugen* never sailed operationally again, and ended her career in 1948 as part of the target fleet in the US atomic test at Bikini Atoll. *Gneisenau* was in dry-dock at Kiel on 25 February, and RAF Bomber Command attacked on three successive nights, damaging the ship so badly that the hull was towed to Gydnia, Poland, filled with concrete and became a stationary gun platform.   *Scharnhorst* was repaired in six months after the Channel Dash, but on 26 December 1943 she was engaged by a British naval force north of the Arctic Circle, and sunk off North Cape, with only 36 survivors from her crew of 1,940 men.

There was little operational flying for 129 Squadron in the first week of March.   On the 8th the squadron flew a fruitless Withdrawal Cover for bombers which crossed out of France north of the planned rendezvous.   This was one of the first two Circus operations for the year, in which attacks were made on Comines power station and the Abbeville marshalling yards.   Three Spitfires were lost, for claims for a Bf109 and a FW190, both later confirmed from Luftwaffe records.   JG26 claimed four victories.   Hugo also was scrambled after some 109s which attacked Christchurch, but they were not caught. Next day, Mazingarbe power station, in France, was attacked.

A damaged RN destroyer was making for Portsmouth on 12 March, and 129 Squadron kept a series of sections of four Spitfires overhead.   No enemy were seen.   Hugo and Sergeant Ted Hiskens RAAF flew the first of these escorts.   Later, Hugo and Ted crossed the Channel to France at 16.15 hours, and flew along the continent coast from Berck to Le Havre.   The weather was foggy, with cloud base at 3,000 feet, visibility about one mile, or 1,700 metres. They saw and attacked an armed trawler.   Hugo saw the 100-ton grey vessel steaming north, and opened fire at 150 metres, pulling up only 20 metres from it.   Ted, from the side, saw the 20mm cannon shells exploding along the waterline, then the Spitfires were past and away.   Crew were seen running to a machinegun, but had no time to get it into action before the Spitfires were gone into the mist.   The two Spitfires landed back at Westhampnett at 17.15.   At the back of his log-book, Hugo drew a small ship with a stick-figure diving off the stern, and *'Otto'* on the hull.

In the way of public relations people the world over, in Press Release No. 19 from RAAF Overseas Headquarters on 26 March, the ship was reported as 'severely damaged.'

Next morning, 13 March, the squadron flew dummy attacks and beat-ups on army convoys in the Chicester area.   In the afternoon, the squadron flew as top cover on Circus 114, when Bostons bombed Hazebrouck marshalling yards.   Heavy flak harassed them at 17,000 feet, and Hugo's Blue Section dived on six 109s, but without success. The Bostons crossed out of France safely, and the Wing returned via Dover.   JG26 claimed eight Spitfires, and admitted one Bf109 damaged.

On the last two Circus operations, ten RAF fighters were lost, and 13 enemy claimed, but no such losses could be found later in Luftwaffe records when these became available to historians. No record could be found of the loss of German aircraft reported by various RAF witnesses to have hit the ground or from which the pilot was reported to have baled out. Despite some movement of aircraft to the north, to support attacks on British convoys, Luftwaffe fighter strength on the Channel coast remained at about 300 aircraft, with 70 in reserve units. This was to be so for some weeks. The RAF decided to continue the air offensive, as in the long run equal losses would be in favour of the RAF. Circus operations were to continue, but were constrained by the lack of range of all available RAF fighters. It was decided that first priority was to be given to attacks on power stations, and then to a list of 58 factories selected in the target area.

A Messerschmitt Bf109F

On 14 March, the Tangmere Wing flew on a Roadstead operation over Le Havre. A 'Roadstead' was an operation in which fighters escorted bombers or fighter-bombers in attacks on shipping at sea or in harbour. Hudson bombers were to attack a German flotilla, and the Tangmere Wing was to provide cover. 41 Squadron flew as low squadron, and after a full throttle crossing of the Channel, reached France north of Etretat at 5,000 feet, with 129 Squadron 2,000 feet higher and behind. There was 7/10 broken cloud at that height, with cumulus higher. The Spitfires turned north-east, and saw the enemy ships 1700 metres off Fecamp. The convoy consisted of a 6000-ton armed merchant ship, with six minesweepers and six other escort boats. The Tangmere Wing circled the ships, but maintained height. Though informed, the bombers could not find the ships. After about ten minutes

129 Squadron: Ted Hiskens RAAF & Pilot Officer Bush RAF.
(Ted Hall)

circling, the Spitfire squadrons saw Bf109s coming in low from Le Havre. These 109s were from JG2 '*Richthofen*'.

At 10.50, 41 Squadron engaged the Messerschmitts some eight kilometres off Etretat, and Squadron Leader Thomas sent Hugo's Blue Section down to assist. Descending through broken cloud, Hugo saw a 109F climbing steeply to a layer of cumulus at 7,000 feet. Using speed accumulated in the dive, Hugo closed on the 109 and fired two 3-second bursts at about 100 metres, just as the 109 slipped into cloud. At that moment, another 109 fired on Hugo from starboard and flew between him and his Number 2. However, Hugo's Number 4, Flight Sergeant V.E. Tucker, confirmed the victory, as he saw the first 109 reappear from the cloud, and dive vertically into the sea in front of Tucker.

The victory over the 109F was marked by another cartoon cross in Hugo's log-book, for '*Kurt*'.

The squadron added another victory, shared between Pilot Officer Bush and Sergeant Edwards, while 41 Squadron claimed seven, of which at least three were seen by other pilots to go into the sea. The Hudsons had not been seen at all.

The Wing took off again at 13.35, for a repeat of the morning operation, but the ships had entered Le Havre harbour and there was no attack. Some 109s were seen, but there was no combat. Hugo's Blue Section was *'jumped by two 109s - squirted a third - missed.'*

Hugo's third sortie of the day was a convoy patrol over 46 ships steaming east past Bognor. He wrote, '*Almost asleep! Four hours ops for the day.*'

There was little operational flying for the next week, and no contact with enemy. Bad weather clamped down, and other activities were arranged to keep the pilots interested. On 22 March, the squadron was visited by Captain Binstead, Trade Commissioner for Mysore, Mr. Goodchild of the India Office, and Sir Frank Brown of the East India Company. After lunch with the Station Commander, the visitors went to the squadron dispersal. Sir Frank made a speech, then presented gold Mysore Medallions to the pilots and to the ten senior NCOs. The AOC Fighter Command, Air Vice Marshal Trafford Leigh Mallory, then arrived and presented the squadron crest to Squadron Leader Thomas. The squadron marched past the AOC, and the pilots later met him in the dispersal hut. Leigh Mallory congratulated them on the squadron record, and also for the fact that 523 hours were flown in February without an accident. At this time, Fighter Command was plagued with accidents which cost many pilots and aircraft. Another sweep was flown next morning to Le Havre, and one in the afternoon to Le Touquet, with no combats.

The visit by the representative of the Sultan of Mysore. (Ted Hall)

Sergeant Bob Good, of the first EATS course, was killed in action in the Middle East with 14 Squadron RAF on 17 March.

On 24 March, after a camera gun test and a wing formation exercise, Hugo was scrambled but could not catch 109s strafing Newhaven. At 14.30, 129 Squadron flew high cover to 41 Squadron on Circus 116, to Abbeville. Once again, the Comines power station and the marshalling yards were targeted.

The Focke-Wulf Expert

The rendezvous was 9,000 feet over Redhill, but when the Spitfires arrived no Bostons were seen. The Wing circled for ten minutes, then set off for the Somme estuary - and there were the bombers, only 16 km off the French coast. Hugo was Blue 3, and with his No.4, became separated from the squadron when Blue 1 returned to the UK with an oil pressure problem, with Blue 2 flying with him as escort. Hugo climbed above the entire formation and tacked on to the top layer. Then, just before reaching the target, several FW190s were seen below, and, with only one other aircraft [Blue 4] to consider in his movements, Hugo attacked at once, came in astern of a FW190, fired a three-second burst, and shot it down. The 190 was seen to crash south of the River Somme; the pilot baled out. There was no other combat by the squadron during the operation.

Luftwaffe records indicate that the FW190 was flown by Oberleutnant Otto Behrens, commander of 6/JG26. Behrens was wounded, landed near Le Treport, and survived. In 1941, as he had a pre-war engineering background, Behrens was detached from JG26, with a team of technical staff, to assist the development programme for the FW190. The excellent airframe designed by Kurt Tank, and the equally excellent BMW 801 engine, experienced many difficulties before the superb entity was complete. Behrens persevered through many dangerous test flights and modifications needed until the outstanding FW190 was ready for operational service. With the technical team, Behrens then returned to the Geschwader and made further contributions to successful adoption of the type by II/JG26.   On 30 June 1942, Behrens left JG26 for the Rechlin testing centre, where he flew the early Luftwaffe jets, and survived the war as last commander of the test centre.

Hugo drew a little figure in a parachute, with *'Erik',* in his logbook.

JG26 claimed seven Spitfires, for loss of two FW190s destroyed and one forcelanded.

There were four Australians mentioned on the squadron in a press release: Hugo and Ted Hiskens, and Sergeants H.K. Barker from Sydney, a former Manly life-saver, and N.R. Caldwell from Adelaide.

An afternoon Circus to Le Trait on the 25th resulted in a combat after 129 Squadron was jumped.   As the Bostons turned onto their bombing run, Hugo's Blue Section was above and behind the squadron. JG2 was directed to intercept by the German control system.   Five FW190s attacked Hugo's formation, but lost two destroyed and one damaged to Pilot Officers Bush and Sherk. Then another bunch of 190s set on Hugo, and the section became separated in individual fights, but all returned safely.

In combat during a Roadstead to Le Havre next day, 26 March, four 129 Squadron aircraft were damaged, and no claims made. *'Flak too good to be funny,'* noted Hugo, who also drove off a persistent Bf109 which was after Pilot Officer Bush. Again, JG2 intercepted the RAF sweep. A Boston crew baled out before reaching the English coast, and one section of 129 Squadron circled them for 40 minutes until leaving because of little fuel remaining. The next aircraft sent out could not find the unfortunate men. More searching next day was unsuccessful.

On the 28th, on a sweep to Le Havre at 10,000 feet, Pilot Officer Hunter, Hugo's No.2, suddenly left the formation in a dive to the sea off Etretat. No one had any idea what caused this loss, but Hugo speculated 'lack of oxygen'.

There were no more combats in March. There had been almost daily operations in the last part of the month, and RAF losses totalled 34, for claims of 55 enemy destroyed. Only 12 were identified in Luftwaffe records.

Hugo was promoted Flying Officer, War Substantive rank dating from 12 January. He flew various sweeps and patrols in the first three days of April, with no contact. These included unsuccessful interceptions, dawn patrols and a sweep inland past Boulogne, plus a shipping reconnaissance which was tactfully abandoned as two Spitfires alone in a cloudless sky flying down the French coast would have been too tempting for the Luftwaffe.

Ted Hall scrapes home

Youthful skylarking. Ted Hiskens and Hugo Armstrong in the Miles Magister. (Ted Hall)

On 4 April, 129 Squadron was tasked to provide cover to two Air Sea Rescue launches off the coast of Kent, and took off at 11.15. The boats were found only 10 miles [16 km] off the French coast, and the squadron split into sections and circled between 2,000 and 8,000 feet. After an hour, Hugo's Yellow Section was detailed to escort one of the boats back to England. Ted Hall was his No.2. The weather in mid-Channel was clear, but closer to France there was 7/10th cloud with its base at about 2,000 feet - cover for a few Luftwaffe fighters to approach. At 12.45, as the relieving section of Spitfires was sighted approaching from England, six FW190s attacked Hugo's section. Hauptmann 'Pips' Priller, commander III/JG26, intended adding another victory to his substantial tally of 61 enemy aircraft.

'Hugo called me to line abreast to dive through the cloud cover below,' said Ted. 'Breaking through at 4,000 feet, I pulled up to hug the clouds, and to look for Hugo. Suddenly I noticed yellow incendiaries passing my right wing. The explosive bullets holed the wing. I pulled back violently to enter the clouds just as a FW190 passed on my left. The black and white cross of the German fighter and the pilot in the cockpit were very clear. Smoke and fumes entered my cockpit and the temperature gauge rose quickly. I knew my glycol was hit.

'Luckily, as Hugo broke cloud, right in front of him was the wing man of the pilot who attacked me. Hugo fired from 50 yards [metres] and the 190 spun to the sea. Hugo got away a decent burst at my attacker as he broke away from me. When my temperature gauge reached 160 degrees, I cut my motor and glided, then re-started the motor until the gauge reached 160, and repeated the procedure many times while heading towards England. Each time, I lost altitude. Somehow, Hugo kept the other two FWs away from me before they turned for home. I nearly baled out twice. First, over some E-boats, and then closer to home, over a British destroyer, but felt I was too low. I did not want to ditch in the sea, or to land on the beaches, as I surmised they had been mined.

'Hugo, flying slightly ahead, called and said it might be possible to belly-land on the edge of the cliff directly in front of us. Exceeding greatly the 160 mark and hoping the motor would not seize, I made the cliff edge without hitting any of the concrete pillars and wire ropes erected to stop enemy gliders landing. Over the radio, I could hear Hugo screaming, "Get out for God's sake! It will blow up!" So, over the side and a very fast sprint to safety.'

After landing, Hugo reported that he swung onto the leader of the second pair, firing from 350 to 150 yards, and saw strikes flash across the port mainplane and on to the fuselage behind the pilot; he claimed a 'damaged'. Hugo then turned back to Ted's damaged Spitfire, and escorted him to the English coast, where Hall crashlanded at old Ramsgate airfield. The squadron records described this as 'a very fine performance' by both pilots, with Ted 'handling with coolness and resource his considerably damaged plane.'

'Hugo,' said Ted, 'received his first DFC and my grateful thanks.'

129 Squadron early 1942. left to right: F/O Chapman RAF, the Intelligence Officer, Sgt Reeves RCAF, Sgt Hiskens RAAF, Sgt Dalton RAF, Sgt Edwards RNZAF, P/O Steen DutchAF, P/O Jones RAF, F/Lt Bowman RAF, Sgt Irish RCAF, P/O Lorrie RCAF, Sgt Engelson NorwegianAF, Sgt Bjornstad Nor.AF, Sgt Frith RCAF, Sgt Jenseen Nor.AF, unknown, squadron adjutant. (Ted Hall)

In his log-book, Hugo drew a running stick-figure, with a large bullet chasing it, and *'190 Dam'*. It seems the damage to the FW190 from Hugo's fire was not heavy enough to be the subject of a report - or, no record of such damage survived.

Meanwhile, Blue and Red Sections of the squadron had turned back, after chasing 190s almost to France. Without warning, Pilot Officer Bush dived into the sea from 500 feet; nothing more was seen of him. Searching found only a patch of oil off North Foreland. There was no indication that Bush had been attacked.

'Pips' Priller duly claimed a Spitfire and was awarded his 62nd victory through the Luftwaffe system. Whether his 'approved' victory was Ted Hall or Bush is not clear.

Earlier, against Circus 119, JG26 claimed 14 Spitfires for admitted damage to one FW190.

To 72 Squadron as a Flight Commander

Next day, 5 April, Hugo was promoted Acting Flight Lieutenant and posted to 72 (Basutoland) Squadron as a Flight Commander. He had flown 30 offensive sorties, and had 228 hours on Spitfires. Hugo arrived at his new squadron on the 6th. 72 Squadron was commanded by Squadron Leader Brian Kingcome DFC*, a Battle of Britain veteran with at least ten victories, and a large number of probables and damaged.   72 at this time formed part of the Biggin Hill Wing, which was led by Wing Commander James 'Jamie' Rankin DSO DFC*, who had at least 14 victories.

Hugo had Spitfire RN-M as his personal aircraft on 72 Squadron   There were more sweeps, but on the 13th, in RN-Q, Hugo *'force-landed at Gravesend.   AND HOW*!' he emphasised the event. Flying as Blue 1 on Circus 124, 15 April, Hugo saw an aircraft in flames spinning south of Boulogne, then the pilot baled out. This sighting confirmed a claim for a FW190 by Flying Officer B.O. Parker RCAF, who led Yellow Section.. *'Jumped about five miles inland by numerous 190s,'* Hugo wrote. *'Fired at two - missed! One hole in port main plane, Number 2 slightly damaged.'*

Off faraway Ceylon, two more members of the first EATS course died in action. The Japanese navy struck at the British naval port at Columbo, and in attacks on the enemy ships Sergeant Hugh MacLennan and Warrant Officer Noel Stevenson were killed on 9 April.

The cross-Channel offensive provided the Luftwaffe pilots in JG2 and JG26 almost daily opportunites for combat, with the result that claims for victories soon reached respectable numbers. While RAF and Commonwealth squadrons rotated through the forward area, or were posted to other theatres, German units remained, with assistance from reserve or training units.   On 17 April 1942, JG2 *'Richthofen'* claimed its 1,000th victory, and a certain amount of celebration followed.

The RAF squadrons flew whenever the weather allowed, but many sweeps had no contact. The defending force was able to refuse combat or engage, depending on the situation being advantageous to them or not. In three days, Hugo flew six sweeps without engaging the Luftwaffe.   His log-book contains small notes which detail the operation, and a comment, such as, *'Saw nothing'*; *'thousands of Spits, nothing else'*; *' Cook's tour around NW France'*.

Then on the 24th, the Luftwaffe reacted to Bostons bombing oil tanks at Flushing: *'Jumped by about 30-plus between St. Omer-Gris Nez.   Blue 2 and 4 missing.   Six second squirt - missed again.'*   JG26 pilots received victory credits for nine Spitfires, including several at this place and time.

On the second sweep on 25 April, the squadron was *'Met at St. Pol by numerous 190s above.   Yellow 4 not yet returned; Blue 4 shot up; chute in water 5 miles off coast.'*   Four wings of Spitfires were engaged by the German fighters.   JG26 claimed nine and JG2 claimed two victories.

There were two more sweeps on 26 April and another next morning, when the Spitfires *'swept to St. Omer and out again.   Saw nothing.'*   This was Hugo's 49th offensive operation.

Circus 141 was flown in the afternoon of 27 April; 12 Boston bombers attacked Lille power station.   72 Squadron provided high cover, with Hugo leading Blue Section. FW190s attacked the Bostons, and Wing Commander Rankin led Red Section down to engage.   Hugo took Blue Section to cover Rankin, but in the dive Rankin passed through another formation of Spitfires.   While avoiding them, Hugo lost sight of Rankin, but then saw three enemy fighters circling the bombers, at 10,000 feet north of Lille. Hugo swung around to the down-sun side of the Bostons, and attacked a 190 which was diving away.   The de Wilde ammunition sparked on the fuselage and tail, but the 190 kept going.   Rather than follow and lose precious height, Hugo pulled up.   He then escorted a damaged Boston, protecting it from a number of predatory 190s.   He fired brief bursts at about six 190s, but missed.   As the Boston crossed the French coast at Gravelines, intense 37mm flak came up; the bomber turned port; two crew baled out and the Boston seemed to be going in for a forced-landing.   *'The flak at 3,000 feet was bloody good*,' noted Hugo.   Short of fuel, he landed at Manston; his Spitfire on this flight, W3168, was a presentation aircraft, "Cawnpore II", paid for by a donation of 5,000 pounds sterling.   His No.2, Pilot Officer Daniel, had claimed a FW190 probably destroyed, and there were many other combats, but no other claims and no squadron losses. Hugo drew another running stick-figure, big bullet behind it, and *'190 Dam'*.

The Tangmere Wing now was led by Wing Commander Piet Hugo, promoted from command of 41 Squadron.   The Wing had escorted Bostons on Circus 143, an attack on Ostend.   On this operation, Piet Hugo had destroyed one enemy, hit another, and decided to fire on a third, despite seeing a distant 190, which seemed too far away to shoot accurately.   Unfortunately for the South African, this German was a good shot, and hit the Wing leader's Spitfire.   Ted Hiskens, still with 129 Squadron, saw the Spitfire under attack, and dived to fire on the 190, but the damage was done.   Hiskens saw the leader's Spitfire in trouble, trailing white smoke, gradually losing height over the Channel, so stayed with it.

'I caught him up and weaved above him, calling up base and giving our position,' Hiskens said later. *'At 5,000 feet the Wing Commander baled out and waved to me as I circled him. When he was in his dinghy, I pin-pointed his position from a sand bank and searched for rescue launches.'*
Hiskens found one, and guided it to the dinghy. Piet Hugo was rescued, but a shoulder wound had him off flying for some time. He continu_ a successful and varied career with the RAF. In August, Ted Hiskens was posted to 24₈ Squadron RAF on Malta.

Next day, 72 Squadron flew two operations, and 'just missed a third show in one day for the first time this year, as a further operation had to be cancelled at the last minute due to the abnormally high wind,' stated the squadron records. The first operation was at 05.50, a Ramrod with eight Hurricanes to St. Omer, but there was no contact and all aircraft returned by 07.20. The second operation returned to St. Omer at 11.10 - a Circus with six Bostons. Flight Lieutenant Woods and Sergeant Robertson each claimed damage to a FW190. The high winds, described as 'violent' in the record, caused the cancellation of the morning sweep on the 29th, but an operation was flown in the afternoon. Before flying, the pilots were inspected by HM King George VI, who watched the squadrons depart on the sweep. To divert attention from Bostons attacking Dunkirk, this was a flight along the coast from Le Touquet to Cap Gris Nez. Two more operations were flown on the 30th, and though Hugo and Pilot Officer Franz Colloredo-Mansfeld fired at enemy on the first sweep, they did not claim anything on return. Colloredo-Mansfeld was an Austrian-born US citizen in the RAF. Hugo was disgusted with his gunnery, and noted, *'Used all cannon on one - missed again - Give it Up!'*

The pace of offensive operations mounted by the RAF in April 1942 increased over the total for March. 29 Circus operations were flown, as well as Rodeos, Ramrods and others. RAF fighter losses were 104, with claims for 67 enemy; only 21 could be confirmed from postwar German Quarter Master records. It has been suggested that these records may not reflect the true loss situation, as, if a unit was in process of re-equipping with a new type or model of aircraft, only loss of that new type needed to be reported, so a replacement would be provided. Loss of an older type was not reported, as it was in process of being replaced automatically in the re-equipment programme. Of course, pilot losses would require replacement. At this time, Air Marshal Sholto Douglas, at Fighter Command, pointed out to the Air Staff that he was urged to go on the offensive to wear down the enemy fighters in the West, in order to help the Russians, but Fighter Command's first line units and reserves were continually whittled away for other theatres. RAF Intelligence analysed information available to them, and found the opposing Luftwaffe force operated in April at 4.5 times the level of March. It also was found that RAF 4-wing operations had more effect and were less costly than smaller but more frequent operations. It may be recognised that this latter finding related to one of the Principles of War: Concentration of Force. Napoleon is reputed to have said that victory goes to the big battalions.

The defending Luftwaffe fighter pilots on the Channel were presented with an almost perfect situation in which to become aces, or, in their own term, *'experten'*. They were operating over or close to their own bases, over friendly territory, with all that meant in assistance in the event of baling out or heavy damage to their Messerschmitt or Focke-

Wulf. In late June and early July 1941, before ordered from operational flying, the great Adolf Galland of JG26 himself had been shot down three times in two weeks, and if the tactical situation had been reversed, each of these occasions would have resulted in death or capture.   The record is, perhaps, held by Major Georg-Peter Eder, who flew from December 1940 to the end of the war:- 78 victories, but 17 times shot down, 12 times wounded; always able to return to his unit.

In the Messerschmitt Bf109F, the Luftwaffe fighter pilots in mid-1942 had an aircraft basically equal to the Spitfire V; in the Focke Wulf FW190, an aircraft superior in every important aspect.   Constant RAF offensive operations provided the most important factor for an aspiring fighter pilot: opportunity to engage in combat.   The continuing expansion of the RAF in 1940-43, and dispatch of squadrons overseas, meant that there was a proportion of inexperienced pilots and junior leaders in RAF formations, while JG2 and JG26 remained in place as 'the home team', with tried and experienced leaders.

However, wars are not won by defence, and the strategic initiative on the English Channel had been surrendered by the Luftwaffe in the winter of 1940-41.   While the RAF - and later the US air forces - developed, expanded and evolved, the Luftwaffe basically remained as it was at the end of the victorious campaigns of 1940-41. A serious weakness in the Luftwaffe fighter arm, condoned by Reichsmarschall Goering and exacerbated by the Third Reich propaganda machine, was the elevation to celebrity status of successful fighter pilots with victories over enemy fighters.   Air power always has been concerned with delivery of bombs to targets, and bombers should have been the primary target of interceptions, but in the first four years of the war the German fighter pilot acquired standing in the fighter fraternity by shooting down enemy fighters.

Also, to put into some perspective the recent adulation of the Luftwaffe and its aces, it should be remembered that, in the final analysis, the Luftwaffe was Hitler's instrument of terror, used to frighten his neighbours, and had taken part in the sustained bombing of towns and cities beginning with the attacks on Madrid and Guernica in Spain, Warsaw, Rotterdam, and the British cities during the 'blitz'. The Luftwaffe and its *experten* flew in defence of an evil regime, whose treatment of political dissenters and others was known by every man, woman and child in Germany.   It has been shown how tissue-thin is the excuse offered by the German military that no one knew what was happening to political prisoners and Jews.   It is impossible to move millions of people across Europe by train without the populations of those towns and cities along the way seeing what was happening, or their neighbours becoming aware of the empty apartments and houses or shops.   The mass murders perpetrated before the death-camps were built were witnessed by thousands of German soldiers, not only in SS units, and as well as witnessing the murders, some were participants in the killing. Some took their own photographs of the scenes.

In addition, there can not be the slightest doubt that Germany was the aggressor, had invaded territories on her borders pre-war, and, since Hitler's refusal to withdraw his invading forces from Poland in September 1939, Germany had attacked and subjugated most of the Western European nations.   Some Luftwaffe leaders proudly painted on their aircraft the flags of nations they had flown against.   The excuse that they were only defending their own country like everyone else is weak when that defence was on the shores of Norway, Denmark, Holland, Belgium, France, North Africa, the Ukraine and over Leningrad.   None of those countries had attacked Nazi Germany.   It was the high point of a military career to be presented to the Fuhrer to receive one's highest decorations. The Luftwaffe flew to the last day of the war for a Germany controlled by the Nazi Party.

On 1 May 1942, 12 Hurricanes were to attack Dunkirk, but 10/10ths cloud forced the squadrons to turn back at the rendezvous point. Later in the day three Spitfire squadrons swept Le Havre, and Hugo noted *'scrap with 190s coming out. Landed West Hampnett for fuel.'* Still later, Circus 150B was flown, as escort for six Bostons to Calais. Hugo saw accurate flak bursting around the Bostons, and many 190s in the area, some at 'great height', but he was not in combats. On return to base he force-landed with a flat tyre, but was able to avoid damage to Spitfire 'M'. On 3 May, two more sweeps were flown, but the squadron did not engage enemy.

A Messerschmitt Bf109 loses its tail

Circus 153 was mounted on 4 May. Six Bostons attacked Le Havre power station, and 72 Squadron provided high cover; Hugo led Blue Section. At 10.40, two of Red Section attacked a Dornier Do217, which went down in a right-hand spiral. Hugo took his section to cover this action, but left to join the main formation when radio chatter informed him that it was in contact. The action was out of sight, but while flying north-west to rejoin, Hugo saw two formations of four each of 109s, and a lone Spitfire attacking the rearmost of the lower 109s. The upper 109s dived from the sun onto the Spitfire, and shot it down just before Hugo was in range.

The victorious 109 was still behind the stricken Spitfire as Hugo fired a short burst from 15-degrees astern; and *'immediately had to take avoiding action to miss the tailplane of the aircraft, which had come off'*. Blue Section then had to turn tightly to avoid the other 109s, and Hugo was able to watch the 109 go into the sea. This was confirmed by Colloredo-Mansfeld, Hugo's No.2. Hugo sent a 'Mayday' call for the Spitfire, also going into the sea, engine stopped, and disabled.

Then another 109 was seen diving onto a Spitfire, and Hugo dived on the 109. The German pilot, keeping a lookout, pulled up in a climbing left turn, but with his speed from the dive Hugo cut across the intervening distance, closed on the 109, and fired a 3-second burst from 200 metres from the port quarter. There was a large flash on the cockpit, then Hugo saw another Spitfire, flown by Pilot Officer Owen Hardy, firing from his left, so broke away. The 109 dived out of the turn, then climbed steeply to the sun; Hugo thought it was about to attack; at the apex it *'fell away slowly onto its back, and I watched it as it dived slightly over the vertical into the sea. In my opinion the pilot was dead.'* Hugo fired 79 cannon rounds for these victories, though the second was shared with Owen Hardy, later a New Zealand ace. These 109s came from JG2.

The list of cartoons in the back of Hugo's log-book grew by two: *'Carl'* was the next grave cross, under *'109E Dest'* and *'Adolf'* was a *'109F Dest (Half)'*. However, in his log-book, Hugo noted next to the brief account of the combat, *'Vic Tucker Doug McPhee not yet returned.'*

On 6 May, six Bostons attacked Caen. The squadron was attacked by 190s over the Orne, and Hugo's Blue Section was split up. He was attacked by six 190s *'all the way back'*, and landed at Tangmere with very little fuel. *'Ever so nice to be back!'* he noted. Later in the day, the squadron escorted six Bostons to Boulogne. Two boats in harbour were attacked, but Hugo noted that the bombs *'missed by miles. Bags of flak.'* It was his 64th offensive operation.

Sweeps went on, but with only infrequent contact. Hugo had given up RN-M and flew a number of squadron aircraft. *'Little flak, no enemy aircraft'; 'saw nothing, came home'; ' toured round with sky to ourselves'; ' dived as soon as they saw us'.*

Then, on 17 May, *'Five blokes in the drink. Two picked up by Jerry boat. Bags of 190s and 109s about.'* JG2 claimed one and JG26 claimed nine victories throughout the day. On the 19th, *'In at Fecamp, out at Dieppe. Jumped by 109s, 133 lost two. None very near us.'* Bad weather affected operations in the third week in May, though the squadrons persisted if conditions eased at all. On the 24th, on a late afternoon sweep, Hugo fired at a FW190 at extreme range, but with no visible result. *'Jumped two 190s - Missed!'* Local flying was possible on the next two days but sweeps had to be abandoned after the aircraft had taken off.

A Messerschmitt loses a wing

On 27 May, 72 Squadron, part of the Biggin Hill Wing, flew a sweep as Rodeo 52 in the Dieppe-St. Valery area. At 11.30, the Wing was flying west just inside the French coast when some Messerschmitt Bf109s were seen approaching, but 2,000 feet below. Squadron Leader Brian Kingcome told Hugo to take Blue Section to attack.

As the 109s passed, Hugo turned port and dived on a pair on the right of the 109 formation, now seen to be 14 aircraft. But the two 109s broke right in a moderate turn, and so that Blue Section remained under the Spitfire top cover, Hugo turned port again, onto another pair of 109s on the left of the Messerschmitt formation. He swung in astern at 300 metres and fired a burst; the 109s turned tightly port; Hugo fired again, full deflection; the 109s dived; one remained. Hugo turned with this 109, for about three full circles, and then the 109 straightened out. Hugo was 200 metres behind, applied slight deflection, and fired. Brown smoke poured back and something came flying away from the Messerschmitt; Hugo thought it was the cockpit canopy. The 109 flopped sideways into a vertical dive, and after losing about 8,000 feet one wing came off and the remainder spun into cloud, followed by the fluttering wing. Hugo's port machineguns had stopped, but he fired 69 cannon and 312 machinegun rounds. This was his 72nd offensive operation. The little cartoon cross carried *'Rudolf'*. Kingcome also claimed a 109 probably destroyed.

On 29 May, Hugo's Distinguished Flying Cross (DFC) was gazetted. The citation read, 'This officer has participated in 29 operational sorties over enemy territory. He has destroyed at least 5 enemy aircraft and damaged a further two. Flight Lieutenant Armstrong has displayed courage and initiative and his judgement and skill as a leader have contributed largely to the successes achieved by his flight.'

On the morning of the 29th, during Rodeo 55, the squadron had a *'perfect jump on 109s spoiled by the top squadron coming through us.'* Hugo's 75th sweep was Rodeo 60 on the 30th, *'Saw nothing'*, and, a touch of humour, *'Chased two Typhoons back to England.'* Next day there was a combat, but Hugo did not claim. May ended with his hours on Spitfires at 321.

Operations in May 1942 cost Fighter Command 61 aircraft, against claims for 45, not all of which could be confirmed after the war. RAF losses still were greater than those of the enemy, and the air offensive was not producing the hoped-for results. RAF losses and lack of better results were due to two things. First, the Focke Wulf FW190 was markedly superior to the Spitfire V. Second, the German defensive system, organised around the radar reporting organisation, allowed their fighters to reach operating height well back from the coast, gain a good tactical position, and attack with the advantage. Fighter pilots of the time had to rely on the unaided human eye to see the enemy. With the advantage of height, with the sun behind them, and the masking effect of summer haze blinding anyone looking through it towards the sun, the German pilots enjoyed a tremendous advantage. If Luftwaffe pilots wished to break off an engagement, basically they had only to dive away eastward, knowing the short range of the RAF fighters did not allow for long pursuits at full throttle.

In the first three days of June, Hugo flew another six sweeps and a scramble. There was no contact, and enemy fighters were seen only once.

By this time, a Circus operation had become a set-piece performance. As soon as the Circus gathered, a climb to the designated height began, and the rising RAF squadrons appeared on Luftwaffe radar screens. The Messerschmitts and Focke Wulfs were alerted and began their own scramble for height, continually guided by their radar control and advised of the RAF location and height. Wing Commander Jamie Rankin, leading the Biggin Hill Wing, thought that a sweep at medium altitude by his squadrons would catch Luftwaffe units while they were climbing to engage the Circus. Rankin intended to stay low, climb steeply at the last moment, and catch the Luftwaffe unawares, before any British fighters would be expected.

Rankin was given permission to try this, and briefed his squadrons on 5 June for Circus 188. He said that while the Spitfires had concentrated on searching the sky above, there probably were many enemy still below who could themselves be bounced. The Spitfires of 133 Squadron were to be led by Rankin, and, with 124 and 72 Squadrons, were arranged for a quick Wing take-off, and soon, below 100 feet, the three squadrons were speeding south-east towards the coast.

Bobby Oxspring, who had first seen the German ships in the Channel on 12 February, was a successful pilot with nine victories in the Battle of Britain, and at this time commander of 91 Squadron. He talked his way onto the operation, and flew as Rankin's No.2. Oxspring recalled the exhilarating low level flight, contour chasing down the valleys to Dungeness, and the inspiring sight of 36 Spitfires low over the Channel. As the squadrons neared France and enemy observers on the coast there soon would report the oncoming formation, Rankin pulled into a climb.

A 109 in flames

Brian Kingcome led 72 Squadron; Hugo led Blue Section. By 15.40, the squadron was at 14,000 feet over Abbeville; Wing Commander Rankin called that he was diving on enemy. Hugo's No.4 called to report 15 enemy below. Hugo turned Blue Section to port, into line abreast to attack; identified the enemy as 109s; but as Blue Section dived another section of Spitfires passed in front of him, and he could not fire. The combat disrupted into individual engagements, and Hugo turned for the coast, but saw a 109F below. Another 109, the No. 2 of the first one, was to starboard, but Hugo dived onto the first Messerschmitt and closed to point-blank range, able only to fire a one-second burst before pulling up violently to avoid both a collision and fire from the 109's No.2, who was trying to protect his leader. Hugo blacked out under the g-forces, but when sight returned went into a steep turn and saw an aircraft below in flames. He fired only 16 cannon and 80 machinegun rounds.

The three RAF squadrons regrouped, amid a sky full of scattered FW190s and Bf109s of JG26 and JG2. Assessing the situation, Wing Commander Rankin realised it was time to go, and ordered, '_Everybody out._'   The Spitfires dived for home; there had not been any losses from 72 Squadron, though 124 and 133 Squadrons lost one each.   Each squadron claimed enemy aircraft destroyed, totalling 4-4-5.   72 Squadron's share was 3-1-2.   Sergeant Hughes, after destroying a 109, had his Spitfire raked by fire when returning alone from France. Wings, fuselage and tail were 'riddled', according to the squadron records, and machinegun bullets destroyed the air pressure system, artificial horizon and radio, while one bullet clipped the side of his helmet without touching him. Jamie Rankin himself had destroyed one 190, from which the pilot baled out, probably destroyed another, and damaged two more with accurate shooting.   Bobby Oxspring faithfully flew as No.2, and, at the end of the day, ruefully regarded his Spitfire's guns - he had not had opportunity to fire while supporting Rankin.   However, many other enemy were seen straggling up from the ground, Rankin's idea was proved, and all wanted to try again.   In his log-book, Hugo named the cartoon grave cross for '_Herman_'.

JG2, in action around Le Havre, claimed 21 Spitfires and these were 'confirmed' by the Luftwaffe system, but in fact only six RAF aircraft were lost.

Another sweep was flown next day, and though radar reported formations of up to 50 bandits, none were seen.   The Luftwaffe, however, took off and climbed hard to the south, then turned back at 25,000 feet.   The RAF squadrons were warned by radar of the approaching horde above, and '_we came home quickly_', wrote Hugo, adding '_VERY!_'

The haze over France was very thick, said to be from fires in Cologne after the first 1,000 bomber raid made by the RAF. To demonstrate that his squadrons could inflict substantial damage on a German city, and to show that it could be done with low losses, the Commander in Chief of RAF Bomber Command, Air Marshal Arthur T. 'Bomber' Harris, sent every available bomber against Cologne on the night of 30-31st May 1942.   Of 1134 fighters and bombers despatched, 44 had been lost.   5,000 casualties had been inflicted on the German population, 45,000 people were made homeless, 36 major factories were destroyed, 70 more badly damaged, and 220 others damaged to a lesser degree.   This was the beginning of serious application of bombing power into Germany.

Later on 6 June, Hugo flew as part of a formation to look for a British bomber crew reported off Ostend.   He found them and guided a rescue boat to the spot.   This was the crew of a four-engined Short Stirling, T-Tommy of 149 Squadron.   Hugo received a thank you note from the crew, all Sergeants or Flight Sergeants: Whitney, Jones, Check, Shields and Martin.

In the first half of June, RAF fighter losses over the Channel zone were 42, against claims for 22, but only seven of these could be verified from German records.   There was still no sign that the Luftwaffe had reinforced the Channel front with units from the east.   In fact, in the Mediterranean and Russia there was quite intense air and ground activity. Air Marshal Sholto Douglas was told that the air offensive would be modified, but pressure maintained - fighter sweeps would engage only when the situation was favourable; deep penetration over France was to be made only when the target warranted; fighter co-operation was to be improved; the new fast Hawker Typhoon was to be used as soon as available.   20 Circus operations were flown in June.   In March, 2,083 sorties had been flown, but this rate increased, with that for June being 5,895, and the four-month total was 21,470. By the end of June, the situation was a stalemate. The aim of the intense air offensive had not been gained, as the Luftwaffe did not reinforce the region, and, with the superb FW190 and a good defensive situation, inflicted heavier losses on the numerically superior RAF. RAF Intelligence, on information available, believed the Luftwaffe on the Channel coast had been badly hurt, and more such operations would continue the serious damage. But, for the four months to 30 June, RAF fighter losses were 259, with claims for 197 enemy. However, German records admit only 58 losses. Every other theatre of war wanted fighters, and serious questions were being asked of the reason to retain such a strong force in England when it was obvious so few Luftwaffe units were in the area. One small bright spot for the RAF was the destruction of valuable trains and rolling stock, with 71 destroyed or damaged in June. The European railway system was a vital part of the German war effort.

One way to force the German defenders to give up some of their tactical advantage would have been to employ a more destructive bomber force against suitable targets, including the airfields. But Bomber Command's heavy bomber policy was devoted to developing a massive punitive force to demolish the German cities at night. While the aircraft could carry a heavy bomb load, their defensive armament was grossly inadequate for daylight operations, and night attacks on Germany were seen as the main way to bring home to the German population the realities of modern war. The RAF did not have an aircraft which could be employed in worthwhile numbers on worthwhile daylight attacks on targets in France, Belgium or Holland.

The Luftwaffe thus enjoyed the advantage of attacking or declining to do so unless the situation was in its favour, and was able to ignore the puny bomber force in the midst of the escort squadrons.

72 Squadron flew more sweeps, and on the 22nd moved temporarily from Biggin Hill for training. There were no more squadron operations to the end of the month. On 23 June, a FW190 was captured intact in England. The pilot, Oberleutnant Arnim Faber, adjutant of III/JG2, became lost during a raid, and, after crossing the English coast south of the Bristol Channel, thought he was back in France, and landed at RAF Pembrey. At last a fully operational FW190 was able to be examined and the results promulgated to the RAF fighter squadrons. At last, after the tests, what every operational fighter pilot in the UK knew was officially accepted - the FW190 was superior in every important aspect of military flying compared to the Spitfire V, not to mention the obsolete Hurricane which some unfortunate squadrons had to fly across the Channel.

The first Mark IX Spitfires, which could cope with the FW190, came off the production line in April, but by June no fighter squadron had been equipped with them. The British aviation industry accepted many compromises during WW2, many lethal to RAF aircrews, and in this instance Spitfire Vs continued to be produced instead of switching to the Mark IX when the need was identified. The Mark VIII, a better version, required extensive alteration, and so was put back on the production schedule, to follow the Mark IX.

Bobby Oxspring took command of 72 Squadron in July; Brian Kingcome was given the Kenley Wing. Oxspring described 72 at this time as the 'best drilled, most experienced and aggressive squadron in the RAF', and was pleased with the 'cosmopolitan bunch of tough operators' he was to lead.   With the new Spitfire Mark IX, in Oxspring's opinion the squadron faced the future and the Luftwaffe with confidence.   On 8 July, a Mark IX was flown by Hugo and Flight Lieutenant 'Timber' Woods, who gave an enthusiastic report, after reaching 480 mph at 25,000 feet. The Engineering Officer said the new Spitfires would be available by the end of July, and the squadron record book stated, 'Then we shall be able to deal with the FW190 and the Me.109F'.

Hugo's first operation in July was on the 12th , when he flew two sweeps without contact. Next day, the 190s were seen coming up from Abbeville, and he *'jumped two but couldn't catch up. Six seconds [burst] from 500 yards.'* Targets of opportunity were strafed on the way home at low level, and Hugo fired at high-tension power lines on several occasions.   On the 23rd, he *'found a Hun staff car - frightened it into a tree.'*   This was the subject of another small cartoon in the back of his log-book: a crumpled staff car at a tree, with two stick figures running away.

On 15 July, in Libya, Pilot Officer John Pottie of the first EATS course was killed in action with 159 Squadron RAF.

A Focke-Wulf head-on

On 26 July, the Biggin Hill Wing flew Rodeo 81, a sweep to the St. Omer area. A Rodeo was an offensive fighter sweep over enemy territory, without bombers.   The Wing was led by Squadron Leader Thomas and 133 Squadron, with 401 in the middle and 72 as top cover.   Bobby Oxspring led 72 Squadron, and again Hugo led Blue Section.   The formation flew to North Foreland below 500 feet, turned on course for St. Omer, and after eight minutes began a fast climb.   The Tangmere Wing was doing the same towards Abbeville, and the Northolt Wing swept from Le Touquet to Gravelines.   Intense flak broke up the 72 Squadron formation, and at 13.40, Hugo's Blue Section was at 10,000 feet, just south of Gravelines, away from the rest of the formation.   Three FW190s were sighted behind, at the same height.   Just as Blue Section rejoined the squadron off Calais, the 190s attacked, but 72 Squadron swung starboard to face them.   One 190 was shooting at Hugo, who fired a one and a half second burst head-on at 20-degrees deflection as Spitfire and 190 sped towards each other.   A single large flash came from the 190, which flicked into a turn towards France, did two rolls while leaving a heavy trail of smoke, and went into a vertical dive, disappearing into cloud.   More 190s turned onto Blue Section, and Hugo could not watch the stricken fighter.   However, Pilot Officer Richard Ratten RAAF, Yellow 3, saw the combat, watched the 190 dive into cloud, and as he himself came out of a turn, Ratten again saw the diving 190, and watched it go into the sea.   There was no parachute visible.   Hugo's port machineguns stopped again, but he fired 29 cannon and 210 machinegun rounds from 200 metres to point-blank range.   Hugo's cartoon tally included a cross with '*Fritz*' and the date.   JG26 records indicate the FW190 possibly was flown by Oberfeldwebel Erwin Leibold, No.2 to Johannes Seifert, commander I/JG26.   Leibold, with 11 victory claims, apparently parachuted but was not found.

Bobby Oxspring himself claimed one FW190 probably destroyed, and several others were damaged. However, Squadron Leader H.R. Tidd RAF, flying Red 2 to Oxspring, was missing.

Hugo's victory was the one of the three claimed in combats at about the same time, and which brought to 900 the enemy destroyed by aircraft from Biggin Hill since the war began. This called for celebration. 72 Squadron adjourned to the 'White Hart' at Brasted, near Biggin, and an instant party developed.

On the 31st, on Circus 201, in which 24 Bostons bombed Abbeville-Drucat, the 190s were seen taking off through bomb bursts, and Hugo ruefully noted, *'perfect bounce on the way out; could not leave the bombers.'* This was his 99th offensive sweep; he had 385 hours on Spitfires. JG26 claimed 15 victories for one slightly damaged FW190, and JG2 admitted the loss of two Bf109s from 11/JG2, one flown by Hauptmann Rudi Pflanz, Knight's Cross. Pflanz, with JG2 since 1938, claimed 52 victories, including six on 23 July 1941.

Operations in July cost the RAF 62 fighters, for claims of 29 enemy destroyed; 16 were admitted lost in Luftwaffe records. Production of the Spitfire IX, which could cope with the FW190, was slow, and only three squadrons had them by the end of the month. In August, only two more squadrons received Spitfire IXs, and again RAF losses of 34 exceeded those of the Luftwaffe, at 13 aircraft [excluding the Dieppe operation on 19 August].

Hugo was told he was to take command of 133 Squadron, but 30 minutes later was stricken with appendicitis. This effectively removed him from operational flying until early September.

While Hugo was recovering from his surgical operation, and not fit for operational flying, on 19 August the Allied raid was made on Dieppe. This raid proved what should have been obvious - first, that an invasion of the Continent had little chance of success if the assault force went ashore at a place that was strongly defended, and second, that it was futile to hope to assault a modern port facility and capture it for further use by the invasion force. However, as in so many human endeavours, the raid had to be made to prove that such invasion tactics were bound to be defeated. A high price in human life was necessary to prove the matter.

The assault force of 6,086 officers and men in Commando and Canadian Army units crossed from England by boat, in 252 vessels, attacked, was held by the defences, re-embarked survivors under intense fire and returned to England. Losses were 494 officers and 3,890 men in the assault force; 33 small ships and landing craft and a destroyer were lost, plus 81 officers and 469 men of the Royal Navy. No tank or other item of heavy equipment landed was saved. RAF losses were 96 aircraft, all details of which are available in public records. Again, however, the only Luftwaffe losses recorded are those for pilots killed or badly wounded.

While the German defenders won a tactical victory, the strategic results were to be not in their favour. A great amount of materials, money and effort was then put into improving defences all along the occupied coast, but, more importantly, the fatal mindset of the German high command was established - that a cross-Channel invasion would come over the narrow part of the English Channel.

For the Luftwaffe, despite victory claims and enhanced reputations of the *experten,* serious faults had been revealed, if anyone had been able to analyse and report on the performance of the German air arm. The Luftwaffe had failed to detect the concentration of ships, the embarkation of the troops, or the night crossing of the Channel. The first indication the defences had of the invaders was by the fortunes of war: a small number of German armed trawlers chanced upon a batch of landing craft inbound to the beach, and when flares illuminated the British ships the land defences were alerted - just in time. The Luftwaffe failed to prevent the landing, failed to influence the course of the battle, failed to prevent the re-embarkation, and failed to prevent the return to England or to inflict serious damage to the mass of shipping.   Only two British bombers are known to have been lost to Luftwaffe fighters, but approximately 68 RAF and US fighters were claimed by German fighters.

30 RAF aircraft were lost to flak, and four Spitfires were shot down by Luftwaffe bomber gunners. Two RAF fighters were destroyed trying to land in bad weather, and about five other aircraft were written off after landing with damage. JG2 claimed some 60 victories and JG26 claimed about 38. Both sides over-claimed, which is entirely understandable given the circumstances, combining bad weather and a large number of aircraft maneuring and fighting in a relatively small air space. But once again the only German losses admitted are for those of pilots killed or badly wounded, some 23 in all.

The RAF had maintained air cover over the battle area and only a relative few Luftwaffe aircraft had been able to attack the ships or beach area, or the returning force. A great deal had been learned and the lessons studied for use in the future full scale invasion of Europe.   The greatest development in air-ground cooperation took place in the Mediterranean theatre. When all this was put into practice on 6 June 1944, in Normandy, the performance of the Allies was at the other end of the scale from the shambles and panic of May 1940, and far in advance of the tentative ideas and procedures employed at Dieppe.

The Luftwaffe, apparently, learned nothing.   As is now well known, on D-Day the best reaction effort the Germans could do was to send a two-plane 'sweep' along one invasion beach by Pips Priller and his wingman.

Hugo was posted to command 611 Squadron RAF, as the first EATS graduate to achieve command of a UK-based RAF fighter squadron.   Clive Caldwell, his class-mate from No.1 EATS Course in 1940, had been given command of 112 Squadron RAF in the Desert in January 1942, the first EATS graduate to achieve squadron command.   Hugo succeeded Squadron Leader D.H. Watkins DFC, who went to Headquarters Fighter Command [Tactics].   The squadrons in the 600- series were raised in the 1930s, as the Auxiliary Air Force, and were named for counties in the UK - for example, 611 was the

West Lancashire squadron. Watkins first joined 611 in 1938, as an Acting Pilot Officer in the RAF Auxiliary. By July 1941 he commanded A Flight as a Flight Lieutenant with the DFC and 300 hours operational flying. After a posting to 57 OTU Hawarden, he returned to 611 as CO in November 1941. With his departure, noted the records, the squadron lost its last Auxiliary officer.

Hugo was the first Dominion officer to command the squadron, and arrived on 12 September. There was no operational flying for four days after Hugo arrived, and Spitfire IX BS435, letter 'F', became his personal aircraft. The Biggin Hill Administration Officer was Squadron Leader Robert 'Bob' Taylor RAF, who described his role as 'head housekeeper'. He saw many squadrons come and go, and recalled Hugo as 'stable and well balanced; an extrovert, but not a show-off; a fine sense of humour and a fine leader, as seen in the high morale of his squadron.' Despite occassional reverses, morale of all at Biggin was, in Bob Taylor's opinion, 'quite high for a very long time.'

611 Squadron contained many Liverpool men in its personnel, and, as Cliff Broadbent recalled, a very strong affinity developed between the ground crews and the pilots, who often were referred to as the 'drivers'. 'The distress was very real,' said Cliff, 'when your

Hugo Armstrong, CO 611 Squadron RAF. (RAAF)

pilot and friend failed to return.' However, the international composition of the wartime RAF was reflected in the Flight Commanders: Flight Lieutenant W.V. Compton DFC, a New Zealander with nine victories, led A Flight, and B was led by Czechoslovakian Flight Lieutenant F. Vancl. Three days later, of three new pilots posted in, two were US citizens in the RAF, and brought to three the number on strength.

On the 16th, the squadron flew on Rodeo 94, with three other Spitfire IX and two US P38 Lightning squadrons from the US 1st Fighter Group of the fledgling US 8th Air Force.

The force flew to Abbeville, circled, then went along the coast, with a combat off Le Touquet.   Two FW190s were claimed damaged by 611 Squadron.   Other similar operations were flown to the end of the month, with no claims by Hugo.   He was somewhat disgruntled by events on the last few days of September.   The squadron took off to escort US B-17 Flying Fortresses to Cherbourg, but was recalled due to weather conditions - 10/10 cloud to 25,000 feet.

'*Next day*', wrote Hugo, '*more or less scrambled to Bolthead [sic] to replace 133, who had been LOST over Brest due to 'hook' trouble on the part of ops.   Sat round in rain for two days.   Finally returned home from all these ops.   My "10,000 hour" hat not yet returned!!*'

A force of 70 US bombers had been tasked to bomb Morlaix, with an escort of three Spitfire squadrons - 64, 133 and 401 Squadrons. With thick cloud below and high winds, the US bombers had been unable to navigate accurately, and had gone almost to Spain, and disappeared off the 10 Group radar plot, yet the formations were not warned.   The escort wing leader was an Australian in the RAF, Squadron Leader Tony Gaze, commander 64 Squadron RAF, who was made to bear the blame for the disaster, which had been caused by the incompetence of 10 Group Operations controllers.   133 Squadron, comprised mainly of US volunteer pilots, had been lost entirely when they decided to leave the returning bomber formation and dive through the thick clouds to give a display of tight formation flying over the town seen below, assumed to be Plymouth or Portsmouth on the south coast of England.   Unfortunately it was Brest, and the German defences were presented with a gunner's dream target.   The only squadron pilot to survive the flak was lost in the Channel through lack of fuel.   This incident is described more fully in the author's *Six Aces*, Banner Books, 1991.   Though greater in scope, this was an incident similar to that which resulted in Oberleutnant Faber landing his FW190 in England.

The bad weather endured for the last ten days of September changed as October opened, 'a beautiful day and quite a change,' wrote the squadron diarist.   Patrols were flown along the English coast on the 1st, with no enemy contact.

Flying Officer David Fulford DFC RAF joined the squadron from 52 OTU, to begin another tour of operations.   Fulford was widely experienced.   He flew in the Battle of Britain as a Sergeant with 64 and 19 Squadrons, and claimed a half share in each of two victories in November 1940. After commissioning, Fulford was posted to 118 Squadron, and claimed a Bf109 Probable and two others Destroyed in July, August and October 1941.   He was awarded the DFC in November.   Fulford was then posted to be a flight commander on 261 Squadron, on Ceylon.   On 9 April 1942 he intercepted a force of Japanese carrier-borne aircraft flying to attack Trincomalee naval base, and was credited with two Mitsubushi A6M Zeros destroyed.   One of these was believed to be the Zero formation leader, Masatoshi Makino, from carrier *Zuikaku*.   In June 1942 Fulford returned to the UK.

On 2 October Circus 221 was flown. This was in support of 43 USAAF B17s of the 97th and 301st Bomb Groups, attacking the French Potez aircraft factory at Meaulte, which was working for the Luftwaffe. Up to this time, only two B17s had been lost on operations; few missions had been flown.   Though the weather was fine, 'the bombing appeared to be rather poor', noted the squadron record.   FW190s engaged the bombers, though none were shot down. US gunners claimed four destroyed, five probably destroyed, and one damaged [4-5-1]. Hugo led 611 Squadron as Yellow 1. At 15.45, 27,000 feet east of Abbeville, they engaged Messerschmitt Bf109s, 11/JG26. Four 109s passed over the Spitfires, climbed into the sun, and one turned to attack Hugo's No.2, flying to the left. Hugo dived a little, and as the 109 passed them in the dive from his attack, Hugo had gained enough speed to remain close, and to fire from 200 metres range. The 109, on its back in the dive, was hit on one wing tip, half-rolled 'smartly', and steepened its dive. Hugo pulled up and returned to escort the bombers. He claimed the 109 as damaged. A running stick-figure fleeing a big bullet was entered in the cartoon list. Flight Lieutenant Bill Compton claimed a FW190 probably destroyed. The squadron landed at 16.15, after a 1 hour 45 minute operation.

left to right, in white pullover, Wing Commander Garth Slater, Hugo Armstrong, Sailor Malan, F/O John Aiken. (RAAF)

The US citizens in 611 Squadron were accepted by the US Army Air Force, and were transferred to that service. However, from 61 OTU three Sergeant pilots arrived to replace them; two were Australians: Keith Clarkson and Richard Due. Dick Due had a total of 251 hours flying, of which 65 was on Spitfires Mark I and II at 61 OTU, and included 25 hours formation flying on Spitfires. He had been assessed as *'Above Average'* at OTU. The arrival of these new pilots may be similar to that of other young men fresh from OTU, joining a squadron at Biggin Hill. The last part of the journey was by bus from the railway station, and included a short walk along part of the perimeter fence. They could see Spitfires in pens, and were excited to note four-bladed propellors, which identified the latest Mark IX.

'This was, to us, the greatest thrill, regardless of who else was on the squadron,' said Dick Due. *'I don't think we even knew who the CO was at that stage. When we did find out, we felt that extra bit of comradeship because he was an Australian.'*

Bad weather prevented much flying for the next week; patrols had no contact. The new pilots were able to start the process of becoming part of the squadron when it was not operating at a high degree of intensity. In retrospect, Dick Due believed the training programme under the Empire Air Training Scheme was 'well conceived and thorough.' Stages of training were broken by long periods travelling or in transit camps, but by the time he arrived at Biggin Hill in October 1942, Dick had spent 50 weeks in flying or class-room training, and 17 weeks travelling or in transit camps since enlisting on 21 June 1941. After joining the squadron, Dick spent another month gaining experience in squadron formation and operational manoeuvring, in a further 16 hours flying. At the end of this time, 'I felt pretty confident that I could give a reasonable account of myself on operations.'

On 9 October, Hugo led the squadron off at 08.50, part of the target support wing to 108 B17s and B24s attacking the Fives-Lille steel works. There was a thin layer of cloud at 15,000 feet over the Channel, and solid overcast at 17,000 feet over France. 611 climbed to 28,000 feet, reached 'somewhere near Douai, and turned for home, leaving the French coast at Le Touquet at 12,000 feet, and landing at 10.30 with nothing to report.' The bomber formations became somewhat ragged as aircraft turned back with mechanical faults. Two US units were on their first operation, their bombing was poor, and civilians were killed and wounded outside the target area. The bombers had been engaged by German fighters which evaded the fighter escort, and lost three B17s and a B24; JG26 claimed four victories. With hundreds of American gunners firing at the attacking Luftwaffe fighters, over-claiming was inevitable. The intial US bomber force claims were for 56-26-20, which RAF Intelligence reports gave as approximately the total Luftwaffe fighter force available to the defence. Bomber claims then were reduced to 48-38-19, and finally 21-21-15 were allowed. Some 500 fighters had accompanied the B17s, but claimed only 5-0-0. Luftwaffe records are incomplete, and show only two fighters lost for the day; JG26 had one pilot killed. Hugo noted in his logbook, *'Yanks claim 47 destroyed!! Ho Ho Bloody Ho!!!'*

Despite poor bombing accuracy and US bomber losses, the US bombing leaders were encouraged. The high claims for Luftwaffe fighters destroyed were more or less accepted, and linked to the facts that US heavy bombers had gone to the target in daylight, fought their way out again despite strong opposition, and lost only four aircraft. The escort fighters, however, claimed only a fraction of the enemy believed destroyed. The glow of a perceived success obscured other aspects of the operation: fourteen B24s turned back with mechanical problems and 40 more B24s and B17s were damaged. One squadron lagged behind and almost every aircraft was damaged as the Luftwaffe concentrated on them.

Press reports presented the raid as a triumph, but the exorbitant US claims for Luftwaffe losses were scorned by the experienced RAF personnel. This situation continued, as the US public relations system fed the national desire for visible progress and results. As US bomber losses mounted alarmingly, claims for corresponding damage inflicted on the Luftwaffe climbed accordingly to assure the American public that the losses were repaid in kind. By deliberate use, from US public relations staffs, of the term 'Allied bombers' when describing RAF night attacks on Berlin and other targets deep in Germany, the US public was given a false impression of the achievements of the well publicised B17 and B24 squadrons.   In fact, USAAF formations did not raid Germany until six months after US bombing operations began from England, and the first US raid on Berlin was in March 1944, 19 months after the commencement of US bombing operations in Europe.   The US public was not told that RAF wooden Mosquitos, unarmed, with a crew of two, with no fighter escort, each carried a heavier bombload to Berlin than the B24 and B17, and Mosquitos raided Berlin regularly and frequently.   But all this was to follow the raid on 9 October 1942.

On 11 October, Hugo led the Wing for the first time, on his 104th offensive sortie, but despite steering to the location of reported enemy, *'they would not come out.'* Other sweeps, scrambles and a B-17 escort also had no contact.

By the end of October, Spitfire IXs equipped only eight of the 49 Spitfire squadrons. Most RAF fighter squadrons were slightly over establishment, but Luftwaffe fighter strength in JG2 and JG26 also had risen, from 250 in June to 320.   Still the situation allowed the Germans to engage on their own terms and refuse combat if it suited them; still RAF losses exceeded those of the Luftwaffe.   It was realised that great assistance to the Spitfire squadrons could be given by radar in England which would be able to see beyond the usual range, to report enemy formations above 10,000 feet, at least 90 miles [144 km] from England, and able to cope with six formations at once.   Tests began in June 1942, at Appledore, Kent.   By the end of October an Operations Room, with Ground Controlled Interception controller and height-finding radar, was established there.

Cliff Broadbent was a long-serving Senior NCO on A Flight, 611 Squadron.   He was impressed when Hugo showed he would listen to NCOs about even minor problems, and when an aircraft was unserviceable for want of a part, would 'use his authority with Station and Group stores, often with dramatic results.'   Both Flights were able to provide the full number of Spitfires when required for operations.   Pilot Officer John Aiken joined 611 in May 1942, and by October was an experienced operational pilot in a squadron which always seemed to contain a variety of nationalities.   Of his six wartime squadron commanders, John Aiken considered Hugo the best.

'He was the finest type of Australian - strong, thoughtful, calm and determined to succeed whatever the circumstances.   These attributes, when set beside his concern for his groundcrew and new aircrew, made him a first class leader and squadron commander.'

1 November began with a 'bright morning' which soon darkened for two reasons. Sergeant Keith Clarkson RAAF crashed the squadron's Tiger Moth on Farley Common, and though uninjured, was sent by Hugo 'to Brighton for three weeks for his effort.'   The air forces disciplinary centre was at Brighton.   Dick Due thought that Clarkson, at this time, was lacking in discipline.   The Tiger Moth was considered very important, as it allowed convenient and unofficial transport for those going on leave around the UK. The time at Brighton was known to be rigorous, but in Dick's opinion, Clarkson was tough, and relieved that no more drastic punishment was awarded.   The second darkening was the weather, which changed at lunchtime, and by 14.00 had reduced visibility to 20 metres; then it rained for the rest of the day.

There had been so many changes in flying personnel that Hugo decided to officially set out the pilot strength by flights.   This listing reinforces the cosmopolitan nature of an RAF Auxiliary squadron by late 1942.   Hugo, an Australian, was Commanding Officer; A Flight was led by Flight Lieutenant Bill Compton DFC, a New Zealander, with the British members of his flight being Flight Lieutenant R.C. Brown, Flying Officer D. Fulford DFC, Pilot Officers P.E. Helmore, J.A. Aiken, G.R. Lindsay, and B.R. Tapley, with Flight Sergeant T. K. Whitfield and Sergeant H.E. Walmsley.   The other nations represented in A Flight were Australian Sergeants K.E. Clarkson, R.L. Due and A.E. Pearce, New Zealander Sergeant A.E. Lissette, and Free France was represented by Lieutenant C.M. DeTedesco. B Flight was commanded by Flight Lieutenant F. Vancl, of Czechoslovakia, whose British members were Flight Lieutenant E.O. Watson and Pilot Officers P.M. Sims, J.C. Minto, V.S. Neill, R.G. Smith, N.G. Lussignea and G.G. White, with Flight Sergeants R.W. Harris and S.O. Appleby, and Sergeants J. North, G.W. Keans and J.A. MacLeod, with Australian Sergeant A.A. Haynes and New Zealander Sergeant J. Badcock.

On 2 November, Rodeo 107 swept the Abbeville area.   The Wing took off at 14.20, flew at zero feet to Beachy Head and, at sea level, proceeded on course for the Somme estuary for ten minutes, then climbed steeply and waited for information from the radar controller in the UK.   There was no cloud and only slight haze over Berck.   At 15.00, Hugo was leading 611 Squadron in circles over Abbeville, when he was informed that radar had detected enemy over Amiens, so he flew to the mouth of the Somme.   Flying Officer David Fulford DFC began to lag, and Lieutenant DeTedesco called that he could see Fulford going down to the sea; nothing was heard from Fulford.   Hugo sent a Mayday call on Fulford's behalf, but the squadron could not go down to sea level in the circumstances prevailing.   Nothing more was known of Fulford; he was swallowed by the sea.   He had been with 611 for exactly a month.

In the 1994 Grub Street edition of *Aces High,* by Chris Shores and Clive Williams, it is stated in the entry for Fulford that his was one of two Spitfires shot down on this day over Le Touquet by FW190s, but this is not so described in the squadron operations log. There was no reference to engagement with FW190s before Fulford left the formation.

A FW190 pilot parachutes

The Free French 340 Squadron, led by Commandant Duperier, engaged FW190s over Berck, so Hugo again turned the squadron north to the battle area.   Four FW190s weaving in line astern were below, so Hugo dived on them, but then saw another eight coming in from over the Channel, so pulled up again.   He climbed past these later arrivals, through 18,000 feet, and found a FW190 committing mortal sin in the combat area by flying straight, and climbing slightly.   Hugo closed from below, unseen, and fired; strikes flashed all over the 190's belly and fuselage; the pilot reflexively jerked the nose up and to port; the 190 climbed steeply, the pilot baled out and the aircraft stalled and spun away below.

'The remaining 190s,' reported Hugo, *'then became hostile and climbed after me.'* However, the second stage of his supercharger ['blower'] cut in and he climbed away from them.   The 190s followed, but gave up and turned back to France.   Hugo went to

32,000 feet, and set course for England. But when he was 15 miles [24 km] west of Le Touquet, he *'was bounced by three ME109s who must have been at a great height.'* The first two missed him, but the third stayed and tried to turn with the Spitfire, guns hammering a long burst which also missed. After several turns, gaining nothing, the 109 straightened out and tried to climb away. Hugo fired from 350 metres range and saw strikes on the starboard wing tip and root; the 109 flicked, then went down *'almost horizontally and rolling slowly.'* Hugo was convinced the 109 *'was absolutely out of control from the way it fell, but was unable to see any more of it owing to the haze and the other two 109s, who were getting a bit keen.'* He set off again for England, weaving, the squadron with him, and the 109s turned back some 24 km south of Dungeness. Hugo and the squadron landed at 15.50, after a 90-minute operation.

In the combat, DeTedesco also claimed one destroyed, and Pilot Officer Sims and Sergeant Keans each damaged one. The latter two, however, set off independently and together for England when the other pilots climbed with Hugo. Over the Channel, a FW190 attacked from behind, shot down Keans into the sea and badly damaged Sims' Spitfire. Sims managed to return to base with the aircraft in what the squadron diary called 'a sorry condition', needing a new stern frame and two new mainplanes.

The FW190 was flown by Unteroffizier Gerhard Vogt, 6/JG26, who had Unteroffizier Georg Granabetter as his wingman. According to Donald L. Caldwell, in his *JG26 War Diary 1939-42,* Granabetter flew between Vogt and the second Spitfire and also was shot down. Granabetter received credit for a victory posthumously, a gesture of respect in the Luftwaffe. Vogt apparently claimed a Spitfire at 15.24 hours 'south-west of Boulogne' for his ninth victory. The French squadron pilots claimed 2-1-2 for the action.

Hugo added another, unnamed, parachuting figure to his cartoon list, with *'190 Dest'.* JG26 admits only the loss of the FW190 shot down by the other. Hugo's claims, however, were witnessed by the rest of the Spitfire squadron.

To Buckingham Palace

Hugo went to London on 3 November, to receive his DFC from King George VI at Buckingham Palace. Low cloud, fog and rain held the squadrons on the ground for three days, and the next operation flown was on 6 November.

In clear weather, at 14.00 Hugo led 611 on Ramrod 22, as a diversion while the main force attacked Caen airfield. The squadron swept from west of Le Havre to the mouth of the Orne, swept back, and returned to base with no contact. Next day, the weather was bad again, and the squadron was confined to patrols by pairs along the coast, with the only matter of interest reported by the first pair, who were shot at by Army anti-aircraft guns at Hastings. The squadron record grumbled at the lack of enemy activity, and included a somewhat envious report about a French pilot of 340 Squadron who intended making a simple cannon test by firing into the sea off Beachy Head, but was attacked by two FW190s, dodged them, and watched as the 190s collided and went into the water.

8 November was described in the squadron diary as a 'brilliant day.' There were early coastal patrols with nothing to report, but at 11.30 Hugo led the squadron on Circus 235, another attack on Fives-Lille by 36 B17s. Hugo noted, *'Bombing bloody good.'* No enemy were seen until the squadron was crossing the Channel back to England, and in a short skirmish Flight Lieutenant Compton damaged a FW190. Hugo wrote, *'Six 190s bounced over Gravelines - missed!'* Fuel shortage led to three squadron aircraft landing at other airfields for petrol before going on to base.

This was Dick Due's third operational sortie.   He was confident of performing well on operations, but the first two flights were uneventful.   In the dive on the six FW190, *'because of my inexperience I lost the rest of the squadron during a tight turn and had to head back for base. Suddenly the sky was empty - not an aircraft in sight. From then on, I learned to keep contact with the rest of the section or squadron, and be aware of everything going on in that three-dimensional arena.   In other words, it is only the real thing and experience that finally is the catalyst which puts all the preliminary training to work.'*

Heading for Manston as required in such circumstances, Dick found himself in dense fog and had to contact Control for instructions.   After a difficult landing at Eastchurch in the fog, guided by Control, and at the end of his fuel, Dick was embarrassed to find that the rest of the squadron had heard 'the whole saga' on radio, while enjoying perfect weather before landing at Biggin Hill.

On 9 November, Hugo flew on Rodeo 109.   This was in conjunction with Circus 136. The squadron, led this time by Wing Commander Thomas, took off at 15.30, and climbed to height while crossing the Channel.   Flight Lieutenant Colloredo-Mansfeld, from 72 Squadron, flew with 611.   The Wing swept St. Omer, then Gravelines, and went to Berck and Boulogne in response to information from the radar controller.   Thomas led the squadron inland.   South of Calais, at 28,000 feet, the squadron saw 15 FW190s 5,000 feet below; 611 bounced them at once.   Hugo took Yellow Section down after the last 190.   He gained speed during the descent, and throttled right back to avoid overshooting the victim.   Hugo fired cannon only from 200 yards astern, and saw about a dozen hits flash on the tail, fuselage and mainplane; large pieces were shot off and Hugo had to pull away to avoid them.   The 190 staggered and went into a dive, past the vertical.   As all the strikes were 20mm cannon, and from the behaviour of the 190 after it was hit, Hugo believed the pilot, if still alive, could not have recovered from this dive.   He only fired 40 rounds of cannon, and claimed the 190 as a probable.   An anonymous parachuting figure was added to the cartoons.   *'Got a perfect bounce on 14 190s - hit one very hard all over but could only claim probable'*, he wrote in his log-book.

Meanwhile, every aircraft in the squadron had opportunity to fire.   However, Red Section found themselves separated from the rest of the formation, and from Cap Gris Nez raced out to sea with seven 190s after them.   Flight Lieutenant Compton claimed one destroyed, and Pilot Officer Lindsey damaged one.   The 190s got in some hits of their own, and Flight Sergeant Whitfield crash landed at Detling with two wounds in the left shoulder, requiring admission to hospital in Canterbury.   Flight Sergeant Harris landed at Hawkinge with small fragments around his left eye.   Both Spitfires were in category 'AC'.

According to Donald L. Caldwell, in his war diary of JG26, the Spitfires had bounced elements of I/JG26, but no Luftwaffe aircraft suffered reportable damage.

Another day of good weather followed on 10 November, and after some usual coastal patrols, Hugo led the squadron on Circus 237, but there was no contact.   Despite frequent poor weather later in the month, intensive air operations were mounted, in support of Operation "Torch", the Allied landings in North Africa.

It was decided to inform the public of the existence of the Spitfire Mark IX, and 611 Squadron was chosen to perform for the filming.   On 8 December, Hugo led four aircraft in close formation low over the field for the cameras; Dick Due was No.4.   Hugo decided to have his Spitfire polished to allow that extra increase in speed which could make a crucial difference in action.   However, after the airmen had worked to make the surfaces so shiny that one's reflection could be seen in them, the aircraft was ordered by higher authority to be re-painted matt, as glittering aircraft would be seen at long distance by the enemy, negating the purpose of camouflage.   Soon, however, the US army would not camouflage aircraft at all, and natural bare metal became standard for US Army Air Force units which operated in daylight. (The US Air Force only came into being as a separate service in 1947.)

At about this time, the commander of RAF Biggin Hill, Group Captain 'Sailor' Malan, introduced a monthly prize for the most training film taken by a squadron on the Biggin Hill base.   This was part of Malan's constant efforts to improve the standard of gunnery. Two Spitfires would take off, the idea being for the second to film the first from behind at different angles and ranges.   The film would them be projected, and a model aircraft introduced before the screen, so that it duplicated the image on the screen.   From this, pilots could be taught deflection shooting before actually flying.   Ranges were at 300, 200 and 100 metres, to correct the common error of firing at too great a distance.   A couple of the ground staff of 611 walked over to the Free French squadron to borrow some part, and were amazed to see the French had jacked up a Spitfire, retracted the undercarriage, and were filming it from the correct ranges, and angles, as if it was flying. At once it was understood how the French were winning the monthly prizes!

On 1 December, during a sweep to St. Omer, 611 Squadron bounced about 20 FW190s, and claimed three destroyed and three damaged.   Hugo again was disgruntled: *'Squirted one 190 over Calais - bloody cannons stopped*!!'   JG26 admitted no losses.   On the 4th, Hugo flew a single reconnaissance to Calais, then two sweeps.   There were combats, but he did not fire.   On 6 December, 60 B-17s bombed Lille with *'bloody good bombing'* according to Hugo.   There was a 100 mph headwind, and the Luftwaffe *'nibbled at us all the way out'*; Crawford claimed one damaged.   Hugo also noted, *'Surely to Christ the Yanks can't claim any for today? They DID!!!'*

On 12 December the B-17s attacked Romilly aircraft park, south-east of Paris.   Heavy cloud foiled bombing attempts and affected navigation, so the Spitfires had to search for the bombers.   The Luftwaffe was up in force, and Hugo noted *'a fair number of 109s about all the way home, a fair number of scraps, no one lost.   My No.2 hit by a B-17 over Mantes - just got home.'*   Two B-17s were lost, and one of these made a safe landing in a French field.   The Germans now had an intact example of a B-17.

On the 13th, the squadron scrambled after a radar plot of 12-plus circling a boat off Cape Gris Nez, but was recalled as Group decided the plot was friendly.   Later it was discovered the aircraft *'were Jerries - Hell!!'* noted Hugo.

Bad weather prevented operational flying for a week, and then the B-17s returned to Romilly on the 20th.   Dick Due flew his eighth sweep on the 20th, as Blue 4, escorting

B17s returning.   A few FW190s were seen, but there was no combat.   All three other members of Blue Section had unserviceable radios, and turned back to land at Ford. Dick hit a tent at the side of the runway and wrote off his starboard mainplane.   On 22nd there was an unsuccessful scramble after a Dornier Do217 which bombed Hawkinge, and a sweep on the 23rd, when, *'on the way home,'* wrote Hugo, *'we tried to intercept two at sea level but had no luck.'*

On 24 December, there was what Dick Due recalled as 'a rather willing Christmas Eve party'.   Johnny Checketts bet Dick and Gus Haynes that they could not stay with him in a chase.   Next day, Christmas, they took off for what was logged officially as 55 minutes of 'Formation aerobatics.'   Checketts found that 'despite the after-effects of the party, we were able to keep with him through the most violent and evasive manoeuvres.   We won the bet and a case of beer.'   By the end of the year, Dick had flown ten sweeps, many as No.2 to Flight Lieutenant Bill Compton; only five sweeps involved sightings of enemy or combat.

Hugo flew his 120th offensive sortie on the 29th, a Rodeo to St. Omer, and climbed through cloud all the way to height.   When the Wing was just inside France, *'two 190s got one of 91 [Squadron] off Hastings.   We tried to intercept, but no go.   Had a hell of a time finding Biggin again'*, noted Hugo.   Next day, he did an air test in FY-F, and saw the first snow of the winter.   As 1942 ended, Hugo had 449 hours on Spitfires.

Rhubarbs and Circus sorties in November and December resulted in RAF claims for 21 enemy destroyed, and for once Luftwaffe figures in their records were higher, and admitted 26 fighters lost.   RAF losses totalled 48 fighters.   For the last three months of 1942, 6,336 sorties had been flown by Fighter Command over the Channel area.   Admitted Luftwaffe fighter losses in the zone for 1942 totalled 197.   On a simple numerical basis, the RAF air offensive had been a failure, as RAF losses at 466 aircraft far exceeded the acceptable one-for-one rate desired by higher headquarters in January.   JG2 and JG26 had not needed assistance from other major units units on a permanent basis, though in 1942 JG26 alone lost 68 pilots killed.   None was over the rank of Oberleutnant.   RAF losses had been severe, but overall pilot numbers had greatly increased due to the enormous training programmes in several distant countries of the British Commonwealth. Of more value to the RAF was the experience and expertise accumulated by individual pilots and leaders up to Wing level.   1943 would see this situation evolve further.   There were now 12 Spitfire IX and eight Typhoon squadrons available to counter the improved Bf109G and formidable FW190.

1943

611 Squadron flew sweeps to Le Havre, Cherbourg and Abbeville in the first week of January.   On the 8th, a Bar to Hugo's DFC was gazetted.   The citation stated that, since the award of the DFC, Hugo had made many more operational flights and destroyed a further four enemy fighters, and continued, 'His great powers of leadership have contributed largely to the successes achieved by his squadron.   This officer's keenness to engage the enemy at all times and his excellent escort work have set an inspiring example to all.'

On 9 January, as Bostons attacked Abbeville, Dick Due was No.2 to Squadron Leader Dicky Milne. The section attacked five FW190s from above and port, and Dick fired at one from 300 yards; a red flash sparked on the port wing root of the 190, which rolled into an inverted dive and Dick claimed it as damaged. Sergeant Walmsley claimed a probable.

Bad weather again grounded the squadron on 12 January, but during the day three RAAF Sergeants arrived from 53 OTU: Ron Mackay, Vernon Lancaster and John Gilbert. Vern Lancaster quickly realised that Hugo 'was very well respected, and popular with all the pilots, as he was a top class pilot and leader.'

Another new arrival, Sergeant Pat Davoren, was the subject of an example of squadron leadership by Hugo. After only a few days on 611, Pat was in the Ops Room when Hugo asked if he had flown a Spit IX. Pat replied that he had not finished the experience needed on the Spit V, but Hugo sent him off in his personal aircraft - something few squadron leaders would even consider. 'I managed to get it up and down without pranging it,' recalled Pat, 'and I was very relieved.'

A more experienced arrival was Franz Colloredo-Mansfeld, from 72 Squadron, to take command of B Flight. A Flight was commanded by Flight Lieutenant Sims, Compton having gone to command 64 Squadron.

Looking back, accepting the losses of a brother and friends in the war, Dick Due recalled that *they were mostly good and happy years, especially with 611 Squadron. It was a thrill at the age of 20 to be flying such a wonderful aeroplane, and the happy atmosphere in the squadron engendered a comradeship second to none. At the age of 20, someone of Hugo's age and with a DFC was looked up to as an older brother, or almost just old!'*

13 January 1943 was fine and clear. At 12.50, Hugo led the squadron on Circus 249, during which 18 Lockheed Venturas were to bomb Abbeville airfield. *'Saw bags of 190s but couldn't get a bounce'*, noted Hugo. Then, twelve FW190 were seen over the target area, and Blue Section attacked. But, wrote Hugo, *'we were bounced good and proper by three cheeky bastards, one of whom shook me no end with a cannon shell on the perspex. However, he didn't live long enough to tell anyone, as Collie [Colloredo] clobbered him in flames.'* Colloredo claimed one destroyed and Flying Officer Johnny Checketts damaged another.

Flying practice took up the rest of the 13th. The 14th had solid cloud and fog all day, and the morning of the 15th was the same, but cleared in the afternoon, when coastal patrols were flown. The 16th was another closed-in day. On days when the squadron was stood down, beer drinking competitions would be organised, with the NCOs pitted against the officers. Hugo employed his sense of tactics here, allied to the sometimes coveted ability to drink without swallowing. He would wait his turn and judge how the NCOs were going, then open his mouth and simply pour down the tankard in a few seconds, putting the officer team ahead. 'I don't think the NCOs ever won,' recalled Pat Davoren. Hugo's drinking ability was recalled by Bob Taylor, the Biggin Hill Admin Officer, who 'attended Hugo's chug-a-lug parties, much to my discomfort on occasion. I do remember him pouring a pint down without swallowing.'

Hugo showed his mettle in another way.   The Sergeants' Mess invited the Commanding Officer and commissioned pilots to be guests.   On their arrival, protocol decreed that the first drink was offered to the Commanding Officer by the Senior Warrant Officer.   In some Messes, this would be in a special pewter, silver or crystal container.   It being wartime, Hugo on this occasion was confronted by the Mess ornamental chamber pot, filled with beer, floating in which were several very well browned sausages.....   Heroically, with eyes open, as Cliff Broadbent witnessed, Hugo managed to drink about half the contents.

On the 17th, weather was better, with 5/10th cloud, and Hugo flew two operations.   At 10.55, 611 Squadron took off on Rodeo 149, to cover Abbeville at 20,000 feet.   Blue Section saw a FW190 taking off, and dived to attack; Flying Officer Lindsey claimed it damaged.   Dick Due, flying as Blue 4, noted in his log book that the enemy was a FW189, a slow army co-operation aircraft.   The squadron returned without further incident. At 14.30, Hugo led three other pilots on Rodeo 154, but returned at 15.20 with no contact. Next day, pairs were scrambled throughout daylight to patrol the coast; there was no enemy contact.   The 19th was another closed-in day, with fog and solid cloud.   Johnny Checketts attempted to patrol Rye, but had to return after five minutes.   After a lecture on night operations, the squadron was released at 15.30.

The Luftwaffe disturbs lunch

20 January was clearer, though there was much cloud.   Practice flying was possible in the morning, and newly arrived Vern Lancaster was able to get in 25 minutes cine-camera practice in Spit VB FY-K.   Dick Due was having a bath.   At 12.00, Vern was sent up for a first flight in a Spit IX, FY-H, to familiarise himself with the aircraft model and with the local area.   It was lunch-time, but Vern was
'enjoying myself doing this, when I heard Fighter Control reporting Bandits crossing the coast 60 miles [100 km] south of Biggin Hill.   I wasn't concerned about this much, until I looked down and saw three FW190s directly below, on the deck.   I then called up Fighter Control and told them the enemy were not over the coast, but were almost over Base. This set the cat among the pigeons.'

At 12.30, 611 Squadron was lunching when the Tannoy base loudspeaker system called that 30-plus bandits were seven miles [11 km] away, approaching from the south-east. Flying Officer John Aiken, on readiness, came out of the crew room and saw FW190s flying low over the airfield buildings.   'A terrific scramble took place', wrote the squadron diarist.   Group Captain 'Sailor' Malan, the Biggin Hill base commander, told a reporter that, 'After the alert the aerodrome went mad.   I never saw anyone on the ground move so fast in my life as those ground crews and pilots when they were getting the machines off.'   The pilots raced to dispersal and saw FW190s at zero feet crossing the northern tip of the airfield.   John Aiken ran to his Spitfire, started up and took off without fastening his straps.   Spitfires took off in pairs as pilots were ready, and 12 were airborne in eight minutes.

The squadron record states that Hugo and Richard Milne were first off, but this was due to the fact that they had a car while everyone else pedalled madly on bicycles! Dick Due believes that the first Spitfires were rolling in about three minutes.   Dick, out of the bath and rapidly dressed, was 'trailing the procession of speeding bicycles, the Mess being a good mile or so from the aircraft.'   When he arrived, only a Spitfire Vb was available, but he climbed in and scrambled.   Control was trying to cope with some 20 individuals calling for instructions.   John Aiken, however, found his radio useless, so independently went at low level to the south coast.

Meanwhile, above it all, Vern Lancaster realised he was the only Spitfire airborne, and *'was agonising as to whether I should have a go at them or not, when I saw the rest of the 25-plus FW190s just behind the first three.   This put the kibosh on any ideas I had of going down on the first three.'*

Unable to mount 'normal' bomber attacks of any strength against Britain, the Luftwaffe had organised fighter bomber units to go in fast at sea level, climb steeply to attack height, bomb, strafe, and get out fast.   These operations by small numbers of speeding fighters had met with some success.   The British defences re-organised, with standing patrols of ten Typhoons on the coast, a more rapid Royal Observer Corps reporting system on the code-word 'Rats', rockets held in readiness to be fired to alert nearby units, and reinforcement of light coastal anti-aircraft defences.

The German force on the raid on the 20th consisted of the fighter bomber FW190s of 10th Staffel JG26, commanded at the time by Oberleutnant 'Bombenkeller' Keller, with an escort of FW190s from I and III/JG26, *Stab* JG2 and Messerschmitt Bf109s of II/JG26. The pilots were briefed to attack anything 'liable to frighten the British people', and this included public transport, groups or gatherings, and flocks and herds of animals. This particular raid was said to be in retaliation for heavy RAF attacks on Berlin, which had commenced on 17 January.   The fast low-flying raiders crossed the coast near Rye, while others confused the well practised Royal Observer Corps network and air raid warning system with a diversionary attack

Hugo, after shooting down two Bf109s, 20 January 1943.   (Armstrong family)

towards Maidstone, and more activity over the English Channel.   In addition, Luftwaffe radio units in France jammed British radar as the raiders crossed the Channel.   The RAF officer who should have been warned of this jamming was not informed.   In addition, as an example of Murphy's Law, part of the British balloon barrage had been lowered to allow calibration of anti-aircraft gunnery radars - the raised balloons would have interfered with the procedures and tests.   To cap matters off, the responsible Air Raid Warning Officer was late in contacting Scotland Yard; no alarm was given before the Focke Wulfs and Messerschmitts were over London.

It was lunch time, and people were going outside; schools were breaking for lunch. One 250kg bomb fell onto the Sandhurst Road School, Catford; 38 children and six teachers were killed, among a total for the raid of 87 killed and 142 wounded.   Survivors and witnesses insisted the aircraft turned back and the bomb was deliberately aimed at the school building.   However, the engine noise of the 'returning' aircraft at low level possibly was that of the approaching second wave, and it is doubtful that any German pilot knew of the location of the school, as a teaching institution.   The truth will never be known.   Other civilian casualties were caused by cannon and machinegun strafing along streets.   In addition, bombs fell on the Surrey Commercial Docks warehouse, starting a large fire, and railways were hit at Lewisham, Poplar, Deptford, Bermondsey and Greenwich.   A gasometer was set aflame by cannon fire, ten of the grounded barrage balloons were strafed, and other damage was inflicted.   The Luftwaffe could claim a success, as a force of aircraft had reached the enemy capital in daylight without the alarm being given.   The Focke Wulfs and Messerschmitts streaked for the coast of Kent, the Channel and France.

A Messerschmitt Bf109 at zero feet

Meanwhile, Hugo quickly climbed to 10,000 feet over London, and while doing so, remembered his new pilot, Vern Lancaster, on his first flight in a Spit IX.   Hugo contacted Control and told them to order Vern to land.   An interested spectator to the activity, Vern was then ordered to
'return to base immediately, repeat, immediately.'   This, recalled Vern, concluded his first *'rather hairy experience with a Spit IX, but also gives an insight into the character of Hugo Armstrong.   In the middle of a scramble like that, he would call Control to order a totally inexperienced pilot to land immediately, to protect him from possible danger.'*

Hugo, meanwhile, was told of bandits at zero feet between Kenley and Beachy, and dived for the south coast.   Colloredo-Mansfeld was with him.   About halfway, he saw five aircraft at Ashdown 'on the deck' heading south, so followed, and watched three of them weave one turn either way, then cross the coast at Pevensey Bay.   Light anti-aircraft fire came up from coastal positions, and the distant aircraft began to weave through it, which allowed the diving Spitfires to close on them.   The time was about 12.45.

With accumulated speed from the dive, Hugo went in to close range on the starboard of the three speeding planes, a Messerschmitt 109, and fired; hits on the wing tip; fired again; hits in the cockpit and the 109 exploded and went into the sea only about 1.5 km off the coast, and two or three km ahead of three minesweepers.   Following pilots saw the oily patch on the sea where the 109 disappeared.

A second Messerschmitt into the sea

The other two 109s were ahead, out to sea; Hugo estimated the range as 800 metres, aimed and fired.   The cannon rounds sent up spurts of foam from the sea; the 109s broke, allowing Hugo to close again.   He aimed and fired from 300 metres, and hit the port radiator of a 109; the other 109 swung back and attacked.   Hugo turned with this aircraft, saw three other Spitfires with him and told them to take care of the German, then looked again for his second victim.   All that was visible was a trail of glycol hanging in the air.   However, coming along behind Hugo, Colloredo-Mansfeld had seen it go into the sea.   Hugo's radio failed, and he returned to base.   He had fired 224 cannon rounds and claimed two 109s destroyed.

Wing Commander Richard Milne, the Biggin Hill Wing leader, also had scrambled, and claimed a FW190 and a 109, bringing his score to 15 destroyed. A pilot of the Free French 340 *'Ile de France'* Squadron, Adjutant Robert Gouby, claimed two more, making Biggin Hill Wing claims six destroyed. Total claims for the combats were for 16 destroyed - eight FW190s and eight Bf109s. Luftwaffe records show a total of 12: three FW190s from JG2, four FW190s from I and III/JG26,

l. to r. W/Cdr Dicky Milne RAF, Hugo, Adutant Robert Gouby, Free French, all victorious after the combat of 20 January 1943. (Armstrong family)

and four Bf109Gs from II/JG26, plus one 109F from *Jagdgruppe Ost*, a training unit. Hugo noted the enemy in his log-book as 109Fs, but there is little external difference between the F and G models.

Dick Due, in his older Spitfire Vb, went to the location as directed by Control, but saw nothing and returned after an hour. John Aiken, without radio contact, did not see any enemy, and returned to Biggin Hill.

Back in London, the appalling result of the raid was becoming known, as rescuers and parents rushed to the school; some families lost all their children. One policeman found the body of his eight-year old son, carried him to the area where the dead were laid out, and then bravely continued with his official duties amidst the destruction. Other parents who rushed to the school found bodies of their children in the rubble. Another school had been hit in a similar raid in September 1942, but the news of that tragedy was not released. On this occasion, there was a large amount of publicity, and feeling against the Germans was intense, especially when witnesses said the bombing and strafing was deliberate.

Next day, the German media described the attack as a victory, and included the unfortunate phrase that the bombs 'went where they were intended to go'. Rather than being a claim for pinpoint accuracy on military targets, this phrase was taken to mean that the German pilots made a definite and intended attack on civilians and school children. It was this type of incident and resulting public feeling that supported the bombing campaign on Germany during the war, and which is so easily ignored by those in safety well after the events, who rant against the destruction of German cities. The German Luftwaffe had bombed towns and cities since the beginning of the war, starting with Warsaw, and continuing with Rotterdam, London, Coventry and Belgrade, to name a few. Deliberate Luftwaffe attacks in 1940 on European roads clogged with refugees had been well documented and publicised. Few people in the Western democracies in 1940-45 protested about Germany receiving the same treatment.

Donald L. Caldwell, the US historian of JG26, admitted to this author that he knew the results of this raid, but 'chose not to mention it' in his history of JG26. He did so in Volume Two of JG 26 War Diary.

The Luftwaffe made 27 low level attacks on south-east England in January 1943, by about 78 aircraft, and only four raids were intercepted. Oberleutnant Keller was killed on 24 March, at Ashford, Kent, when his bomb apparently was detonated by ground fire.

There was a certain amount of media publicity for successful pilots of Fighter Command who reacted to this attack, as the British Press constantly sought stories of success, but often to the dislike of the pilots concerned. As a result of newspaper reports of the interception after the attack, Hugo received several letters from members of the British public, thanking him for his efforts on the day. Some of these were pinned in the Ops Room for the squadron to read.

There was another sweep next day, and immediately after landing from a sweep on the 22nd, the squadron was scrambled, but with no interception. Hugo flew two more sweeps on the 25th and 26th, and ended January with 478 hours on Spitfires, and 130 offensive sorties. He did not count scrambles and other defensive operations in the total.

On 27 January, Vern Lancaster was at dispersal to see off the other two newly arrived Aussies, Ron Mackay and John Gilbert, who were to climb through the cloud and practise formation flying. Vern walked back to the Mess, and was greeted with the news that both were dead, apparently having collided in the climb through the cloud cover, and spun out of cloud into the ground. They had been with the squadron for two weeks.

'This was a hell of a shock to me,' said Vern, 'because Ron Mackay and I had become good friends during our training period.' Dick Due recalled that the day of the funeral was wet and miserable, and the mourners had to stand in the rain for 30 minutes, as the long low-loader bearing the coffins could not negotiate the turning into the lane beside the church, and made a detour. In Dick's time on 611 Squadron, Gilbert and Mackay were the only pilots buried in this way. Everyone else lost went into the sea or into France. At this time, anyone lost was referred to as being duty pilot over Dover or Calais.

Early in January 1943, the Luftwaffe had 320 Focke Wulfs and Messerschmitts positioned for defence against cross-Channel

Vern Lancaster RAAF, 611 Sqn RAF 1943.
(Vern Lancaster)

operations. RAF claims for enemy destroyed in January came to 26, for a loss of 26 aircraft and pilots. Admitted Luftwaffe losses were 27, with 17 damaged. Bad weather limited days on which cross-Channel operations could be made, but on 13, 21 and 22 January significant actions were fought during Circus and Ramrod flights. For the first two dates, Luftwaffe records confirmed loss of five of the total of six claimed, but none of the six claimed on the 22nd.

The pendulum had begun to swing against the Luftwaffe. Up to late 1942, the German higher command had been able to juggle available fighters from crisis point to crisis point, but then Allied pressure began to mount at all points. In Africa, the Battle of El Alamein in October and November marked the beginning of the end there; in Russia the encirclement of the German 6th Army at Stalingrad resulted in the surrender of the tattered freezing remnants on 31 January 1943. On 27 January, the US 8th Air Force attacked Wilhelmshafen, the first German target bombed by US air forces - despite earlier careful US media phrasing which implied otherwise. The Luftwaffe was to be forced on to the defensive everywhere.

Bad weather continued into February 1943. On the 1st, there was local flying in 'the brighter periods.' Next day, weather was better and Hugo led 611 Squadron on Circus 257 in the morning, there was practice flying in the afternoon; Sergeant Robert McLay RAAF arrived from 58 OTU. The 3rd was 'a good day - never more than 3/10th cloud.' At 10.15, Hugo led the squadron on Circus 258 (a), to Ypres, but no enemy were engaged. At 14.45, Hugo led the Wing on Circus 258 (b), to Abbeville. Once again, despite information from the radar controller of enemy nearby, none were seen. Next day, though overcast, the squadron took off at 12.00 on Rodeo 162 to St. Omer. 611 climbed to 38,000 feet, and though enemy were reported at that height, none could be found. Distant vapour trails were seen, but no enemy aircraft appeared. The weather prevented flying after lunch.

A Fighter Pilot's Appetite For Action

5 February was a rather miserable day, with 'low cloud and only fair visibility'. The pilots were sitting in the crew room, and John Aiken entered as Hugo came in from the small operations room. Pat Davoren had noticed that 340 Squadron scrambled first one section of four aircraft, then a second - it seemed something was on. He mentioned this, and Hugo checked with Biggin Hill Sector Operations from the small squadron ops room: there was Luftwaffe activity over the Channel. Hugo was spurred to activity, and said, 'Who is coming? You and you, get your gear.'

At 11.30, with Franz Colloredo-Mansfeld and John Aiken as his Blue Section Numbers 2 and 3, Hugo took off, in theory for some 'local flying'. However, soon after becoming airborne, he heard the section of 340 Squadron vectored onto aircraft over the Channel. Hugo set off to the French coast through the clouds.

'The weather was very poor,' said John Aiken. 'We found ourselves in and out of low frontal cloud with solid layers above. There were patches of mist at sea level.' Cloud base was at 800-1,000 feet, with layers of cloud above, and frequent heavy showers of fine rain. John Aiken was on Hugo's left, and Colloredo-Mansfeld on his right, but often the broken cloud hid the other aircraft from either pilot. Just after noon, Hugo was leading the other two through the cloud layers at 4,000 feet when he called to say they were returning to base; there had been no enemy reported. The Spitfires turned port, on course for England, speeding through the low broken cloud. Suddenly a FW190 attacked from astern.

Unteroffizier Heinz Gomann, from II/JG26, had taken-off after the rest of his unit and was looking for them. He believed he was alone. Through broken cloud, he saw a Spitfire, then lost sight of it, but suddenly saw three Spitfires behind him. Gomann broke into a tight turn and, as the circle was completed, found himself behind a Spitfire; he fired.

As fate had it, at that moment the Spitfires were lost to each other's sight by patches of cloud. Hugo was hit, and as John Aiken broke he saw thick black smoke pouring from the leading Spitfire. Reacting like lightning, Colloredo-Mansfeld swung onto what he thought was one of a formation of 190s - Hugo had led them out to look for a formation - and fired a four second burst as the Focke-Wulf made a steep climbing turn port; Colloredo-Mansfeld thought strikes flashed along the fuselage and white smoke streamed back from the engine, then the 190 disappeared into cloud. Colloredo-Mansfeld heard Hugo call that he was hit and baling out. John Aiken turned and fired at a 190 just as it flitted up into the clouds, looked down and

Heinz Gomann, JG26
(Gomann via Donald Cladwell)

again saw Hugo's Spitfire, black smoke pouring from it. Aiken tried to dive to Hugo, but, he reported, two 190s attacked and he had to pull up into cloud to shake them off. He heard Hugo repeat that he was going to bale out, and add, *'There is a 190 on my tail.'*

'All this happened not very high above the ground,' recalled Gomann, 'Armstrong's Spitfire hit the water very quickly.' He saw the Spitfire hit the water and that the pilot did not leave the cockpit.

Aiken and Colloredo-Mansfeld dodged in and out of cloud, looking for Hugo, but reported they were continually bothered by 190s. Heinz Gomann tried to call the rest of Sternberg's staffel, but the radio conditions were not good and he could not contact Sternberg, who was over the French mainland. Gomann set off low for France. John Aiken later saw a 190 at sea level, going towards France, so climbed into cloud and followed for a time, then dived out and saw the 190 about 600 metres ahead. Aiken aimed, fired, and believed he saw strikes on the fuselage ahead of the tail fin. The 190 did a sluggish turn to port and to starboard, then kept on to the coast. Gomann recalled that he was followed for a time by two Spitfires as he flew towards the French coast, but was not hit. Aiken turned back to look for Hugo. Nothing was found. Meanwhile, Wing Commander Dicky Milne was organising a thorough air-sea rescue operation, and aircraft flew from

12.40 to 14.15 over the area where Colloredo-Mansfeld had sent a May Day call. The weather worsened, with wind and rain; visibility fell to zero. Despite assistance from 91 Squadron and a Walrus flying boat, nothing was found. Dick Due escorted the Walrus, but *'search fruitless'* he noted in his logbook.

Listening to the RAF radio chatter, the Germans thought the Biggin Hill Wing Leader was missing. No attempt was made to interfere with the search. Without a witness to the combat, Gomann could not expect his claim to be accepted, but the RAF response confirmed the loss of a Spitfire. This was the only Luftwaffe claim in the area that day. Until contacted by the author in 1995, Heinz Gomann believed he had shot down an English wing leader.

'Hugo was highly regarded by all on the squadron,' said Pat Davoren, 'and was sadly missed when he didn't come back.' 'It was a sad day,' recalled Wing Commander Milne. 'Hugo, ever full of bounce, enthusiasm and a real fighter pilot's appetite for action, was very much a friend to us all and a very inspiring leader. We missed him greatly.'

Flight Lieutenant Franz Colloredo-Mansfeld assumed command of the squadron until a new CO arrived, and also completed the February entries in Hugo's log-book. In Vern Lancaster's opinion, Colloredo-Mansfeld was a thorough gentleman and a fine leader. Patrols and sweeps continued; 611 carried on; Squadron Leader Charlton Haw DFM was posted in to take command. Being nearly at the end of a tour, he was succeeded in April by the Canadian Jack Charles.

John Aiken's opinion, expressed independently of any contact with Gomann, is correct: that Gomann saw Hugo in the patchy cloud, and made an instant accurate and successful attack. Leutnant Horst Sternberg led his 5/JG26 up on the day, but in Heinz Gomann's opinion, there were only three Spitfires and one FW190 in the combat, and he was not damaged.

Hugo Armstrong's body was never found, and he is commemorated on the Runnymede Memorial in the UK. It is, perhaps, pointless to wonder what the future held for Hugo, if he had not decided to fly that day. After a rest, he perhaps would have returned to lead a Wing later in 1943, possibly to become an Australian contemporary of Al Deere from New Zealand, Sailor Malan from South Africa, and Johnnie Johnson of England. Probably, though, Hugo would have been recalled by RAAF Headquarters in Melbourne for service in Australia and the South West Pacific Area, for the wasteful employment of Spitfires strafing patches of Japanese-occupied jungle. How Hugo would have accepted this is unknown.

Postscript.

As described, on 26 July 1942, Hugo Armstrong was credited with the 900th victory by aircraft from Biggin Hill. The 1,000th claim came on 15 May 1943; Circus 299, an attack on Caen. The score that morning stood at 998, a victory claimed by Vern Lancaster a few days before. It was a fine day, with good visibility, and anticipation was high. Several leading fighter pilots had themselves included on the flying order. The Biggin Hill Wing was led by Canadian Squadron Leader Jack Charles, eight victories, commander 611

Squadron, as Blue 1, with Sergeant A.R. Betts as his Number 2, Flight Lieutenant Johnny Checketts as his Number 3, and Lieutenant R. Teadings as Number 4. Flying as Red 1 in 611 Squadron was the New Zealand-born wing leader, Wing Commander Al Deere, 15 victories, who had shot down a FW190 on 4 May as the 995th victory. Group Captain 'Sailor' Malan, the great South African ace with 27 victories, flew as Deere's Red 3. Commandant Rene Mouchotte led the Free French 341 *'Alsace'* Squadron, with Yellow Section led by Captain Martell and Blue Section by Captain Boudier.

The Wing was to free lance - go anywhere a combat might result. At 16.21, the Spitfires took off, and crossed over Cabourg at 21,000 feet ahead of the bombers: B25 Mitchells and RAF Typhoons which were to attack Caen. The Luftwaffe reacted, and 611 saw what was later reported as 'a melee taking off below.' Jack Charles led Blue Section down and engaged FW190s. Rene Mouchotte swung his squadron west, to bounce stragglers leaving the fight with 611 Squadron; he saw a lone FW190. Three victories were claimed in a few seconds: two FW190 by Jack Charles and a FW190 by Commandant Mouchotte. At least four parachutes were seen by Al Deere and Red Section, and Rene Mouchotte said he saw one of Jack Charles' victims in a parachute before he fired at his own target. Luftwaffe records list 12 fighters destroyed on this date, but it is not clear how many were lost to the Biggin Hill wing, other units, or on the ground to bombing. One Luftwaffe 'expert' was lost: Oberleutnant Horst Hannig, Knight's Cross, commander 2/JG2, with 98 victories - 90 on the Russian Front - was shot down, and killed when his parachute did not open or he was unable to do so because of injuries. He was awarded the Oak Leaves to the Knight's Cross posthumously.

The important matter of who destroyed the 1,000th enemy for Biggin Hill was subject to much scrutiny, and it was decided to share the honour between Jack Charles and Rene Mouchotte. An enormous party was organised at Grosvenor House, London. In addition, the two successful pilots shared a prize of 300 pounds, the result of an unofficial sweep on the 1,000-destroyed 'race'. Vern Lancaster never forgot that he had missed out on the 'nice little sum.'

In May 1943, RAF claims were for 70 destroyed and 19 probables, for a loss of 45; Luftwaffe figures show a loss of 89.

Few of the Australians who flew with Hugo Armstrong survived the dangers of a tour of operations on fighters. Flight Sergeant Ted Hiskens was killed in action over Malta on 15 October 1942; Pilot Officer A.R. Menzies was killed with 453 Squadron RAAF over the Channel on 11 October 1942; Pilot Officer J.W. Macdonald was killed with 72 Squadron RAF on 5 December 1942 in North Africa; Sergeants J.R. Gilbert and A.R. Mackay were killed in the collision on 27 January 1943, as described; Flight Sergeant A.E. Pearce was killed when his Spitfire hit the sea on 11 February 1943; Flight Sergeant R.M. McLay was killed in action with the squadron on 14 March 1943. Keith Clarkson overcame the wrecking of the Tiger Moth, and ended the war as a Flying Officer with the DFM, but was shot down and killed in the Korean War on 5 November 1951, as a Lieutenant in the RAN Fleet Air Arm.

Ted Hall survived operational flying both from the UK and over Darwin with 452 Squadron RAAF against the Japanese, and at time of writing lived near Junee, NSW. Vern Lancaster left 611 Squadron in April 1944, and went without a rest straight to 453 Squadron RAAF to commence another tour of operations, in time for the D-Day landings in Normandy.

He survived the war with the rank of Flight Lieutenant with Distinguished Flying Cross and Mention In Dispatches (DFC MID).   Richard 'Dick' Due and Angus Haynes also survived the war, but Gus Haynes was killed in a car accident.   Dick was commissioned, attended a fighter leader's school, and when he left 611 Squadron in May 1943, his logbook was endorsed by Squadron Leader Jack Charles with *'well above average in every respect'*, and *'will make a good flight commander.'*   At time of writing, Dick lived in Melbourne.   Gary Herbert, who knew Hugo in West Australia and was on the first EATS course with him, survived the very dangerous Blenheim strikes from Malta in December 1941, did a second tour in the UK on Mosquitos with 105 Squadron RAF, was awarded the DFC, became a Path Finder, then, at the end of the tour of 42 bombing operations, returned to Australia to instruct on Mosquitos. He flew post-war with Australian National Airlines, but retired from flying for medical reasons in 1956, and went to West Australia to live in 1975.

Of the first EATS course, Clive Caldwell became the leading RAAF fighter ace of WW2, with 28 victories, six probably destroyed and 15 damaged Italian, German and Japanese aircraft between 26 June 1941 and 20 August 1943, the date of his last combat.   After Hugo's death, only one more member of the first course died in the war, when John Broderick was killed, with the rank of Flying Officer, at No.2 Aircraft Pool, Richmond NSW, on 20 December 1944. Nineteen men on that course at 2SFTS died in the service of their country; eighteen survived the war.

Franz Colloredo-Mansfeld went on to command 132 Squadron, but was killed in March 1944 by coastal anti-aircraft fire while crossing out of France.   Robert Gouby, the Free French pilot who claimed his fifth and sixth victories on the 20 January raid, brought his score to 10, but was killed by flak on 14 August 1944.   Richard Milne RAF was shot down soon after Hugo was killed, but survived as a prisoner.   Bill Compton, a New Zealander in the RAF, went to command 64 Squadron, to various other postings, and survived the war with 21.5 victories, as New Zealand's most highly decorated fighter pilot, with DSO and Bar, DFC and Bar, and died in 1988.   Owen Hardy RNZAF, who shared a Bf109 with Hugo Armstrong, later claimed seven victories, survived the war with a DFC and Bar, joined the RAF after the war, and retired in the UK.   Petrus 'Piet' Hugo, a South African in the RAF, the Tangmere Wing leader when Ted Hiskens followed him to bale out point over the Channel and then sent a Mayday call, ended the war after a varied career with 22 victories, went to farm in southern Africa, and died in 1988.   Bobby Oxspring also enjoyed a varied wartime career, with victories over France, Africa and four V-1s over England, but died in 1989.   Johnny Checketts RNZAF survived the war with 15 victories and lived at time of writing in New Zealand.   Jamie Rankin RAF survived the war with 17 victories, remained in the RAF, but died after retirement in Scotland.   John Aiken RAF flew his second tour of operations as a flight commander with 548 Squadron RAF, in the defence of Darwin.   He remained in the RAF, became Air Chief Marshal Sir John Aiken KCB, and at time of writing lived in London.

Few Luftwaffe opponents in the cross-Channel operations survived the war.   However, Pips Priller, who gave Ted Hall's Spitfire a hammering over the Channel, became commander of JG26, did survive, wrote a unit history, but died of a heart attack in 1961.   Otto Behrens, shot down by Hugo Armstrong, went to Argentina with Kurt Tank, but in 1951 was killed demonstrating the Tank-designed *'Pulqui II'* jet fighter to General Peron - he failed to recover from a deliberate spin before a wing touched the ground.   Kurt Tank's comment could serve as epitaph for many fliers:
'If he had another 50 metres height, he would have been all right.'

Gerhard Vogt, 6JG26, was killed on 14 January 1945, as leader of 5/JG26, with 48 victories. On 4 September 1943, Vogt shot down Australian ace Tony Gaze, but Gaze escaped to the UK.

Heinz Gomann served with II/JG26 almost to the end of the war, with 12 victories, then was posted to fly jets. Internal chaos in Germany was such that Gomann could not report to the assigned unit, and went home to await the end of the war. He survived, went into politics, and today lives in Austria.

Appendix 1
Aircraft flown by Hugo Armstrong to gain victories.

129 Squadron

[records do not identify individual aircraft]

21 Sep 41	Spitfire V	1 Bf109	destroyed
14 Mar 42	Spitfire V	1 Bf109	destroyed
24 Mar 42	Spitfire V	1 FW190	destroyed
4 Apr 42	Spitfire V	1 FW190	damaged

72 Squadron

Flight Commander

27 Apr 42	Spitfire Vb W3168	1 FW190	damaged
4 May 42	Spitfire Vb W3429	1 Bf109	destroyed
		1 Bf109	destroyed
		[shared with P/O O. Hardy RNZAF	
27 May 42	Spitfire Vb BM345	1 Bf109	destroyed
5 Jun 42	Spitfire Vb W3168 'Cawnpore II'	1 Bf109	destroyed
26 Jul 42	Spitfire IX BM271	2 FW190	destroyed

611 Squadron

Commanding Officer

squadron letters FY-

2 Oct 42	Spitfire IX S116/N	1 Bf109	probable
2 Nov 42	Spitfire IX BS435/F	1 FW190	destroyed
		1 Bf109	destroyed
9 Nov 42	Spitfire IX BS435/F	1 FW190	probable
20 Jan 43	Spitfire IX BS435/F	2 Bf109	destroyed
5 Feb 43	Spitfire IX BS435/F	shot down; killed.	

Appendix 2
Text of Citations to Awards
Award of Distinguished Flying Cross, Date 29 May 1942, London Gazette No.35577.

This officer has participated in 29 operational sorties over enemy territory.   He has destroyed at least 5 enemy aircraft and damaged a further 2. Flight Lieutenant Armstrong has displayed courage and initiative and his judgement and skill as a leader have contributed largely to the successes achieved by his flight.

Award of a Bar to Distinguished Flying Cross, Date 8 January 1943, London Gazette No.35855.

Since being awarded the Distinguished Flying Cross Squadron Leader Armstrong has participated in many sorties over enemy occupied territory during which he has destroyed a further 4 enemy fighters and probably destroyed 2 others.   His great powers of leadership have contributed largely to the successes achieved by his squadron.   This officer's keenness to engage the enemy at all times and his excellent escort work have set an inspiring example to all.

Appendix 3
Nominal Roll of No.1 EATS Course
Ranks on graduation 12 January 1941

Pilot Officers

R.M.	Achilles	
H.T.	Armstrong	first EATS graduate to command a UK-based fighter squadron
G.D.	Avery	KIA 22/10/42, F/O, 100 Sqn RAAF, Townsville
C.R.	Caldwell	leading RAAF fighter pilot WW2
M.F.	Dekyvere	
H.D.	Foot	CO 92 Sqn RAAF 1945
A.A.	Hogarth	
J.F.	Kent	KIA 30/6/41, P/O 250 Sqn RAF
R.J.	Lea	KIA 13/6/41, P/O 11 Sqn RAF, Syria
S.F.	Lawson	
D.A.	Munro	KIA 18/6/41, P/O 250 Sqn RAF, Libya
P.C.	Nangle	KIFA 20/10/41, F/O 88 Sqn RAF, UK
R.M.	Rechner	survived, Wg Cdr, DFC

Sergeants

C.K.	Berriman	KIA 22/8/41, Sgt 39 Sqn RAF, M.E. (Middle East)
J.J.	Broderick	KIFA 20/12/44, F/O 2 Aircraft Pool, Richmond NSW
A.C.	Cameron	'Tiny' Cameron, F/Lt, DFM, POW
J.M.	Campbell	
W.S.	Campbell	
F.F.	Clowry	KIA 14/7/41, Sgt 38 Sqn RAF M.E.
T.B.	Comins	
N.A.	Evans	KIFA 5/6/41, Sgt 3 Sqn RAAF, M.E.
D.R.	Gale	KIA 26/6/41, Sgt 250 Sqn RAF, M.E.
C.R.	Gallwey	
R.J.	Good	KIA 17/3/42, Sgt 14 Sqn RAF, M.E.

G.W.	Hartnell	
H.C.	Herbert	
G.E.	Hiller	Died of wounds as POW 2/12/41, 3 Sqn RAAF, M.E.
W.A.	Hopkinson	KIA 8/11/41, Sgt 107 Sqn RAF, Greece
J.M.	Kirkman	
L.L.	Maundrell	
H.A.	MacLennan	KIA 9/4/42, Sgt 11 Sqn RAF, off Ceylon
H.	McMaster	
A.R.	Noseda	KIA 9/1/43, P/O DFC 105 Sqn RAF, France;
P.L.	Payne	
J.C.	Pottie	KIA 15/7/42, P/O 159 Sqn RAF, Libya
S.J.	Prentice	
F.B.	Reid	KIA 15/2/42, Sgt 3 Sqn RAAF M.E.
R.	Secomb	KIA 23/9/41, Sgt 38 Sqn RAF, M.E.
D.	Scott	
N.L.	Stevenson	KIA 9/4/42, W/O 11 Sqn RAF, off Ceylon
H.E.	Tyzack	

W/O Warrant Officer; P/O Pilot Officer; F/O Flying Officer; Wg Cdr Wing Commander; DFC Distinguished Flying Cross; DFM Distinguished Flying Medal; KIA killed in action; M.E. Middle East.

This list of the course at graduation at 2SFTS, Wagga Wagga, 9 January 1941, was supplied from RAAF Historical Section, Deptartment of Defence.   The detail of deaths came from the Roll of Honour at the Australian War Memorial, available on the Internet at www.awm.gov.au.

Sources:

Australia

Perth: Elaine Throssell and Bernie Bellanger; W. 'Bill' Edgar, Archivist of Hale School; Gary Herbert spoke of his bike race with Hugo, their time together in training, in W.A. and aboard ship to the UK; *Melbourne*: Hugo Throssell Armstrong, nephew; Russell Guest, aviation historian and very helpful colleague; Dick Due, ex-611 Squadron pilot; Bob Taylor, Biggin Hill Admin Officer; *Canberra*: the Australian War Memorial: AWM 65 collection, files on HT Armstrong, ET Hiskens and VA Lancaster; AWM 220 collection, the RAF Historical Branch studies, Roll of honour cards available on the Internet at www.awm.gov.au. Kev Ginnane, expert photographer, provided his usual first class assistance. *Sydney:* Norman Rankin, Secretary of the Spitfire Association, kindly assisted in my search for people who knew and flew with Hugo Armstrong. Vern Lancaster in *Victoria*, Pat Davoren in *SA*, and Ted Hall in *NSW* provided personal detail of their time on RAF squadrons with Hugo Armstrong.

UK: PRO Kew, squadron operations record books of the squadrons and pilot's individual combat reports. 611 Squadron Association kindly provided detail of Hugo's time with them. Assistance which could not be faulted came from Phil Wigley DFC, RAF fighter pilot, who kindly agreed to search at Kew for me.   Thanks again, Phil.

USA: Donald L. Campbell, author of a history of JG26, was helpful with detail from his records of JG26.

Austria: Heinz Gomann kindly provided detail of his combat on 5 February 1943, and made comments to the draft of this chapter.

Bibliography

"Aces High"; Christopher Shores & Clive Williams, Grub Street, 1994

"*Die Ritterkreuz Trager Der Luftwaffe*"; Ernst Obermaier, Germany, 1966.

"Fiasco"; John Deane Potter, William Heinemann, UK 1970.

"JG26"; Donald L. Campbell, Orion, New York, 1991.

"JG26 War Diary Volume One"; Donald L. Caldwell, Grub Street, 1996

"Nine Lives"; Alan C. Deere, Hodder & Stoughton, London 1959.

"Spitfire Command"; Bobby Oxspring, Grafton Books, London 1987.

"The Greatest Air Battle"; Norman Franks, William Kimber, 1979.

"The Mighty Eighth"; Roger A. Freeman, Macdonald, 1970.

"The Mouchotte Diaries"; Staples Press, London 1956.

"The Ship Busters"; Ralph Barker, Chatto & Windus, UK 1957.

Chapter 3.

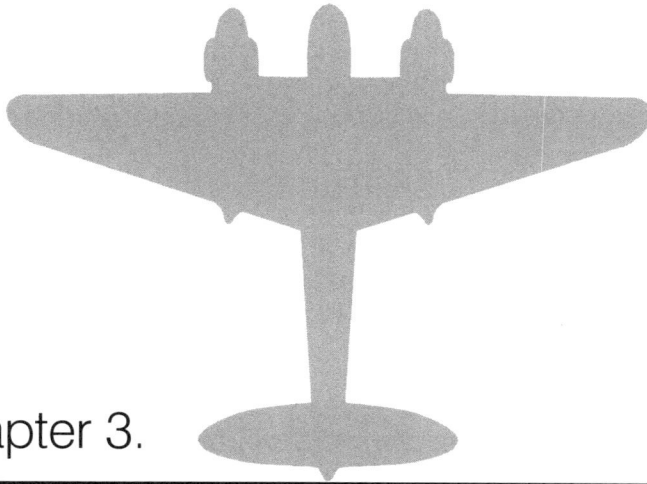

OUT OF THE SHADOWS
Mosquito Intruder

Wing Commander Gordon Panitz DFC RAAF
Flight Lieutenant Richard Williams DFC RAAF

Peter Panitz joined the RAAF in 1940, and by 1944 was a squadron commander in the UK, with the rank of Wing Commander. Panitz was the youngest of nine children born to Fred and Janet Panitz, who owned a bakery in Boonah, southern Queensland. Actually, "Peter's" given names were Gordon Hamilton, but he was generally called Peter, at the instigation of his sister Nell, who said that there were too many Gordons in the family - Janet Panitz was a Gordon. The 'Hamilton' was said to have been included as the British commander at Gallipoli was Sir Ian Hamilton, a Gordon Highlander. As Gordon/Peter was born on 21 September 1915, the events of the Anzac landings were quite topical.

Fred Panitz, wary of anti-German feeling during that war, claimed that the family came from Poland. This was accepted by his children, and presumably the population at large, and it was only later research which showed the Panitz forebears came from Salzgitter, Lower Saxony, in Germany. Peter Panitz was educated at Southport State School, in Queensland, and was a high-jump winner, as well as being a good swimmer. He was a good shot, played golf, as a teen-ager was a drummer, and in addition was learning the baritone to be in the Brass Band. All the Panitz men for several generations were bakers, except one. Peter worked at various times with his father and brothers in bakeries. After extra study to reach the required standard, Peter learned to fly with the Royal Queensland Aero Club, and gained his 'A' Licence.

The young Peter Panitz
(Panitz family)

Things aviation were a little more informal in those days, and Peter would fly a Moth aircraft to Surfers to visit his parents, who had retired there. He would land on the beach at low tide, near the end of Cavill Avenue, and walk to his parents' home. Peter's girl friend lived on a farm at the southern outskirts of Beaudesert, and he would fly low over the main street, looping over the farm to let her know he had arrived. To go with the dashing pilot image, Peter drove a red Ford convertible.

When war came, two other brothers enlisted in the Army, in the Second Australian Imperial Force (2nd AIF). Colin was in the campaigns in Greece and Crete, was captured, and spent the rest of the war in Stalag XIIIc, Hammelburg. George served in the AIF in New Guinea.

Peter began his flying training on 7 February 1941, at Amberley. After only two flights with Pilot Officer Cameron on the 8th, and a two-day break, on the 11th he was given a 'solo test' by Flight Lieutenant Meehan, and then sent off, in Tiger Moth A17-23. Obviously, Peter's pre-war flying experience allowed this very quick progress. However, there was still a lot to learn, and the following weeks were filled with instructional flights interspersed with solo practices of what had been demonstrated. It is now not known how or why, but Peter was allocated to twin-engined aircraft training. In 1941, almost all pilot trainees wanted to fly Spitfires or Hurricanes, which so recently had won the Battle of Britain. Peter first soloed in an Avro Anson on 11 April, two months after doing so in a Tiger Moth. Training on Ansons continued to 21 July, by which time Peter had 167 hours, over 80 of which were as pilot in command of the aircraft. He had been graded as *'Average'* or *'Average Plus'* throughout his training so far.

Peter was the first wartime volunteer from the Wondai area to graduate as a pilot. On his return after receiving his pilot's brevet, or 'wings', a dance and public farewell was quickly organised in the local Memorial Hall. Councillor A.C. Philps, Chairman of the Wondai Shire Council and Zone Patriotic Committee, congratulated Peter, farewelled him, and hoped for his safe return. Other speeches and dances followed, and Peter was presented with a wristlet watch. After supper and the singing of the National Anthem, and 'Auld Lang Syne', the evening concluded. While not every volunteer was guest at such events, there were many such, which demonstrated the wide patriotic support for the war against the Axis.

To England and 456 Squadron RAAF

Peter was commissioned a Pilot Officer on 29 July, and left Australia on 1 August 1941. He arrived in the UK on 21 September, and was posted to 54 Operational Training Unit (OTU) at Church Fenton, Yorkshire, to complete his training before going to an operational squadron. Coincidentally, Hugo Armstrong claimed his first victory on 21 September.

Throughout 1940 and 1941, Luftwaffe intruder aircraft had operated at night against the RAF over England. 91 RAF aircraft were damaged or destroyed by *I Gruppe, Nachtjagdgeschwader 2* (I/NJG2). However, in October, soon after Peter began flying at 54 OTU, Adolf Hitler ordered the intruder flights to cease, so that all RAF losses would fall on Europe, and be witnessed by the local population, particularly Germans. Of the 91 RAF aircraft destroyed, seven were from 54 OTU and 28 from other training units.

The Luftwaffe lost 32 aircraft on these operations. The RAF was to bring the techniques of intruding to a high standard before the war ended, to the extent that Luftwaffe personnel spoke of 'Mosquito panic', and almost every aircraft lost, regardless of cause, was attributed to RAF Mosquitos.

On leaving 54 OTU on 17 February 1942, Peter had just under 261 hours total flying time. He had an *'Above Average'* pass in the night vision tests, and was graded *'Above Average'* as a night fighter pilot.

On 24 February 1942, Pilot Officer Panitz arrived by train at 456 Squadron RAAF, stationed at Valley, Isle of Anglesey, with his observer, Pilot Officer T.R. Cloke, and the Sergeants Gatenby/Melrose crew. Gordon Gatenby had come from 1 OTU Cranfield. Born in 1919 in Sydney, Gatenby enlisted in the RAAF in January 1941, and trained at Narromine, NSW, and in Canada. Being an officer, Peter was able to telephone for transport from the railway station to the airfield. Gordon Gatenby was pleased to find that Peter was good enough to include the other crew in the RAF vehicle - Sergeants had to find their own way, which usually meant walking.

456 Squadron RAAF was the only Australian nightfighter unit to serve in the European theatre in WW2. Formed at Valley on 30 June 1941, the squadron was first commanded by Australian Battle of Britain veteran Wing Commander C.G.C. (Gordon) Olive DFC RAF, who claimed four victories during the battle flying Spitfires while on 65 Squadron RAF. 456 Squadron at first was equipped with single-engined Boulton Paul Defiants, which had all armament in a turret behind the pilot, a design stemming from the 1930s concept that enemy bomber formations would have to attack England from Germany, beyond fighter escort range, and the firepower of the .303-inch calibre four-gun turret of the Defiant would be adequate to destroy aircraft in such situations. No one had thought that the Germans would occupy France and the nearby coastal airfields, and attack from such short range with fighter escorts. Gordon Gatenby's future wife, a member of the British WAAF, had been stationed during the Battle of Britain in 1940 at an airfield in the south of England. She had seen the slaughter of the Defiant squadrons, then used in daylight, as soon as the Luftwaffe fighters realised the only weapons aboard a Defiant were in a rear-facing gun turret. Apart from a few successes, the Defiant had proven useless in previous campaigns. The aircraft were replaced at 456 Squadron by twin-engined radar-equipped Bristol Beaufighters, Mark II models, from September 1941.

The squadron was declared 'operational' on 5 September 1941. Its only victory before Peter Panitz arrived was a Dornier Do217 destroyed on the night of 10-11 January 1942 by the Squadron Leader J.S. Hamilton/Pilot Officer D.L. Norris-Smith crew. On 27 March 1942, Wing Commander E.C. Wolfe DFC RAF, from 141 Squadron, assumed command of 456 Squadron.

Peter was allocated to B Flight, and Gordon Gatenby to A Flight. Gatenby recalled that when they arrived, squadron morale was not good, as it was well understood the Defiants were useless by day or night, and the new twin-engined Bristol Beaufighter was proving hard to master. The 456 Squadron pilots, accustomed to the single-engined Defiant, were sent for about 20 hours twin-engine training, then were expected to fly solo in the big Beaufighter II. This Mark of Beaufighter was described by Gordon Gatenby as the

'Merlin-engined Brute'. It was fitted with Rolls Royce Merlin liquid-cooled engines rather than the radial engine Bristol Hercules for which the Beaufighter had been designed originally. As production of the Hercules engine had not reached its peak, some production runs of Beaufighters were modified to accept the Merlin XX.

The original design accommodated the Hercules engine, which rotated the propellors anti-clockwise, and the aircraft fin was offset slightly to counteract this effect on take-off. But the Merlins rotated clockwise, and the combined effect produced a pronounced and vicious swing on take-off, resulting in many accidents on squadrons with Beaufighter MarkIIs. The technique which evolved called for the port engine to be opened up first, then introduce power to the starboard until directional control was gained. 456 suffered a number of such crashes, with aircraft written off or badly damaged. The hypothetical balance sheet for prosecuting the war indicated a steady succession of losses without any damage inflicted on the enemy.

Having more recent experience on twin-engined aircraft, Panitz and Gatenby made successful solos in the Beaufighter, and Gatenby believes that this demonstration of ability by two new arrivals might have 'stopped the rot.' Apart from a short period of dual instruction on a Beaufighter at OTU, Peter had no experience on the type. However, regardless of individual initial ability on arrival at 456 Squadron, both Panitz and Gatenby had to reach operational standard before being let loose on the German enemy. The hazards of weather and night-flying, combined with minimal training and experience, were killing more aircrew than the Luftwaffe. At the end of February 1942, the squadron had 15 crews graded as proficient for night operations, and 11 under training. But mid-way through March, the operationally qualified crews had been reduced to 13 of a total of 23, and only 18 Australian pilots and observers were on strength. A constant stream of postings into and out of the unit affected the situation. The squadron War Diarist recorded that because of the frequent moves, some were of the opinion that the squadron was regarded only as 'a glorified OTU', and added a hope for more successes soon.

On 20 March 1942 the station was treated to a sight of comedy mixed with drama. Sergeant David Spring RAAF was taking off on his third solo flight in a Beaufighter, but clipped the steel post supporting the wind-sock. The speeding Beaufighter was flicked around, rolled end over end for 300 yards [metres] and proceeded to burn. Spring escaped with burns and was taken to hospital. The comedy began when the fire-engine was unable to close with the wreckage, as the cannon shells were exploding and fuel tanks detonating in spectacular fashion, and the airman responsible for using the hose turned it toward the fire-engine and covered it with a mountain of foam....

For ten weeks, March, April and half of May, Peter flew the necessary training exercises as a member of B Flight, in a variety of Mark II Beaufighters, with Pilot Officer Cloke as his operator. On 2 April, in Beaufighter T3036, Peter made a less than successful cross-wind landing and the port wing and undercarriage were damaged, reducing the aircraft to Category B. The squadron diary soon included the happy comment that Hercules-engined Mark VI Beaufighters were to arrive.

The second victory for 456 Squadron fell on 18 May. During a daylight convoy escort, Pilot Officer Bernie Wills RAF, with Sergeant Ron Lowther RAAF as his radar operator, was just east of Bardsey, a Welsh island. They saw a Ju88, which evaded them for 20 minutes in the clouds, but eventually Wills was able to open fire and saw hits on the Junkers. Later the German crew were rescued from their dinghy in Cardigan Bay. The Ju88, 4U+FL, was from the Luftwaffe reconnaissance unit 3(F)123 - Third Longrange Staffel of Reconnaissance Gruppe 123.

Peter's first operational patrol was flown on 22 May, in aircraft R2371. At the end of the month, he had a total of 310 hours. Further training continued to the end of June, and included an *'Average'* grading at the Blind Flying School. On 1 June, Wing Commander Wolfe assessed Peter as *'Average'*, and yet more training followed through July, with a second operational flight on the 29th, in R3042. More training flights continued in August, with several operators, until on the 17th he flew with Pilot Officer R.S. Williams, who was to remain as his observer throughout most of Peter's operational career. Peter's flying time had risen to 424 hours.

In June, the squadron was informed that the MarkII Beaufighters were to be replaced with Hercules-engined MarkVI models, and these were anticipated with interest as being better to fly than the MarkIIs.

Dickie Williams makes up the team

Richard Sutton (Dickie) Williams, from Patonga Beach, NSW, had been in business for ten years before joining the RAAF, for two of those years running his own family business in a general store and estate agency, and using his earlier training and experience as an accountant and statistican. Born at Leeton on 12 August 1915, his parents were Ernest and Evangeline (Hickey). Ernest migrated to Australia from the UK via Canada and joined the NSW Education Department, was posted to Mudgee, and there met and married Evangeline. After working at Leeton and Guildford, they moved to Patonga in 1918. Ernest intended farming, but several floods destroyed the venture, so he helped build, then purchased and opened the general store at Patonga Beach, which expanded into a Post Office Agency. Dickie's schooling began at Coogee, and was completed at Sydney High. Ernest was stricken by rheumatism in the early 1930s, and from 1933 Dickie took more and more interest in the store. However, he started work at Greater Union Theatres in Sydney, then moved to the mail system in Qantas, and studied accountancy.

Dickie had been able to make a few annual shooting excursions to the Moree area in 1935, '36 and '37. In September 1938, he and Geoff Warren decided to build a boat and sail to the Northern Territory for the adventure, then perhaps sail around the world. 'That is,' he wrote

Dickie Williams as an aircrew cadet (Williams family)

in his diary, 'if War does not intervene.' Dickie thought the next war involving Britain and Australia against Nazi Germany would be the result of a demand by Germany for the return of former colonies, taken as war reparations by the victorious Allies at the end of World War 1, in 1918. Dickie noted that the veterans of the 1914-18 war could still be seen - on crutches or named on memorials, then added,

'It only needs a few military bands to swing down George Street today, and with a little wise propaganda, the bloody mugs (including probably myself) will rush to the recruiting office and sign on the dotted line. Time will tell. Date 7/2/39.'

Dickie and Geoff Warren began building the boat, but also studied signalling, radio, navigation, prospecting, and seamanship. This was in addition to normal work and his own accountancy studies, which he hoped to complete in the two years allocated to building the boat. Dickie was depressed by the economic hardships inflicted on Australia by the Depression, and wrote in his diary of a radio interview he heard on 2FC. The young men involved in the interview were too old at 20 years of age to be considered for an apprenticeship, had 'dead-end' jobs, or were unemployed and had no prospects of work. Dickie realised that in a few years there would be 'a horde of untrained, unskilled workless', who had no hope for a better future with Jack Lang and his followers leading the Labor Party. In his diary entry for next day (9 March 1939), Dickie noted that 'unless a miracle happens' the country would be burdened with enormous Social Service payouts to the unskilled unemployed, but he did not believe that the United Australia Party (UAP; forerunner of the Liberal Party) would do anything to solve the problem.

Ernest Williams died on 24 April 1939, and Dickie returned to Patonga to run the growing business, which included the general store, post office, real estate and insurance agencies, telephone exchange, library, motoring and petrol requirements, general carrier and deliveries of coal, coke, wood and ice.

Dickie began RAAF training in April 1941, married Joyce Ewer, and left for Canada. He was originally a Sergeant, but was commissioned on 17 June 1942. He had done some flying training in Australia, but most had been in Canada. His interests were listed as yachting, golfing and hunting, and with those interests and his business training and experience, Dickie Williams probably was the perfect partner to Peter Panitz.

The Australian nightfighter crews, operating over the western areas of Britain, had very little opportunity for contact with the enemy. Only two victories had been gained in the life of the squadron. On 30 July 1942 Wing Commander Wolfe destroyed a Heinkel He111. Wolfe had four radar or visual contacts, but was only able to close with the fourth, and fired from 50 yards [metres] range. The aircraft was a twin-engined Heinkel He111, F8+LW of 12/KG40, which crashed on Lleyn Peninsula, Wales. This was the last success for 10 months. On the debit side, Pilot Officer P.A. Dey and Sergeant E.W. Mitchell engaged a Ju88 on 26 June, but the Luftwaffe gunner put a bullet right through the fuel line between the two inner tanks, and the cockpit began to fill with petrol. Despite some firing by Dey, the Ju88 escaped. Eventually, out of fuel, Dey had to ditch the Beaufighter, but both men were picked up next day.

September 1942 passed without any operational contact on Peter's 16 flights, but another 30 hours flying time was gained.   Peter made five operational flights in October, during which contact was made with the target aircraft, but no claims were lodged for damaged or destroyed enemy.   November and December saw more similar flying and by the end of 1942, Peter's hours totalled 529.

Accidents continued to plague the squadron.   On 14 September, David Spring had to forceland with engine trouble and the Beaufighter blew up and burned, fortunately after the crew had escaped.   This was one of those events in which the aircraft was totally destroyed, making it a convenient time and place for certain items on the stores account to be certified as destroyed, and so tidy up some loose ends. Apparently six parachutes had been aboard X8205 when it burned.   On 6 October, in X7896, Peter had to land with the starboard undercarriage leg not locked down, the Beaufighter ground-looped and was extensively damaged, but neither Panitz nor Williams was hurt.   The aircraft was reduced to Category AC.   On 8 October, the Norm Scott/Grahame Wood crew died when they mistakenly tried to make a night landing on one engine, after the other failed, at a dummy airfield built to delude enemy aircraft.   On 28 October, an older MkII model was destroyed in a landing mishap through brake failure.   Doug McGregor and Leo McCormack went into the sea while practising radar interceptions, and it was surmised that they were struck by lightning.   Such events were not confined to 456, as the nominated incoming CO, Wing Commander J. McDougall DFC was killed in a flying accident on 16 December.

Adverse weather was frequently the subject of comment in the squadron diary, and on 10 December a gale struck the airfield, damaging the flimsy wartime huts, and rain flooded much of the accommodation, to the extent that fears were held for the health of squadron members if warm and dry conditions in the accommodation could not be achieved.   Squadron strength on 31 December 1942 stood at 112 RAAF and 128 RAF members.   The weather, about which little could be done, again was the subject of a special reference in the diary.   'A lovely typical Valley day. Wind up to 100 mph in gusts. [170kmph]   Horizontal rain in the morning, clear by lunch.'   As for the operational reason for being of 456 Squadron, at the end of 1942 the Luftwaffe bomber force made infrequent appearances in strength over the UK, being mainly engaged in the east against the Soviets and in the south against Mediterranean targets.   Heavy losses had been inflicted on the German bomber units in both theatres since the serious losses suffered in the Battle of Britain and the night 'blitz' of the British cities.

1943

In January 1943, 456 Squadron received its Mosquito Mark II aircraft, fitted with Mark V radar.   The entire squadron was involved in mastering the maintenance and operation of this very different type of fighting machine.   On 1 February, Wing Commander M. H. Dwyer RAF assumed command.   Due to the lack of enemy action, 456 was informed on 28 February that it also would operate as long range day fighters and fly Ranger sorties over France.

A Ranger operation was defined as,

'Offensive patrols by day or night involving deep penetration of hostile territory with the object of destroying enemy bomber, reconnaissance, training and communications aircraft in rear areas, of disorganising enemy low-flying training, and of attacking enemy transport targets in rear areas.'

To Middle Wallop and effective operations: Intruding over France

Seven RAF crews arrived to reinforce the Australian aircrew complement. On 16 March, a flight moved to Colerne for Ranger operations. The radar equipment was removed from aircraft allocated to Ranger flights, as it was a matter of policy that recent developments in radar would not be permitted to fly over enemy territory.

The first RAAF Ranger sorties were flown on 21 March, by the Harry Smith/Jack Ross crew and V.P. 'Red' Ratcliffe/Ron Lowther crew, but thick ground haze prevented the crews from seeing any trains. Peter and Dickie Williams set off on their first Ranger flight over France on 23 March, but, with two other crews, were forced back by the weather.

The role of the navigator on these flights was important. Both men were constantly scanning the sky and ground for enemy, particularly enemy fighters and anti-aircraft fire directed at them, and for sightings of important items such as airfields not yet known to the RAF, defensive positions, radar and signals installations, tanks, artillery and truck parks, training installations, headquarters, supply areas and vehicular traffic. The navigator also had to master the topography of the area, be able to locate the position of the aircraft very quickly, make a note of the time and location of sightings of interest, and inform the pilot of changes of course which might be planned, and course back to base in emergency. Some pilots of these low-level fast sorties admitted that the navigator had the more difficult job of the two.

Vern 'Red' Ratcliffe and Peter Panitz,
456 Squadron RAAF, at dispersal hut, Valley,
August 1942 (Panitz family)

The squadron had no enemy contact on these Rangers, and at the end of March was transferred from Valley to Middle Wallop. This move brought 456 into 10 Group, and to a base which was well placed for operations over France.

'Middle Wallop proved to be a splendid station', stated the squadron historian. The Station Commander was Group Captain Stephen Hardy RAF, who was described as 'unforgettably impressive... huge, stern, just and enormously competent' and with 456 Squadron, made a good working relationship. 'The station was a model of convenience and smooth running', added the historian, with a clear description of the adequate grass airfield, clean quarters, and the convivial atmosphere of the nearby "The Pheasant". No one, it seemed, regretted leaving Valley.

By the end of March 1943, Peter had a total of 622 hours, and in April was to begin inflicting damage on the King's enemies.

10 Group required six squadron aircraft be on readiness each night, as the enemy could still make small but concentrated attacks without warning. The attempts to intercept such enemy as did appear showed conclusively that the Mark V radar was not adequate for successful night interceptions. The equipment showed the target height and bearing on one screen and its range on a second. Range indication was limited by altitude, and the radar was unable to efficiently hold low-flying targets. The Mark VIII radar was much better, but 456 did not have the priority necessary to have it allocated - the needs of Bomber and Coastal Commands were more urgent.

Wing Commander Mickey Dwyer RAF, who had replaced Wolfe as the squadron commander, flew a Ranger patrol on 16 April, searching for trains, but was unsuccessful, though intense light ground fire was noted. Next night, Warrant Officer Red Ratcliffe found and strafed two trains, leaving one halted and clouded in steam.

On 20 April, with Dickie Williams as observer in Mosquito DZ269, Peter Panitz departed Middle Wallop at 22.25 for a three-hour sortie. They crossed the French coast at Cap D'Erquy at 700 feet, and searched for targets along the railway to Argentan. Nothing was seen, but while en route back to the coast, a 20-wagon train was spotted near Villers Bocage station. Three strafing runs were made, with strikes each time on the engine, which exploded with a burst of steam and smoke. There were no ground defences, and the train was claimed as destroyed. It was 26 months since Peter began flying training with the RAAF. The squadron historian later wrote of Peter that 'night fighting did not afford adequate scope for his impatient genius.'
On both nights of 24 and 28 April the squadron had been unable to engage enemy aircraft which attacked England, due to the limitations of the Mark V radar. A Mark VIII-equipped Mosquito of 85 Squadron was successful against one enemy who had evaded 456 Squadron.

Peter flew another uneventful Ranger on 30 April, but the Ranger flight on 6 May was to be quite successful. Again in DZ269, Peter and Dickie Williams set off for France, this time in mid-afternoon. They departed Portland Bill at 14.29, and crossed the enemy coast at zero feet, again looking for trains, along the Paris-Brest line. A single engine was seen near Combourg, and a dummy run made, to allow the French crew to abandon the train. Cannon and machinegun strikes brought steam spurting from the boiler, and the Mosquito turned right to Caulnes, where the machineguns scored hits on a goods train just out of the station, again with steam pluming from the punctured boiler. Further down the line many cannon and machinegun strikes were seen on a train near Doi. The cloud cover necessary for these Ranger operations, by hampering German fighter opposition, was beginning to break up, but Peter Panitz went on, and made an effective but short attack on another train east of Lamballe. At Lamballe itself, three trains were found in the station, and yet another was halted after an attack, with the usual cloud of smoke and steam billowing upwards. There was no ground fire, but a flak position was seen on a train at Lamballe. They crossed out to the Channel and climbed into cloud to conceal them on the return to England. A claim for six trains damaged was made on return to base. When interviewed by the Public Relations staff, Peter said, 'We had quite a good time over there. On our way in at nought feet, French fishermen waved to us.'

The individual attacks on trains, while perhaps regarded as pinpricks to the Axis war machine, became of reat significance when linked to heavy bomber attacks on the repair facilities. As the war continued, and results of all these attacks were assessed, it was realised that attacks on trains, repair facilities and rail stations combined to produce a very effective means of slowing the movement of military equipment, supplies, individual personnel and entire units.

Oxlade and Shanks - a difficult interception

There was more airborne success for the Australian squadron on 7 May. Flying Officer A.G. (Geoff) Oxlade and Flying Officer D.M. (Don) Shanks were scrambled at 23.10 against enemy aircraft flying north. Despite very bad weather, Ground Control guided them onto an enemy aircraft, but cloud was so thick they never did see it. Don Shanks later described Oxlade's flying during the sortie as 'the most wonderful piece of flying I have ever seen. It was also the most violent I have experienced.' Cloud base was at 400 feet, and cloud went to 17,000 feet, with rain all the way. Oxlade, guided by Shanks' directions from the radar set, flung the big Mosquito fighter (HJ650) through the murk, refusing to give up the chase, and they glimpsed what were thought to be aircraft lights just before the other aircraft seemed to explode as it hit the ground while trying to evade them, near Shaftesbury, Dorset at 23.25 hours. It was the first victory by 456 on the Mosquito.

The Luftwaffe crew probably were alerted by their rear-warning radar, dodging whenever the fighter was detected on their tail, and flew into the ground by pilot error. Five minutes later, Oxlade and Shanks were directed by ground control onto another contact, and chased the enemy through the anti-aircraft barrage firing over Portsmouth, through the cloud, with static electricity flaring around the propellors. This time, as they came in range the enemy bomber went into the sea off the Isle of Wight, leaving no trace. The Australian crew and squadron knew it would be pointless claiming the destruction of this second victory, and there was some doubt that the first would be allowed, as no firing had occurred. However, it was later found that Junkers Ju88A-14 No. 144078, 3E+KL of 2/KG6, crashed near Rectory Farm, Winfrith, Dorset; pilot Unteroffizier P. Czonner and crew were all killed. 40 minutes earlier, the staffel commander of 2/KG6 had been killed with his crew near Ringwood, Hampshire; there were no other losses around the time Oxlade and Shanks chased their quarry.

Geoff Oxlade was congratulated next day by the Air Officer Commanding (AOC) 10 Group for his fine flying.   Oxlade was born in 1920, at Echuca, and graduated as an *'Above Average'* pilot.   He gained an enviable reputation among both ground and air crews, as the man who never made a mistake on the ground or in the air; he never damaged an aircraft.   After training, he flew with 256 Squadron RAF before going to 456.   His first tour of operations would be 22 months.

Peter Panitz and 'Red' Ratcliffe were forced back from France by good weather on 11 May.   Fine weather meant the faster Luftwaffe day fighters could intercept them; prudence dictated a return.   Next day, on a flight in the early afternoon, from 12.30 to 14.25, Peter, with Dickie Williams navigating, attacked two more trains near La Hage du Puits and Polligny, causing each to throw off dense clouds of smoke and steam.   Ratcliffe also hit two other trains, causing one boiler to explode, but was hit in the tail wheel by a 40mm anti-aircraft shell.   The next Ranger was at night, departing base at 22.20 on 15 May.   Peter strafed two electric trains, and a truck crashed off the road and caught fire after being hit with the four cannon and four machineguns in his Mosquito.   This time there was accurate light flak and searchlight activity, but the Mosquitos returned safely.

On 16 May, the Ratcliffe/Lowther and Oxlade/Shanks crews flew with 26 other night fighters to harass German night fighter bases to assist the returning Lancasters of 617 Squadron on the famous Dambusting raid.   Neither RAAF crew engaged the enemy.

On the 17th, Flight Sergeant C.S. Samson heavily damaged three more engines near Lamballe.

On 22 May, Peter was promoted (Acting) Flight Lieutenant.   Next day, Flying Officer Hitchcock and Leading Aircraftman Roberts were killed when the squadron Magister light aircraft spun in from 1500 feet.   In the last two weeks of May, 456 also began flying Intruder patrols over enemy airfields in Holland and Belgium, to hinder Luftwaffe night-fighter operations.   In addition to these duties, 'normal' night defence operations were flown.

On 30 May, Wing Commander Dwyer, the commanding officer, had engine failure when returning from a day Ranger south of the Brest peninsula, and had to forceland in a field near Crediton.   The aircraft was destroyed and both Dwyer and his navigator, Don Shanks, were injured. Shanks was unable to resume operational flying for more than six months.   A new CO was appointed, Wing Commander George Howden DFC, an Australian in the RAF.

Then, on 2 June, the aggressive Ratcliffe, with Flight Sergeant Ron Lowther, failed to return from a day Ranger, with which he had pressed on though the clear weather conditions were not suitable.   Ratcliffe and Flight Sergeant C.S. Samson set off at 13.20, but Samson prudently turned back when the weather began to clear. The squadron historian described Ratcliffe as 'a fine and utterly fearless pilot', and his observer, Lowther, as 'experienced and very competent.'   Lowther had flown with Wills on 18 May 1942 when a Ju88 was destroyed.   They were the first crew lost on operations.

As Gordon Gatenby said, 'You can't take on a brace of FW190s without cloud to hide in.' Of Gatenby, the squadron historian wrote that he 'was well known for his incredibly keen eyesight and vigourous and skilful piloting.'

To the Bay of Biscay

On 5 June, the squadron was ordered to provide three aircraft, plus flying and ground crews, to Predannack for an unspecified period.   This detachment began flying Instep patrols in the Bay of Biscay, a counter to the Luftwaffe air activity there.

An Instep operation was defined as,
'Offensive fighter sweeps to intercept enemy seaplane or long range land fighters interfering with the operations of Coastal Command aircraft in the Bay of Biscay.'

Germany could not win the war without winning the Battle of the Atlantic, stopping the flow of men, materials and supplies across the ocean from the Americas. The Allies could not win the war unless that flow was sustained. The campaign in the Atlantic went on for every day of the war, fought by day and night, almost regardless of the weather. German U-Boats had access to ports and facilities along the Atlantic coast of France, and particularly on the Biscay coast, where entire flotillas were based. Courage, personal initiative, determination and technological advances were required by boths sides in the struggle for success in the Bay of Biscay and the far reaches of the Atlantic.

RAF operations against U-Boats crossing the Bay of Biscay had been intensified with good result: six U-Boats had been sunk in the first two weeks of May, more than for the period January to April.   RAF Coastal Command was tasked with attacking the U-Boats on passage out to the Atlantic or back to port, and a variety of twin- and four-engined bombers and flying boats were sent to perform this duty.   On 19 May, the son of Admiral Donitz, head of the German U-Boat service, was lost in U-954 to air attack.   Admiral Donitz had made repeated requests for air cover for his U-Boats crossing the Bay, and after the increase in submarine losses, the hard-pressed Luftwaffe complied. The effect of the Luftwaffe fighter sweeps over the Bay was soon felt by the RAF, and aircraft losses began to mount.   In response, RAF long range fighters also swept the area.   10 Group had sent these sorties on an ad hoc basis for some time, but now it was decided to form a squadron-sized unit from the available night-fighter squadrons.

Though in theory neutral, Spanish fishing boats in the Bay had been reported with radio aerials, which led to the deduction that they were used to assist the Luftwaffe by sending sighting reports of RAF activity.   On 20 April the Spanish were warned that after 1 June, all ships seen in designated areas on the high seas would be considered to be enemy.

The most dangerous of the Luftwaffe forces countering Coastal Command operations in the Bay were formations up to squadron strength of twin-engined Junkers Ju88s, though other aircraft had gained some success.   The 30 or so Ju88s were from 5th *Gruppe, Kampfgeschwader* 40 (V/KG40), had a three-man crew of pilot, navigator and radio operator, and were armed with three fixed forward firing 7.9mm machineguns and three 20mm cannon in the nose, plus other machineguns defending the rear and sides.

Operating mainly from Kerlin Bastard at Lorient, and Bordeaux-Merignac, the Germans could fly in the knowledge that they were likely to find RAF bombers at almost any time. However, the Instep patrols could not be so sure of locating the Germans, so many Instep flights were without result.

The famous film star, Leslie Howard, who played 'Ashley' in *Gone With The Wind* was aboard a KLM DC3 passenger aircraft G-AGBB *Ibis* on 1 June 1943, flying from Lisbon to England. It was shot down over the Bay of Biscay by two of a formation of eight Ju88s from V/KG40. There were many rumours and stories about this tragedy, and it was claimed the DC3 was shot down apparently because one passenger was thought, by German Intelligence in Portugal, to be British Prime Minister Winston Churchill. However, the Luftwaffe crews were junior officers, and had never been told that civil aircraft flew the UK-Portugal route, and in addition the KLM liner was painted in RAF camouflage pattern, with only white lettering denoting civil registration. RAF DC3s of Transport Command had been flying to Gibraltar and North Africa across the Bay, and were legitimate targets. When it was realised the aircraft under attack was a civil airliner, the Luftwaffe leader called to cease fire, but the DC3 already was on the way down with port engine and wing on fire, and no one was seen to survive the crash into the sea.

A well-known example of the Luftwaffe-Coastal Command combats was fought on 2 June 1943. Sunderland 'N' of 461 Squadron RAAF was attacked by eight Junkers Ju88s, which made about 20 separate attacks. Four 88s were claimed by the RAAF crew, though the Sunderland was riddled and three members of the crew were killed or wounded. The pilot, Flight Lieutenant C.B. Walker, flew back 350 miles [560 km] on three engines. One of the Luftwaffe pilots, Herbert Hintze, later said that the Ju88s 'could not down the big bird, because it made good its escape into the "official cloud".' A 236 Squadron RAF Beaufighter was badly damaged on the next day by a pack of 88s, and more such combats followed on the 5th. A mixed formation from 456 and 25 Squadron RAF engaged eight Ju88s on 11 June, and the formation leader of 25 Squadron destroyed a Ju88 of KG40. Flying Officer John W. Newell, with Flight Sergeant A.J. Keating as observer, claimed two of these enemy damaged.

Peter Panitz, in HJ702, had to return with engine trouble. Newell flew DZ269, Peter's mount on earlier successful operations. Newell, from Mareeba, was born in 1917, joined the RAAF in September 1940, and also was trained at Narromine and in Canada. The squadron diary noted that, 'All the pilots here are wildly excited and inclined to be jealous that they are not there themselves [at Predannack].'

Another claim for a 'damaged' was submitted by [now] Warrant Officer Gordon Gatenby, after a combat on 19 June; other aircraft from 151 Squadron RAF claimed one destroyed. The flight had gone well down the Bay of Biscay, almost to Spain. Gatenby saw what he thought to be barrage balloons low on the water, but then realised he was looking at eight Ju88s circling a fishing trawler. The Mosquitos attacked, and again the formation leader, from 151 Squadron, destroyed a Ju88, while Gatenby saw his fire hitting his target. The Ju88s escaped in cloud.

The Ranger Flight, 456 Squadron, September 1943. l. to r. are:
F/O Merv Austin, W/O Arthur McEvoy, F/O Dickie Williams, F/Lt Peter Panitz, P/O
George Gatenby, P/O J.M. Fraser, F/O John Newell, P/O Alec Abbey, F/O Stew
Smith, (front) F/Sgt Alan Keating. (Panitz family)

On the 21st, Gatenby and three other Mosquitos from 151 Squadron strafed a U-Boat, and though it was not sunk, U-462 was badly damaged and suffered casualties among the deck crew.   The submarine had to abort its important resupply mission to other U-Boats in the Atlantic, and return to Bordeaux for repairs.   It was not every day that nightfighters could influence the Battle of the Atlantic.

The policy of constantly harassing the U-Boats, though often not of immediate value to the RAF aircrews, paid a cumulative dividend.   The submarines of the era required time on the surface to charge batteries and introduce fresh air into the hull.   The longer they could be forced underwater, the better, and if crews could be wounded, or damage force a return to port, so much the better for the Atlantic convoys.

A series of intense combats erupted in mid-June, as the U-Boats tried a new tactic, ordered by Donitz, of fighting their way across the Bay on the surface, in formation, relying on massed anti-aircraft weapons to bring success.   Groups of five submarines challenged the air and naval forces, generally with losses to both sides.   However, Peter Panitz flew nine Instep patrols in June, without contact.

Some of the squadron's night defensive patrols were 'Bullseye' exercises with Bomber Command, and the Luftwaffe knowingly or otherwise sent four bombers which slipped though the activity on 21st June, to bomb Winchester.   Exploding bombs were the first intimation that the enemy had arrived.   There was a flurry of activity, but only four enemy were among a larger number of friendly aircraft, and the Germans escaped.

More Intruder operations

456 Squadron returned to intruder flights over France.   On 12 July, with Flight Lieutenant B. Howard/Flying Officer J.K. Ross, Peter Panitz and Dickie Williams attacked a transformer station at Guerledin.   This operation was carefully planned and well executed. The Station Intelligence Officer, Squadron Leader R. Frost MBE RAF, gave frequent invaluable assistance in preparation for this and other operations.   He had great knowledge of Ranger operations, and provided what was described as 'a magnificent series' of coastline photos, from which the crews were able to identify their routes, and Frost personally marked target maps, which assisted the crews in locating the small objectives.   Ground haze made it necessary to make three passes over the target to identify it correctly before firing.   Dickie William's navigational ability was vital to the success of such precise attacks at night on a darkened continent.

Strikes were seen exploding on the building, then it gave a big electical flash.   Light flak came from a position about 1000 metres away.   Peter then searched the railway near Guincamp, and strafed two trains, both of which halted and were shrouded in steam and smoke.   As they left for England, what looked like a burning aircraft was seen near Minard Point.   On 26 July, they had another success, flying with Flying Officer R.G. Pratt/ Flying Officer S.D.F. Smith, in Mosquito Mark VI aircraft.   Again, the operation was planned with a great deal of assistance from Squadron Leader Frost, the Intelligence Officer.   Departing base at 21.40, the pair easily found the target and attacked, because, apart from good navigating features en route, a light was on in the power-house.   Each crew saw flashes and explosions, and the building was left in flames.   There was no enemy reaction during the flight.

The squadron had received some MarkVI Mosquitos, which did not have radar fitted, but were equipped for fighter-bomber tasks, with long-range fuel tanks and strengthened structure for carrying bombs.

The war in the Bay of Biscay continued.   The RAF persisted in anti-U-boat operations, despite the dangerous Ju88 sweeps, and despite losses.   The Luftwaffe could not claim air superiority over the region - the U-Boats were to be attacked whenever possible.   On 8 July, a Liberator was attacked by seven Ju88s over the Bay of Biscay, but survived at least 30 separate attacks and escaped into cloud.   Herbert Hintze took part in an attack on a B24 on this day, claiming it shot down into the sea after a head-on pass at 150 feet. One Ju88 was lost in this combat, when Leutnant Wittmer-Eigenbolt went into the sea during a steep turn.   On the 18th, another Liberator was attacked by five Ju88s, but survived.

Other combats occurred frequently, and the hapless crews flying twin-engined Armstrong-Whitworth Whitleys from 10 Operational Training Unit (OTU) took their obsolete aircraft out into the search areas, knowing that they had little hope of survival if intercepted.   The squadrons operating Vickers Wellingtons fitted with Rolls-Royce Pegasus engines knew that these aircraft could not maintain flight on one engine for more than a short time - but crews were sent in these on long patrols over the ocean.   RAF Bomber Command was demanding all four-engined bomber production to expand its force and replace the frightening losses suffered in its campaign to demolish the German cities, with the result that Coastal Command had to fly in its own vital role of convoy protection and anti-U-Boat operations with a mass of lesser quality aircraft and a handful of modern Liberators.

On 30 July, there was another epic combat in the Bay of Biscay, a six-hour battle between three surfaced U-Boats, aircraft of Coastal Command and the US Army Air Force, and ships of the Royal Navy.   All three U-Boats were sunk, but it was obvious that the Germans were going to fight for superiority in the Bay.   In the six days from 28 July, nine U-Boats were lost in the Bay.   Some of these were vital supply boats tasked to meet those U-Boats already in the Atlantic.   25 RAF and Allied squadrons, with 358 aircraft available, flew 9690 hours on Biscay sorties in July.   86 U-Boats crossed the Bay, in one direction or the other, and the aircraft made 90 sightings and 63 attacks.

Admiral Donitz presumably regretted his words to a gathering of U-Boat commanders at the beginning of the war, that 'the U-Boat has no more to fear from aircraft than a mole from a crow.'

Donitz' frequent requests for more air support were met in August, but he already had ordered a change in tactics, away from the 'fight-it-out' stance, and U-Boat losses fell. Air battles increased.   Forty Ju88s, some Arado Ar196 single-engined float-planes and Focke-Wulf FW190 single-engined fighters began to sweep the coast and Bay more intensively, and had some success against the relatively cumbersome four-engined and twin-engined anti-submarine aircraft hunting U-Boats.   For a Luftwaffe loss of five Ju88s and a FW190, 16 RAF anti-submarine and six RAF fighter aircraft were lost in August. On 3 August, a 10 Squadron RAAF Sunderland flying boat was attacked for an hour by seven Ju88s; one was claimed destroyed, but the Sunderland crew suffered one killed and one wounded.   Sadly, most of the 461 Squadron crew who had survived the epic combat on 2 June were lost on 13 August.   Between May and August, a total of 31 British and five US squadrons, plus 10 OTU, were involved over the Bay.

By the end of August, six fighter-bomber Mark VI models of the Mosquito had arrived at 456 Squadron, to form a Ranger flight.   These aircraft were not fitted as night-fighters, but had long-range tanks, could carry bombs and had the Gee navigational aid.   Peter Panitz was selected to lead this flight, with six chosen crews.   The choice was between him and Bill Hyem, but Peter's seniority as an officer predated Hyem's by one day. Before specialised training for the Ranger crews could commence, the flight was detached to Predannack.

The Ranger Flight

The squadron normally operated two flights, A and B, but the Ranger Flight was given its own identity, as C Flight, and its own radio callsign, Didus.   The flight members, as crews, comprised:

> Flight Lieutenant G. Panitz/Flying Officer R.S. Williams
> Flying Officer J.W. Newell/Flight Sergeant A.J. Keating
> Flying Officer R.G. Pratt/Flying Officer S.D.P. Smith

Pilot Officer C.S. Samson/Pilot Officer A.M. Abbey
Warrant Officer G.F. Gatenby/Flight Sergeant J.M. Fraser
Warrant Officer A.S. McEvoy/Flying Officer M.N. Austin

The first operations were without great results, but power stations and trains were attacked. On 7 August, Samson led four Mosquitos to attack Luftwaffe mine-spotting aircraft expected off La Rochelle, but none were found.   However, two armed trawlers were strafed; one had its superstructure blown off and was 'smoking furiously' when last seen.   More Instep patrols were flown with no contact.   Gordon Gatenby recalled that on some of them, not even a seagull was seen.   On 17 August, 151 Squadron RAF, with the better Mark VIII radar in its Mosquitos, and so more likely to be successful against the low-level German raiders, replaced 456 at Middle Wallop, and the RAAF squadron moved to Colerne.

September brought the first successes for 456 Squadron over the Bay.   Peter Panitz arranged that the six crews of the 456 Squadron Ranger flight be regarded as a separate unit, that aircraft and crews would not be part of a mixed formation with RAF squadrons, and that four RAAF crews be rostered for such operations as were ordered.   The four Mosquitos would spread into a line abreast formation and sweep across the Bay of Biscay for up to five hours.   Rather than fly at wave-top height, they would patrol at a few hundred feet, to relieve the strain on the pilots.   Low flying kept them below enemy radar, and also allowed the pilots to see other aircraft silhouetted against the sky, while they themselves were partly hidden due to the grey-green camouflage pattern on the Mosquito.   In normal day fighting, every effort was made to gain height, as the first aces of World War 1 had found that the combatant with height controlled the battle, but the Rangers used the opposite tactic, relying on speed and camouflage to assist them to avoid the more formidable foes such as the Messerschmitt Bf109 and Focke-Wulf FW190.

On 7 September, with Flying Officer Smith as observer, Peter was one of four aircraft which machinegunned a fishingboat, and all crews reported seeing strikes on the hull and sails.   These boats, as explained earlier, were believed to be used by the Germans to send sighting reports of Allied air activity over the area, and so were sometimes designated as targets.   Also, they had been warned to stay within certain areas, and had sails riddled as warning for straying.   This declaration of bounds, though harsh and required by wartime, assumed that the boatmen were accurate navigators who operated from charts.

Two more Insteps were flown, without contact for Peter Panitz.   However, the Luftwaffe was quite active in the area, and on 9 September a 224 Squadron RAF Liberator was attacked by seven Ju88s, who persisted for over an hour, but eventually left after losing one shot down and three so badly damaged that they were reported to have crash-landed in Spain.   The crew of the Liberator were awarded three Distinguished Flying Crosses, one Conspicuous Gallantry Medal and two Distinguished Flying Medals. Another RAAF crew was having a period of intense operational activity.   Flight Lieutenant Dudley Marrows RAAF, 461 Squadron, had been awarded the DFC for sinking a U-Boat in the battle on 30 July.   On 16 September, his Sunderland was attacked by six Ju88s, and gradually shot out of the sky.   One 88 was seen to turn for France with a smoking engine, and three others were hit, but their attacks left Marrows with only one of his four engines working.   He landed in the sea successfully, and the 11-man crew crowded into the sole remaining usable dinghy.   Fortunately, next day they were rescued; Marrows received the DSO.

A Junkers Ju88 destroyed

On 21st September, four Mosquito VI led by Peter Panitz left Predannack at 14.50.   Two and a quarter hours later, Gordon Gatenby saw the enemy well above: eight aircraft at 8,000 feet and to starboard.   The Mosquitos climbed after them, lost them in cloud, saw them again.   Then they were identified: Junkers Ju88s.   The 88s were in line astern, climbing for higher cloud.   They split into two formations; Gatenby went for the highest.   Peter attacked the lower formation, and closed on the last Junkers, he fired at 200 yards [metres]; hits sparked on the cockpit and starboard engine - smoke streamed back and the rear gunner stopped shooting; Peter fired again.   More hits flashed on the starboard engine, the 88 started to go down, and Flying Officer Samson hit it on the port engine, the fuel tank there burst into flames and the 88 was seen to crash into the sea.   Flying Officer Newell fired on another from 600 yards, and it disappeared into cloud with smoke coming from the starboard engine.   Gordon Gatenby engaged another, with four bursts from slightly above and dead astern, strikes flashed all over it, and it also disappeared into cloud, but this one was smoking from wingtip to wingtip.   The Mosquitos returned to base.   Peter reported that if there had not been cloud, he thought that all the Junkers would have been destroyed.   These Junkers were from V/KG40.

It was decided to send a Royal Navy cruiser fitted with radars and fighter control radios into the Bay, to assist the sweeps to contact the enemy.   On 25 September, 307 [Polish] Squadron RAF, with 12 Beaufighters covering a wide swathe, engaged eight Ju88s, claiming three destroyed.   The Aussies could only listen to the aggressive Poles chattering on the radio as they hammered the invaders of their homeland.   By the end of September, there had been 25 combats over the Bay, with six enemy destroyed.   This intensity of action was to fall sharply in October, to seven combats with three enemy claimed, but with three friendly aircraft also lost.

The inherent dangers of flying were witnessed by many in the squadron area on 29 September.   A Mosquito flown by Flight Lieutenant E.H. Griffith, the squadron gunnery officer, with Corporal W.H. Blakely in training as an observer, went into a dive, did not recover, and crashed near one of the hangars; both men were killed.   The starboard engine had parted from the wing, and itself fell into the airfield, while the aircraft fell close to a hangar and burst into flames.   It was found that the engine mounting bolts had stripped, and all others had to be checked and replaced.

Lake Biscarosse and a Ju88 destroyed

Eager to give his crews some action to balance the unsuccessful Bay patrols, Peter requested permission to fly a Ranger operation as well as the Instep sweeps.   He selected the Luftwaffe flying boat base at Lake Biscarosse, and took three other crews there late on 3 October.   There were no aircraft to attack, but despite intense light flak, a refuelling launch, a tender and flak barge were strafed.   As they left the French coast, they strafed an armed trawler, leaving it on fire.   Then Peter saw, in the dusk, an aircraft at 200 feet.   He swung in behind it to identify it, and at only 100 yards [metres] saw it was a Ju88, with two bombs slung between the fuselage and each engine.   At 75 yards [metres] range, he fired.   The unfortunate Junkers blew up and hit the sea as a mass of flames.   'We found ourselves flying through falling bomb splinters and wreckage,' Peter said later.

The excitement was not over - three aircraft had intermittent engine problems which made the return flight over the sea somewhat stressful.   Engine trouble had plagued the Mosquitos, and this flight was to be the last for some time.   Eventually, it was found that salt water and salt air had been entering the engines on the low level flights.   The salt tended to build up in the fuel lines and eventually clogged them, with potentially lethal results in an aircraft flying low over the sea.

Command of B Flight and DFCs

On 20 October, Peter was promoted Squadron Leader, and appointed to command B Flight.   This took him from the Ranger operations, back to a Mark II night-fighter Mosquito.   On the 28th, he and Dickie Williams were awarded the Distinguished Flying Cross (DFC).   The citation to Peter's award stated that in the previous four months he had damaged 13 trains and several electrical installations, and had
 'at all times displayed fine leadership, skill and devotion to duty.'

Dickie Williams' citation stated that his work as navigator had
'been faultless and had contributed much to the success' of the operational sorties, during which he 'invariably displayed great courage, dash and determination.'

The full texts of the citations are in Appendix 2.

In November, Peter made several flights in a variety of Mosquitos, and in DZ681 made a single-engined landing, as well as an unsuccessful Intruder flight to Biscarosse - the weather was unsuitable.   On 4 December, Pilot Officer J.L. May and Flying Officer L.R. Parnell did not return from an operation.   Gordon Gatenby fell victim to tuberculosis, which ended his RAAF career, and resulted in some 10 years in hospitals and under Repatriation care.

At the end of December, with 911 hours flying time, Peter was graded '*Exceptional*' as a twin-engined pilot, and '*Above Average*' as a pilot-navigator.   Peter was posted to HQ 9 Group, and later was to be posted as a flying instructor, but these postings were cancelled.   However, his operational tour with 456 was over.   Several pilots were posted at the end of the year, and command passed on 14 December to Wing Commander Keith Hampshire, who had come from the Pacific theatre.   On 27 December 1943, Peter left for a Fighter Interception School course at Lulsgate Bottom, and a posting to 63 Operational Training Unit (OTU) at Honiley.

1944

January 1944 and the first week in February were spent qualifying as an instructor, for which Peter was graded as *'Average'*, and classified in the category of 'Q (ME)'.   He then commanded 1 Squadron at 60 OTU, and later became Chief Flying Instructor.   By 13 June 1944, he had 1018 flying hours.   On 22 June, he arrived at Thorney Island to command 464 Squadron RAAF, equipped with Mosquito FBVI bombers.

464 Squadron RAAF

464 Squadron formed in September 1942, and flew for a year with Lockheed Ventura twin-engined bombers before re-equipping with Mosquitos.   464 had been involved in some epic operations with the Venturas.   Its first was the daring low level attack on the Philips radio factory at Eindhoven, Holland, in which 13 aircraft were lost, including three from 464.   Almost every aircraft was damaged, either by flak or bird strikes.   464 was to continue to make its mark with the Mosquito.   In February 1944, 464 Squadron took part in the famous attack on the jail at Amiens, in which the walls were breached to allow as many as possible of the Resistance people held there to escape.   After Operation 'Overlord', the D-Day invasion of Normandy on 6 June 1944, the squadron moved on the 18th to Thorney Island, near Portsmouth.

The air offensive in support of the Normandy invasion was at full strength.   The lessons of the earlier war years had been learned, and it was realised that a powerful air force would be necessary to assist the ground forces to fight their way across Europe, as well as battle opposing German Luftwaffe units.   The heavy bomber forces were attacking strategic targets deeper into Occupied Europe and Germany, though on occasion they would be diverted to targets in support of the invasion.

The RAF organisation which provided the battlefield support was titled 2nd Tactical Air Force (2TAF), commanded by Air Marshal Arthur Coningham, commander of the Western Desert Air Force([North Africa) in 1942.   As D-Day neared in the spring of 1944, 2TAF was a powerful force of 100 squadrons of reconnaissance, fighter, fighter-bomber, bomber and observation aircraft, with two objectives:
        firstly, to achieve air superiority, which would allow Allied bombing, reconnaissance and ground attack operations in support of the land forces;
        secondly, to provide a high degree of air support to the land forces, constrained only by weather.

The aircraft in the 2TAF squadrons were Spitfires, Typhoons, Mosquitos, Mitchells, Wellingtons, Tempests, Mustangs and Austers.

2TAF was made up of a Headquarters, with 2, 83, 84 and 85 Groups, plus some attached squadrons and flights.   2 Group was commanded by the legendary Air Vice Marshal Basil Embry DSO***, who continued to fly operational sorties despite his high rank, but as a 'Wing Commander Smith'.

Preparing Mosquito FBVI bombers of 464 Squadron for operations. (RAAF)

2 Group, of four Wings, included 140 Wing, which was made up of 21 Squadron RAF, 487 Squadron RNZAF and 464 Squadron RAAF.

It was as part of this great Commonwealth expeditionary air force that Peter Panitz returned to operations. The D-Day landings had been successful, despite great cost, particularly in the US sectors. The enormous Allied air effort blanketed German attempts to counter the landings, and German field commanders at all levels knew that the war was lost. However, the Allies demanded unconditional surrender from the Axis enemies, and the leaders and functionaries of the Nazi regime in Germany knew that they would be held responsible for crimes unsurpassed in the history of the Western Democracies. The Italian Fascist regime, led by Benito Mussolini, had surrendered in September 1943, despite the vainglorious bombast and military posturing of Mussolini and his colleagues. Only Germany and Japan remained and neither would surrender.

On D-Day, the German Luftwaffe could mount only 319 sorties of all types of aircraft against the Allied force. For the first month of the invasion, the Luftwaffe formation in France, Luftflotte 3, received as replacement aircraft a total of 998 fighters, 83 bombers and 24 reconnaissance types. Losses were 458 single-engined fighters, 224 bombers and seven on supply flights, plus there were 137 destroyed and 212 damaged on the ground - a total of 826 aircraft destroyed. All this was later reported by the Luftwaffe's own historical staff, who also found that fighter losses were 3:1 in the Allies' favour and personnel losses 2:1 in the Allies' favour. Post-war accounts of the campaign by Luftwaffe individuals and unit histories portray them as small bands of experts piling up victories shot from the waves of Allied aircraft, but their own studies done at the time by their own staff members show this was not quite the case. The experienced and flexible Allied air forces, employing tachnological advances and tactical procedures conceived and developed since 1941, had brought the Luftwaffe in Western Europe to battle and showed the German Wehrmacht how air power should be employed.

Not only were the German commanders in the West confronted with Allied material superiority, but they were saddled with inept orders and directives coming from Adolf Hitler's field HQ in Poland.   The combined success of the Allied deception plan, the pre-invasion bombing campaign, and the landings themselves, are beyond the scope of this book.   However, the Germans continued to resist and fought expert defensive battles in the Normandy battle area, where the terrain favoured such actions.   With the Luftwaffe on the defensive, and stretched to provide some sort of presence in the four main theatres - France, Italy, Russia and the defence of Germany itself against the US and RAF heavy bombers - the German ground forces had to rely on camouflage, concealment and ground fire to counter Allied air superiority.

With that self-deprecating humour which so often is to be found in front-line troops, the German ground forces parodied the Nazi propaganda which promoted 'the German salute' - the the stiff-armed 'Heil' - and constant other references to things German, referred to 'the German glance', which was a constant look over the shoulder at the sky - for Allied aircraft.

Meanwhile, in the build-up to the invasion and to the end of June 1944, 456 Squadron had begun to amass a respectable victory score.   Peter's victories in September and October had been the last for the squadron in 1943.   On 25 February 1944, the long drought without successes had broken, with a Ju88 destroyed by Samson, and by 30 June another 27 enemy had been claimed as destroyed, plus four probably destroyed and two damaged.   Six destroyed and two 'probables' were claimed by the CO, Wing Commander Keith Hampshire DSO DFC RAAF.

464 Squadron, under Wing Commander Bob Iredale's leadership, had achieved a high standard of professionalism, and flew over 250 sorties in June.   The squadron had lost four crews in June: Flying Officers R.A. Faulafor/R.W. Wilkins on the 2nd, sent to attack Laon; Squadron Leader Geoff Oxlade/Flight Lieutenant Don Shanks (formerly of 456 Squadron) on the 5th; Captain A.M. Wakeman (USAAC)/Flying Officer G. Holmes on the 10th and Flight Lieutenant J.L. Martin/Sergeant H.L Morgan on the 21st.   On the 11th, Flight Lieutenant S.T. Sharpe/Flying Officer A. Mercer had to crashland at Tangmere, and both men were injured, requiring hospital treatment; the Mosquito was written off. Many operations had been against the IInd SS Panzer Corps, a battle hardened force from the Eastern Front, re-equipping in France, and which was advancing to the Normandy battle area.
In February, Oxlade and Shanks had brought back a damaged Mosquito, after two 40mm flak hits shot away 2.2 metres of the starboard wing, and made a 1.3 metre hole in the rear fuselage.   Shanks' opinion of Oxlade as a 'consummate pilot' was reinforced, when they flew back across the deadly freezing waters of the English Channel, with Shanks throwing his body weight on the control column to keep the port wing down until they could land at base.   On first seeing the damage, when still over France, Shanks asked if they were going to bale out, but Oxlade emphatically replied in the negative, indicating the snowy ground: 'Too cold!'   As related earlier, in May 1943, Oxlade and Shanks had driven a Ju88 into the ground without ever seeing it.

Damage to the Mosquito after Geoff Oxlade brought it back across the English Channel in February 1944. (RAAF)

Geoff Oxlade's sacrifice on the eve of the invasion

Don Shanks returned to the squadron in September, and related the events of the last operation over France with Squadron Leader Geoff Oxlade. It was their 13th operation of the second tour. Flak from Brionne airfield, firing along searchlight beams, hit the bottom of the Mosquito as they were going to their assigned patrol area, and Shanks could see the glow of flames reflected from below in the engine nacelle. Geoff Oxlade decided to go on, as 'this is the all-important night', before the invasion. There was nothing to report in the patrol area, and they turned for home - then the engines failed. First the port engine failed for lack of glycol coolant lost to the flak damage earlier, and then the starboard engine began to burn; they were at 1500 feet. Oxlade told Shanks to bale out. Shanks did so successfully, through the single small lower hatch by his seat, and thought Oxlade would try to land the Mosquito, but after his parachute opened he saw the aircraft hit the ground and explode. Shanks spent some time with the local French people, in the area of a V1 flying bomb launch unit. If discovered, he and the French assisting him would have been summarily killed.

Wing Commander Iredale flew his 63rd and last operation on the 21st, and handed over to Peter next day, but did not actually leave until the 28th.

There were many experienced crews with 464 at this time, and without wishing to select one to the detriment of others, Flight Lieutenant Wilbur Parsons from Tasmania might be a good example. Parsons, from Burnie, was born in March 1919, joined the RAAF in January 1941, trained at Somers in Victoria, in Tasmania, and at 17 OTU Upwood, UK.

He had flown ten intruder operations in Blenheims, including one to Norway, and 15 bombing operations in the Venturas.   On 13 June 1943, in a Ventura, he survived a combat with FW190s off the island of Guernsey.   The squadron was tasked to attack the viaduct at St. Brieuc, but thick layered cloud made it impossible, and the squadron had just aborted the operation when four FW190s appeared out of the clouds, presumably directed by radar.   They attacked the second box in the squadron formation.   In the first pass, the 190's shells and bullets shattered the Ventura's turret, wounded Sergeant B. McConnell and threw him out of the turret, shot away the port elevator, damaged the hydraulics, jammed the trim-tabs and punctured the tyres.   But McConnell forced his way back into the turret, and then, ignoring his wounds, gave concise and timely directions to Parsons which allowed him to evade more attacks.   The Ventura was brought safely back, despite the above damage and 1.3 metres of tailplane shot away.   Parsons made a forced landing; one other Ventura was shot down and two others damaged, one of those also force-landing.   Parsons was awarded the DFC and McConnell the DFM.   It was men of this calibre Peter Panitz was to lead in 464 Squadron.

Bill Hyem, formerly of 456 Squadron, also was back on operations, commanding B Flight 464 Squadron, with John Brayne as his observer.   Both men had been rested in September, but went back for a second tour on Mosquitoes.   As a senior Squadron Leader and experienced flight commander, Hyem had some hopes of taking command when Iredale departed, but these were dashed when Peter Panitz arrived.

Bad weather reduced much operational flying in the first days of July, so Peter flew his first operation as CO 464 Squadron on the 3rd, and left three enemy transport vehicles burning north of Blois; four others were attacked and bombed.   The railway station at Cloyes was attacked and a train left in a cloud of steam.   The squadron had 13 Mosquitos airborne, sweeping north of the Loire; all attacked similar targets of opportunity.   The next day 14 squadron aircraft flew a similar operation, Peter's share being a train damaged.

Flying Officers B.M. 'Ern' Dunkley and H.P. Woodward had to bale out near Caen, after flak damaged their aircraft while they attacked a train near Tours.   An engine caught fire, and the flames restarted every time Ern tried to feather the propellor.   Finally, with not enough fuel left to reach the UK, he decided to abandon the Mosquito.   Woodward jettisoned the cabin door, but stuck on a 'wear strip' just at the entrance; Dunkley assisted Woodward's exit by the use of his boot on Woodward's back.   Ern followed, but both men were shot at on the way down by Polish troops.   When Ern landed his foot went into a cart rut in a field, resulting in a broken ankle, and in addition he was regarded suspiciously by the Canadians among whom he landed - they somehow thought he represented a German paratrooper attack.   After a few days in a casualty clearing station in France, Ern was flown back to the UK.   He was off flying until September, but was very pleased to be visited in hospital by Peter Panitz, who was regarded by Ern as 'a great morale booster', and very popular as squadron commander, despite following an outstanding leader like Bob Iredale.   On the 6th, twelve Squadron Mosquitos flew on operations; lights in a wood near Coutance were bombed; Flying Officer D.V. Avery and Warrant Officer J.J. Williams had to crashland at base after flak damage.   It was a landmark day for Peter - he was promoted Wing Commander.   Similar sorties followed on the 7th, 9th and 11th.   Flying Officers R.G. Rowell and C.E. Davidson had to crashland at Ford airfield on the 8th, after flak damage to their starboard engine when over Angers.

Pinpoint bombing against a German barracks

On the 14th, a German barracks at Bonneuil Matours and a train were attacked, 'with good results' as Peter noted in his log-book. This barracks was reportedly a 'Gestapo' building, but more accurately housed Waffen-SS troops, and the RAF formation comprised aircraft from all three squadrons in 140 Wing. The briefing was by Air Vice Marshal Basil Embry, who used a scale model of the target, explained why it was being attacked, gave routes to and from the area, and the bomb-load detail - high explosive and napalm. There were six buildings, in an area of only 170x100 feet (52x32 metres) on the north-east corner of Mouliere forest, close to a French village; accuracy was essential. The scale model was studied by all crews, aided with air photos of the area. The formation was led by Group Captain Peter Wykeham-Barnes DSO* DFC*, a very successful pilot, with 15 victories gained during several tours on fighter and intruder aircraft.
The Australian squadron representation in this Wing operation was

> Peter and Dickie Williams in NS994/F;
> Squadron Leader R.W. Hyem/Flying Officer E.J. Brayne in HR187/X;
> Flight Lieutenant Wilbur D. Parsons/Flying Officer Ramsey in NS926/Y;
> Flying Officer Bob Walton/Flying Officer C.H. Harper in HX919/Z.

Walton, from Maryborough in Queensland, joined the RAAF in October 1941, three months before his 20th birthday. The attack on the German barracks was Bob's 27th operation; he had 1053 hours, 210 on Mosquitos. He already had flown on two Wing daylight bombing operations, releasing from 20,000 feet on the signal from Path Finder Force aircraft equipped with radar, but preferred operating at lower level alone, in pairs or in sixes.

The SS barracks at Bonneuil in the black rectangle on the left bank of the river. Close proximity to the village required accurate bombing to avoid French civilian casualties.
(RAAF)

Bill Hyem was to lead the second flight, to attack some ten minutes behind the first. However, on take-off both the side windows of the Mosquito cockpit 'blew out', exposing Hyem and John Brayne to the noise and wind, which made conversation almost impossible.   They decided to go on.

The squadrons formed up and set course along the coast, down the Channel, through accurate 88mm flak from the Channel Islands while passing Alderney and Sark, and crossed the French coast in the Gulf of St. Malo.   Wykeham-Barnes led the formation at 2,000 feet, but weather conditions hid the barracks, so he went down to 1,000 feet, saw the target, and dived to attack at 800 feet.   Though the squadrons were forced to split to allow individual attacks, all attacks were finished in a short period.   Dusk was falling as Bob Walton made his run-in, flying at the 'tremendous fireball' already created in the barracks.   He was so low that he had to pull up to clear the flames, and he thought destruction was so complete that he did not fire his guns.

The attack was successful, with all bombs seen to hit in the target area, which was left in flames.   Bob Walton climbed to 3,000 feet near the Brittany coast, and off the Cherbourg peninsula flashed past a Messerschmitt Bf109 going in the opposite direction.   He hauled the Mosquito around but lost sight of the 109 in the turn, and the German flew on, apparently not knowing the Mosquito was near him.   Peter Panitz and Bill Hyem also strafed a train each for good measure.   Hyem and Brayne found trains at Le Creusot, but the flak, and Red Cross painted on some wagons, reduced their scope for strafing. All the squadron aircraft returned safely.

Decorated by King George VI

An indication of the pace of the times can be gained by the following: in the morning of that day, Peter, Dickie Williams and another squadron member received their DFCs from King George VI at Hartford Bridge, then flew the operation in the afternoon.   That night, five squadron aircraft continued the usual harrassment.

Lights behind the German lines at Caen were bombed on the 18th, and a similar sortie flown on the 20th.   Meanwhile, in Hitler's HQ, another in the inept series of assassination attempts on him also failed.   As usual in a totalitarian regime, vengeance was widespread and terrifying; people of all ranks and occupations were arrested, interrogated and killed brutally.   The German armed forces fought on all fronts as best they could, but again their efforts were weakened when several generals and other officers were included in the search for the plotters.   On 22 July, Caen was captured, six weeks after D-Day. Field Marshal Bernard Montgomery, commanding the British force, had consistently attacked, and drawn onto his northern front the greater part of the available German forces, particularly the dangerous Wehrmacht and Waffen-SS tank divisions.   To the south, on the Allied right, and now faced by fewer enemy divisions, the US armies under Generals Omar Bradley and George Patton prepared a great offensive and 'break-out' into southern France.

The SS barracks at Bonneuil after the attack. Bomb craters can be seen around the buildings. (RAAF)

With massive Allied air support, which involved 1500 four-engined bombers, twin-engined bombers and fighter-bombers, three US army corps burst out to the south of the Normandy beach head positions. German defensive efforts failed, and a huge US force plunged further into their rear. Some US units also began to swing east, to the Seine River. Disaster in France now stared the Germans in the face. This was 'blitzkrieg' as they had performed it in Belgium, Holland and France in 1940, the Balkans in 1941 and Russia in 1941-42. However, the levels of mechanisation, firepower and air support in Normandy 1944 far surpassed anything achieved in earlier campaigns.

Peter Panitz had a break from flying for a week. Sometimes, if there was no operational flying required, Peter would load his station wagon with other members of the squadron, and they would roar off to Bognor Regis or somewhere else nearby for a party. 'He was a very popular C.O.', recalled Gordon Nunn. 'He fought hard and played hard.'

On the 26th, Bob Walton, who flew on the attack against the Gestapo barracks, was shot down, but with his navigator, Charles Harper RAF, later returned to England. However, Bob then was repatriated to Australia, classified unfit for operational flying. He had been tasked to patrol near Orleans, with a 500-pound bomb under each wing and two clusters of three one-million candlepower flares in the bomb-bay. These flares were dropped from 3,000 feet, and burned for 90 seconds, in which time the attack had to be planned and made. One set of flares had been dropped near Giens, at 02.15, and Walton was climbing for a second run, when the Mosquito was hit in the bomb-bay and belly by light flak. The flares there began to burn and filled the cockpit with dense acrid smoke; normal breathing would have been impossible, but crews routinely flew on oxygen. Opening the side windows drew off some of the smoke, and Bob could see again. However, the controls gradually became less effective, and then the 20mm cannon ammunition stored under the cockpit began to detonate. He knew it was 'time to go', so gave the order to abandon the Mosquito.

'Flying Officer Harper seemed to take a long time to depart,' Bob recalled. *'First he had to unplug his head phones and attach his chest pack, after groping for it in the smog, then jettison the door and squeeze through the small opening.'*

Bob meanwhile had stopped and feathered the port engine, and prepared to follow Charles Harper, but was hampered by his parachute and dinghy in getting around the control column and lining up with the escape hatch. He believes he was blown out by a fuel explosion, narrowly missed the starboard propellor and collided heavily with that engine nacelle. Aware that the aircraft must have been close to the ground, he pulled the ripcord and the parachute snapped open, assisted by the slipstream of the starboard propellor. The violence of the opening severely bruised Bob, as well as inflicting permanent damage to some joints and vertebrae. Almost instantly he crashed through a tree and thunked onto the ground, or, in his words,

'arrived in France minus a flying boot which served as holster for my Smith & Wesson, and most of my lung capacity, which had not withstood the impact.'

Bob had landed in an orchard, and also sprained an ankle. He hid his parachute and other equipment, then crawled west for about two miles [3.5 km] and hid in a hayfield. Late next day he hailed a passing Frenchman, who came back and escorted Walton to his home, where he was passed to the local Resistance. He was delivered to Maria, code named 'Belette', and given shelter, a false identity card, a 9mm Mauser pistol, moral support and First Aid. 'The remainder of my journey was arranged for me,' as he said on return to the UK.

Helping 'Blood and Guts' Patton

On the 29th, Peter Panitz returned to operations with an attack on lights seen in a wood behind the battle front; an explosion followed his bombing. The hapless Germans had to insist on absolute obedience to light discipline - any flash of a torch to find the way, or to allow work in the night, resulted in a swift attack with bombs and cannon. These sorties by the squadron at the end of July were south of the British area, in support of General Patton's US 3rd Army, for the great mechanised thrust by Patton's US forces south through German-occupied areas. The developing destruction of entire German formations called for combined Allied air and land operations around the clock, and the RAF's 2TAF squadrons were tasked as heavily as the US 9th Air Force units. Destruction from the air was tremendous, and in ground actions, the US 1st Army alone took 20,000 prisoners in the last six days of July.

The pressure of operations continued in August, with sorties by Peter on the 2nd, 4th, 9th, 15th, 17th (2), 18th (2), 20th (2) and 22nd. Crews were flying two or more sorties a night. On the 5th, the Flying Officer A.E. Crellin/Flight Sergeant T.A. Orr crew failed to return; no trace of them was found. On the 8th, the Flight Sergeants G.M. Miller/A. Lister crew failed to return, and later were found to have been killed over the Orne River bridgehead. On the 13th, the squadron flew 34 sorties, and on the 17th, the Wing flew 104. By this time, comments began to appear in the squadron diary about the lack of rest for all ranks and musterings, what with aircraft coming and going at all hours. Nothing could have been done without prodigious efforts by the unsung ground crews - no aircraft could so much as start an engine without them. In addition to the operational flights, there were night-flying tests and formation and bombing practice flights with the squadron. As well as all this, some crews were tasked to fly two sorties in one night, to maintain maximum pressure on the Germans.

On 2 August, the squadron diary noted it was the first fine day in a long while. That night, fourteen squadron Mosquitos again set out for the battle area. In moonlight, a train south of La Rochelle was hit with a bomb, halted, and strafed; Peter had flown about 1,000 miles [1600 km] on the sortie, saw the train when he was at only 200 feet but managed a direct hit. On the 4th, a railway bridge at Briare on the Loire was hit with a bomb; 'a lucky hit', said Peter. The moonlight was so bright, pieces of the bridge could be seen flung into the air after his hit on the centre span. Flight Sergeant Miller, of Croydon, also was in the area hunting trains, and suddenly saw Peter's bombs explode on the bridge in front of him. 'It was a lovely sight', he said.. On the 15th, Peter hit a road bridge with a bomb. By this time, Peter's score stood at 22 trains destroyed or damaged, which contributed to the resulting great disruption to the German war effort. It has been calculated that in 1944 85% of French rail traffic was devoted to taking produce from French agriculture and industry to Germany. In six nights, the squadron flew 120 sorties. By the end of August, it had flown 3,969 operational hours, of 1,776 sorties since 6 December 1942.

At the beginning of August, Hitler ordered a counter-attack, and Field Marshal Kluge faithfully carried out the task. This only hastened the destruction of the German forces in France. The 'Ultra' signals organisation had been providing valuable information to the senior Allied commanders since before D-Day, and this German move also was reported. The Germans were swamped with high explosive and another debacle began. By 16 August, seven German corps were trapped in a giant 'pocket', the entrance to which was to the east, at Falaise. By the evening of 19 August, in the ever-shrinking area, continuously pounded by artillery and air power, were two Army headquarters, four Corps headquarters, ten divisions, and a huge collection of support and other units. Next day, the pocket was sealed. 50,000 prisoners were taken; 10,000 dead littered the area; equipment of all kinds was everywhere. The scenes of destruction and mass killing were indescribable - not only men had been slaughtered, but also thousands of horses still used by the Germans. Advance US elements crossed the Seine, and the British prepared their own break-out to the north. A decisive battle had been won; France was almost liberated.

Daylight operation to Chagny

On 22 August, 464 Squadron was to attack in daylight what was described as 'the Chagny marshalling yards', south-west of Dijon. A number of ammunition and supply trains were gathered there. The 2 Group records describe the target as 'petrol trains between Chagny and Paray'.

About three-quarters of the way to the target, Peter's aircraft began to slow down, and he waved the squadron on; Squadron Leader Taute took over. Strict radio silence was maintained, and no one knew what the problem was in Peter's Mosquito. The squadron attack was successful, but, further south-west, intense light flak was met over Le Creusot. From heights of 20 to 200 feet, 17 trains in the area were attacked, nine were destroyed or seriously damaged, and 140 Wing noted that the operation 'was most successful.' Peter did not return from the operation. The squadron diarist wrote that it was sincerely hoped he and Dickie Williams had been able to hide somewhere. Peter's squadron command had lasted two months. Operations continued; the squadron flew on against many targets in northern Europe. Two more successful attacks on Gestapo offices were made, in October 1944 and March 1945.

On 25 August, Paris was liberated. Soon after, most of France was free. At the time, this was the greatest defeat suffered by Hitler's Third Reich, surpassing the previous disasters at Stalingrad in February 1943, in North Africa in May 1943, and the total destruction of Army Group Centre in Russia in June 1944. Stalingrad had cost 20 divisions; North Africa, eight; Army Group Centre, 28 divisions completely destroyed. During the Normandy battles, German HQ in the West had 50 infantry and 12 panzer divisions under its command. By September 1944, only remnants of 24 infantry and 11 panzer divisions retained any sort of organised presence in the field. 2,200 tanks had been lost in France, and only 120 remained on strength in the battered panzer regiments. 500,000 German soldiers had been killed or captured. Though German units remained in occupation of some Atlantic ports, the port facilities were not able to be used by U-Boats, and the garrisons were left to 'wither on the vine'; surrender was inevitable. In the air war, the Germans had lost the advantage of forward locations for their radars, and the Luftwaffe was more than ever unable to cope. Apart from battle losses, the enormous contribution made by French agriculture and industry to the Nazi war effort also was lost.

22 August 1944, Chagny rail yards. Fires starting among the rail wagons.
(RAAF)

Yet, Germany fought on. The Allied demand for unconditional surrender, the vivid memories of the cruel treatment inflicted on Germany after surrender in WW1, and the perceived horrors of a Russian occupation, complemented with internal control exercised by the Nazis, combined to allow no alternative. Germany fought on until May 1945, when Hitler suicided, and every square metre of German soil came under the command of the Allies.

Peter Panitz and Dickie Williams at rest

After the war, the bodies of Peter and Dickie Williams were located in the cemetery of the village of Bona, north-east of Nevers. The local people reported that at 18.44 on the 22nd, the aircraft, flying very low, had struck a hill; both men were reported to have been killed instantly. Jules Millot, the local policeman, reported in his daily log that one aviator was burned beyond recognition, but an identity disc, with '411.411, Williams RS, RAAF - RC' was found on the body. The other man had no identity disc, but was not burned. There was no reference to wounds inflicted on either man prior to the crash. Also, there was no reference to German troops firing on the aircraft to cause it to crash. It is believed that there were no enemy troops in the immediate area, as a large-scale withdrawal was in progress from southern France. Despite orders to the contrary by the regional German commander, the villagers organised and performed a full burial ceremony, attended by some 300 people. The bodies were shrouded in their parachutes, and placed in coffins paid for by the population. The aircraft propellors were placed diagonally over the grave, and behind the cross was a silk-wrapped fire-extinguisher with a ribbon, inscribed "To our valiant Allies". The grave was well cared for, and on the day that Japan surrendered a thanks-giving service was held by the entire population. The grave was completely covered with flowers.

In 1950, Peter's sister, Mrs Walter Gray, visited Bona and spoke to the village priest. The cure said that Peter was in the aircraft when it crashed, but Dickie Williams had parachuted, though was dead when found. The cure dragged Peter's body from the Mosquito before it burst into flames. (This, of course, differs from Jules Millot's report.) The cure added that both bodies were hidden from the Germans, then taken to the village church, and buried in the early hours of the next morning. Mrs Gray later said that though no one in the village apparently knew she was coming, the grave had fresh flowers on it. The people of Bona still cared for the resting place of the Australians who had come so far to fight the Nazi regime.

UNDISMAYED
INTO THE BRIGHTNESS OF DAY
WITH THE FLAG OF LIBERTY UNFURLED
YOU WENT AWAY

Brian Panitz

The grave of Peter Panitz and Dickie Williams, Bona, 1952, on the visit of Peter's sister. (Panitz family)

The grave of Peter Panitz and Dickie Williams, Bona, with official Commonwealth War Graves headstone. (Panitz family)

456 and 464 Squadrons fought on to the end of the war, and both were disbanded soon after hostilities ceased.   As well as interceptions of enemy aircraft, 456 Squadron destroyed 29 V-1 flying bombs.   Personnel losses had continued to the end and after it. Sadly, John Newell was a passenger in the aircraft carrying the party of General George Vasey, when it crashed at Cairns on 5 March 1945, killing all aboard.   Wing Commander Bas Howard, the CO, on 29 May 1945, suffered consecutive engine failures and had to ditch into the Blackwater River.   Howard, much respected by all, drowned.   The Mosquito's entry and escape hatch was a double door affair, on the starboard side, below the level of the cockpit seats.

IInd SS Panzer Corps, comprising 9th and 10th SS Panzer Divisions, target of the squadron in Normandy, in early September 1944 was dispersed in the Nijmegen area of Holland. When the now-famous great Allied airborne operation 'Market Garden' was launched to capture all the bridges to the Rhine, it was the battle-hardened units of IInd SS Panzer Corps who inflicted the crippling delay on the ground advance, and who first rushed to the bridge at Arnhem and fought the British paratroops in that town.

Appendix 1
Aircraft flown by Peter Panitz on notable operations or flights.

456 Squadron RAAF

Mosquito NFII
20 April 1943	DZ269 Ranger; train strafed
6 May	DZ269 Ranger; 6 trains strafed
12 May	HJ702 Ranger; 2 trains strafed
15 May	DZ269 Ranger; 2 trains strafed
12 July	DO751 Ranger; electricity station attacked

Mosquito FBVI
26 July	RX*E/HJ817 Ranger; hydro-electricity station attacked
21 September	RX*L/HJ818 Instep; 1xJu88 destroyed
3 October	RX*E/HJ817 Instep; 1XJu88 destroyed

464 Squadron RAAF

3 July 1944	SB*F/NS994	1st operation.
	Flew 'F' on all ops this month, except:	
11 July	SB*K/HX977	
29 July	SB*G/NT229	
2 August	SB*G/NT229	
	Flew 'G'/NT229	on all ops, except
18 August	SB*G/NT177	(may have been re-lettered)
22 August	SB*G/NT229	missing; crashed at Bona.

464 Squadron formation in the attack on the Gestapo barracks, 14 July 1944.

Panitz/Williams	SB*F/NS994
Hyem/Brayne	SB*S/HR187
Parsons/Ramsey	SB*G/NS926
Walton/Harper	SB*P/HX919

Appendix 2
Text to Citations for Awards

     Award of Distinguished Flying Cross, Date 20 October 1943, London Gazette No.36226.

Flight Lieutenant Panitz has taken part in many operational sorties. In operations during the last 4 months he has damaged 13 trains and several enemy electical installations. He has at all times displayed fine leadership, skill and devotion to duty.

     Award of Distinguished Flying Cross, Date 29 October 1943, London Gazette No.36226.

Flying Officer Williams has flown as navigator on a number of operational missions. His work has been faultless and has contributed much to the success of these sorties. He has assisted in damaging many trains and transport in enemy territory and has participated in raids on transformer and power stations which have proved most effective. This officer has invariably displayed great courage, dash and determination.

Sources:
Personal log-book and family records, courtesy of Royston Panitz, Australia, and Gordon Panitz, UK.

Personal contributions from John Brayne; Ern Dunkley; Gordon Gatenby; Gordon Nunn; John Newell's log-book, courtesy of Bob Newell; Bob Walton.
Squadron records in the Australian War Memorial AWM 64 collection for 456 and 464 Squadrons, and the RAAF Historical Section records. Some personal details for various aircrews came from the AWM 65 collection. Background to the operations and other detail from the AWM 220 collection.   Translations of Luftwaffe historical studies are in the AWM 54 collection, 423/4/103 [164 parts]; that describing the Normandy battlefront is Part 22.   From Germany, Herr Herbert Hintze, V/KG40, gave some detail of the Biscay operations.

In France, Bernard Baeza kindly assisted with information from French sources, including contact with the national police archives and local authorities of Bona.
David Vincent kindly gave permission to use relevant information from his "*Mosquito Monograph*", a detailed history of the Mosquito in RAAF service.

For a thorough account of the Bay of Biscay campaign in May-August 1943, see Norman Franks, "*Conflict Over The Bay*", William Kimber, London, 1986.   Luftwaffe intruder operations over England 1940-45 are detailed in Simon Parry's "*Intruders Over Britain*", Air Research, UK, 1987.   The history of 456 Squadron is told in *Fighter Nights* by John Bennett, Banner Books, Australia, 1995.

Index
The index has been confined to persons named in the text.   The structure of the book is such that references to aircraft types, units and place names would serve little purpose. The index also is structured to represent that of the book.

P-40 All rounder P. 1 - 44

Spitfire Sweeps P. 45 - 105

Mosquito Intruder P. 106 - 139

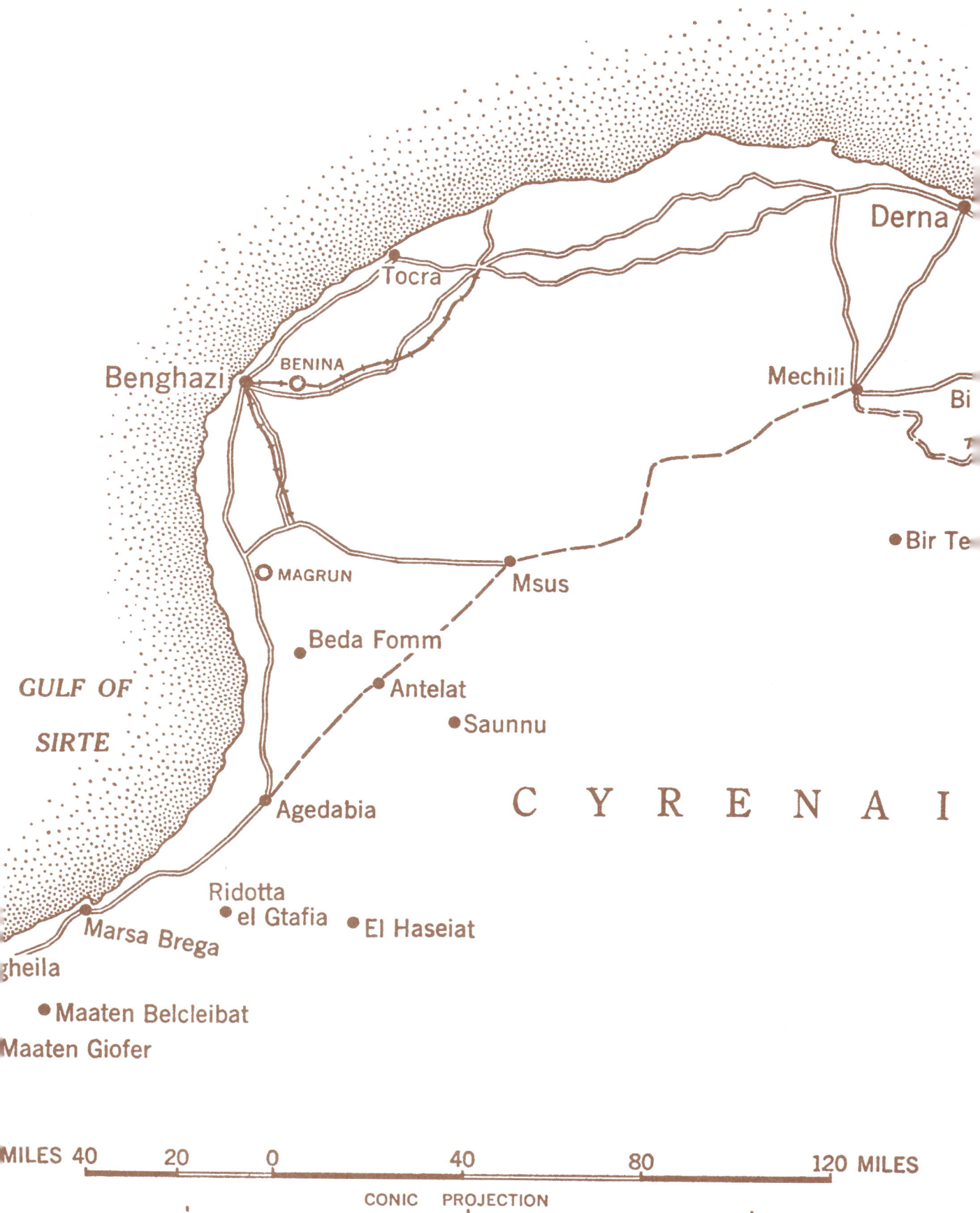

M E D I T E R R A N E

Derna

Tocra

Benghazi O BENINA

Mechili

Bi

Bir Te

O MAGRUN

Msus

Beda Fomm

GULF OF

Antelat

SIRTE

Saunnu

Agedabia

C Y R E N A I

Ridotta
el Gtafia   El Haseiat

Marsa Brega

gheila

Maaten Belcleibat

Maaten Giofer

MILES 40   20   0   40   80   120 MILES

CONIC   PROJECTION